Retail Milestones

Englisch für Verkäuferinnen und Verkäufer | Einzelhandelskaufleute

von
Arnd Nadolny

Ernst Klett Verlag
Stuttgart · Leipzig

So arbeiten Sie mit Retail Milestones

Einsteigen

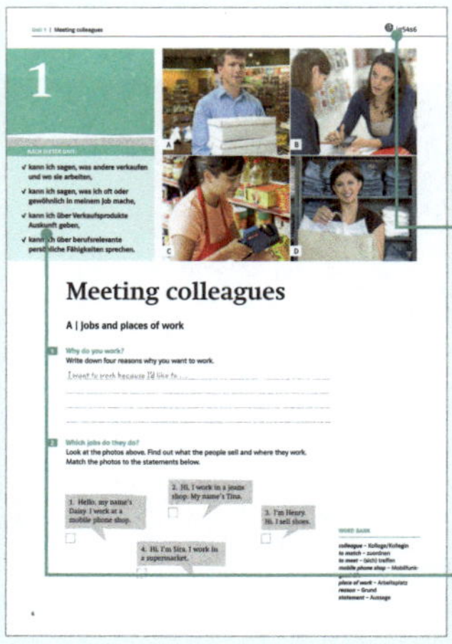

Check in
Bilder und Aufgaben zur Einführung in die Unit

Milestones-Code zu den Audios und ergänzenden Materialien im Internet

Überblick über die Lernziele

Überprüfen

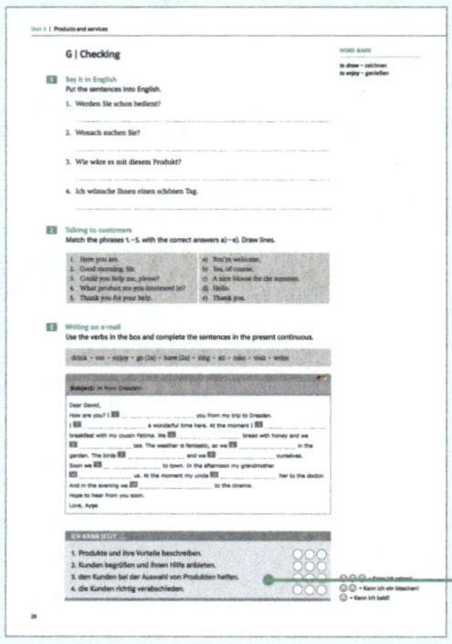

Check out
Aufgaben zur Überprüfung des Lernstandes

„Ich kann jetzt…“ Selbstevaluation

Erarbeiten, üben, anwenden

Language Box
Grammatik und sprachliche Besonderheiten

Intercultural Box
Informationen zur Förderung der Interkulturellen Kompetenz

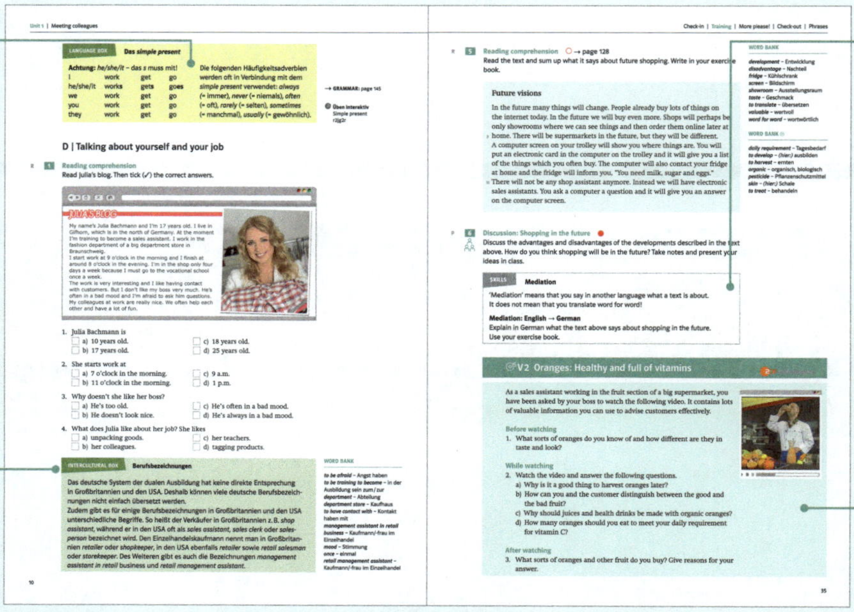

Skills Box
Training ausgewählter Fertigkeiten

Video Lounge
Authentische Videos mit Aufgaben zum Hör/Sehverstehen

Unitelemente

NACH DIESER UNIT:	Lernziele	LANGUAGE BOX	Grammatik und sprachliche Besonderheiten
WORD BANK	Schlüsselvokabular	SKILLS	Training ausgewählter Fertigkeiten
→ **PHRASES:** page 17	Verweis auf *Phrases*	INTERCULTURAL BOX	Interkulturelle Kompetenz
→ **GRAMMAR:** page 136	Verweis auf Grammatikanhang	VIDEO LOUNGE	Authentische Videos mit Aufgaben zum Hör-/Sehverstehen
ICH KANN JETZT …	Selbstevaluation		

Erweitern, vertiefen

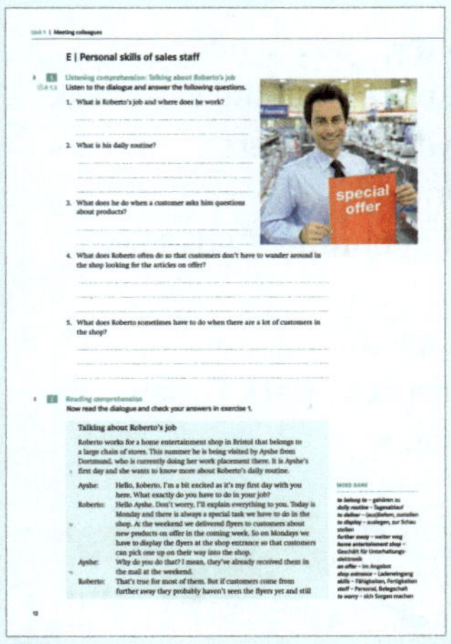
E | Personal skills of sales staff

More please
Längere Texte und anspruchsvollere Aufgaben bis B1-Niveau

H | Phrases: Serving customers

Phrases
Nach beruflichen Situationen geordnete Redewendungen

Anhang

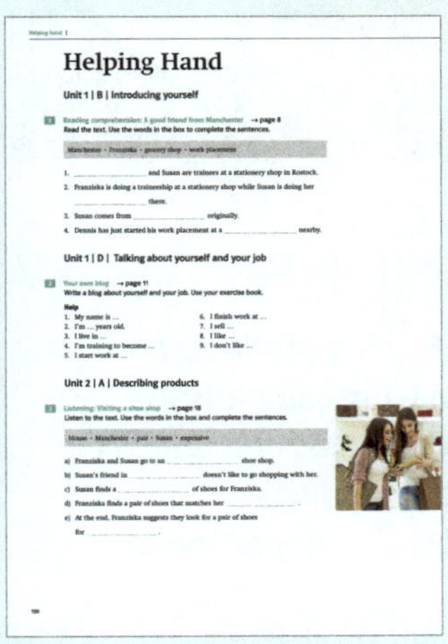
Helping Hand

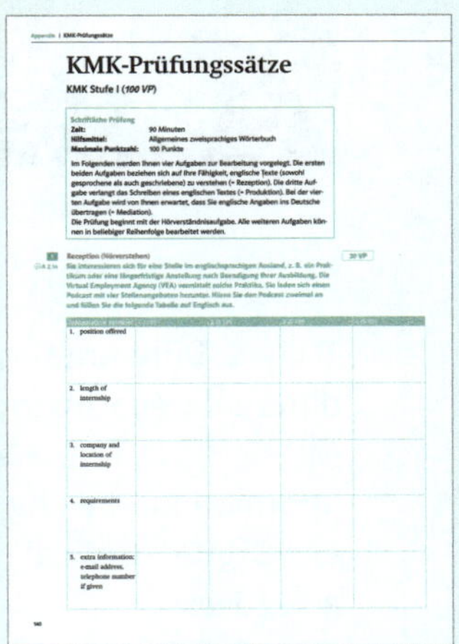
KMK-Prüfungssätze

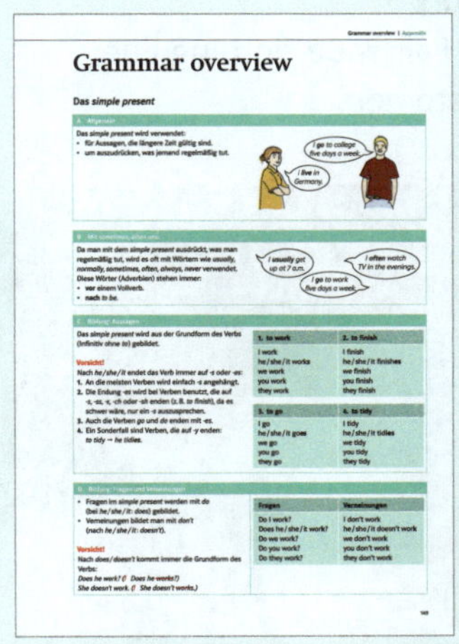
Grammar overview

Chronological word list

Helping hand
Leichte Zusatzaufgaben und Hilfestellungen zur Differenzierung

KMK-Musterprüfung
Aufgaben zum Erarbeiten, Üben und Trainieren

Grammar overview
Kompaktgrammatik zum Nachschlagen und Lernen

Vocabulary
Chronologische und alphabetische Wortlisten

Symbole

◎ A 1.4	Verweis auf ein Audio mit Angabe der Tracknummer (CD1 – Track 4). Alle Audios sind im Internet über den Code der jeweiligen Unit abrufbar.
○ → page 126	Verweis auf eine einfachere Aufgabe oder eine Hilfestellung auf den *Helping hand*-Seiten im Anhang
●	Anspruchsvollere Aufgabe
👥	Partner-/ und Gruppenaufgaben
P, M, I, R	Produktion, Mediation, Interaktion, Rezeption
🌐	Aufgabe mit Internetrecherche
🌐 ig54s6	Geben Sie diesen Code auf www.klett.de ein, um zu den Zusatzmaterialien im Internet zu gelangen.
🌐 Üben interaktiv r2jg2r	Geben Sie diesen und die weiteren Codes auf www.klett.de ein, um zu den interaktiven Grammatikübungen zu gelangen.

40% OFF
SAVE $10
I ♥ COUPONS
free

1

NACH DIESER UNIT:

- √ kann ich sagen, was andere verkaufen und wo sie arbeiten,
- √ kann ich sagen, was ich oft oder gewöhnlich in meinem Job mache,
- √ kann ich über Verkaufsprodukte Auskunft geben,
- √ kann ich über berufsrelevante persönliche Fähigkeiten sprechen.

A

B

C

D

Meeting colleagues

A | Jobs and places of work

1 Why do you work?

Write down four reasons why you want to work.

I want to work because I'd like to …

____

____

____

2 Which jobs do they do?

Look at the photos above. Find out what the people sell and where they work. Match the photos to the statements below.

1. Hello, my name's Daisy. I work at a mobile phone shop. ☐
2. Hi, I work in a jeans shop. My name's Tina. ☐
3. I'm Henry. Hi. I sell shoes. ☐
4. Hi. I'm Sira. I work in a supermarket. ☐

WORD BANK

colleague – Kollege/Kollegin
to match – zuordnen
to meet – (sich) treffen
mobile phone shop – Mobilfunkgeschäft
place of work – Arbeitsplatz
reason – Grund
statement – Aussage

B | Introducing yourself

R/P **1** **Listening: A good friend from Manchester**

◎ A 1.1 Listen to the text and sum it up in one or two sentences.

____

____

____

2 **Meeting people**

What do the people say when they meet each other? Underline the phrases in the text.

A good friend from Manchester

Susan, 17, comes from Manchester and is an exchange student at her friend's vocational school in Rostock. Twice a week, Franziska and Susan go to school together but the remaining days of the week they both work at a stationery shop just opposite their school in the city centre of Rostock. Franziska is currently doing her traineeship there and Susan is doing a work placement to find out if she likes the job. If she does, she might start an apprenticeship like Franziska's back home, too.

Today is Monday and, as school has recently started, Franziska, the trainee, and Susan, the intern, are preparing a special sales area for stationery items which students might need to buy.

Franziska: Look, Susan. This is where we hang up the pencils.

Susan: We should put the mechanical pencils at the front because customers don't need to sharpen them.

Franziska: Good idea, Susan. We should also put complete writing sets on the shelves, too. They contain everything that students need to survive a school day.

Susan: Wow, that looks like a complete school survival kit!

Franziska: You and your funny remarks! Oh, look Susan. That's Dennis and Paul over there. I know them. They come from Bristol and have just started their work placement at a grocery store nearby. They probably need some school items.

Dennis and Paul come over to them.

Dennis: Hi, you two. How are you doing, Franziska? You look as if you need a few days off.

Franziska: Very funny, Dennis. Nice to see you, too. May I introduce you to my friend Susan? She's from Manchester originally and is doing a work placement here.

Paul: Pleased to meet you, Susan. I'm Paul.

Dennis: Pleased to meet you. You look great.

Susan: Pleased to meet you, too. Thank you for the compliment, Dennis. Sorry, but Franziska and I are very busy at the moment.

Dennis: No problem. Come on Paul, let's go!

WORD BANK

apprenticeship – Ausbildung
to contain – beinhalten
exchange student – Austauschschüler/in
to have a few days off – ein paar Tage frei haben
grocery store – Lebensmittelgeschäft
to hang up – aufhängen
intern – Praktikant/in
to introduce sb to sb – jdn. jdm. vorstellen
item – Artikel
mechanical pencil – Druckbleistift
nearby – in der Nähe
opposite – gegenüber
originally – ursprünglich
phrase – Redewendung
Pleased to meet you. – Schön Sie / dich / euch kennen zu lernen.
remaining – verbleibend
remark – Bemerkung
sales area – Verkaufsfläche
to sharpen – anspitzen
shelf, (pl.) shelves – Regal
stationery shop – Schreibwarenladen
to sum up – zusammenfassen
survival kit – Überlebensausrüstung
to survive – überleben
traineeship – Ausbildung
twice a week – zweimal pro Woche
vocational school – Berufsschule
work placement (BE), internship (AE) – Praktikum

R **3** **Reading comprehension** ○ → page 130

a) Read the text on page 7 and find out if the statements are true or false. Tick (✓) the right box.

	true	false
1. Dennis and Susan are trainees at a stationery shop in Rostock.	☐	☐
2. Franziska and Susan are both trainees.	☐	☐
3. Susan comes from Manchester originally.	☐	☐
4. Dennis has just started his work placement at a stationery shop.	☐	☐

b) Correct the false statements on an extra sheet of paper.

I/P **4** **Role play: Introducing yourself**

Work in groups of three. Complete the conversation and act it out.

→ **PHRASES:** page 17

Partner A	Partner B	Partner C
Hello. My name's …		
	Hello. I'm … May I introduce you to … (C)?	
Hi …, pleased to meet you.		Pleased to meet you, too.
Are you a trainee, too, … (B)?		
	Not yet. But I'm hoping to start my traineeship as a(n) … What do you want to do?	
I'd like to start as a(n) …	And what are you doing, … (C)?	I'm a trainee … I work for …

INTERCULTURAL BOX **Begrüßung**

Bei formellen Begrüßungen verwendet man *"How do you do?"* („Guten Tag."). Erst dann folgt z. B. die Frage *"How are you?"* („Wie geht es Ihnen?") mit der möglichen Antwort *"I'm fine, thanks."* („Danke, gut.").
Bei gegenseitigem Vorstellen beginnt man formell mit *"May I introduce you to …?"* („Darf ich Sie … vorstellen?") oder *"May I introduce …"* („Darf ich Ihnen … vorstellen?"), worauf die Antwort folgt *"Pleased/Nice to meet you."* („Ich freue mich, Sie kennen zu lernen."). Unter Freunden begrüßt man sich mit *"Hello."* oder *"Hi."*

5 **Vocabulary work**

Complete the sentences with the words from the box.

contain • interns • introduce • items • meet • traineeship

1. Pleased to ______________ you, Mrs Yilmaz.
2. The writing sets ______________ a fountain pen each.
3. May I ______________ you to Mr Winter?
4. Many young people work as ______________ in stationery shops.
5. I started my ______________ two years ago.
6. Every morning I put different ______________ on the shelf.

WORD BANK

to complete – vervollständigen

C | Job duties

R **1** **Listening: People with different jobs**

A 1.2 Listen to three people talking about their jobs. Then fill in the table.

	Torsten Schneider	Ferhat Yilmaz	Jasmin Wesemann
1. Age			
2. Town			
3. Job			
4. Company			
5. Duties			

2 **Job tasks**

Match the tasks in the box to the photos and write a sentence about what each person does. Use the simple present.

serve customers • weigh fresh food • tag products • unpack goods

1. Andrej often ____________________.
2. Brian usually ____________________.
3. Lin always ____________________.
4. Orhan rarely ____________________.

P **3** **Your job duties**

Write about your own job duties. Use a dictionary and the sentences in exercise 2. Look at the Language box on page 10 for help.

____

____

____

____

____

WORD BANK

company – Firma
customer – Kunde/Kundin
fresh food – Frischkost
goods – Waren
job duty – Arbeitsaufgabe
to serve – bedienen
table – Tabelle
to tag – auszeichnen
task – Aufgabe
to unpack – auspacken
to weigh – (ab)wiegen

WORD BANK

branch manager – Filialleiter/in
cashier – Kassierer/in
retail chain – Einzelhandelskette
shop assistant – Verkäufer/in

LANGUAGE BOX **Das *simple present***

Achtung: *he/she/it* – das *s* muss mit!

I	work	get	go
he/she/it	work**s**	get**s**	go**es**
we	work	get	go
you	work	get	go
they	work	get	go

Die folgenden Häufigkeitsadverbien werden oft in Verbindung mit dem *simple present* verwendet: *always* (= immer), *never* (= niemals), *often* (= oft), *rarely* (= selten), *sometimes* (= manchmal), *usually* (= gewöhnlich).

→ **GRAMMAR:** page 149

Üben interaktiv
Simple present
r2jg2r

D | Talking about yourself and your job

R **1** **Reading comprehension**

Read Julia's blog. Then tick (✓) the correct answers.

JULIA'S BLOG

My name's Julia Bachmann and I'm 17 years old. I live in Gifhorn, which is in the north of Germany. At the moment I'm training to become a sales assistant. I work in the fashion department of a big department store in Braunschweig.
I start work at 9 o'clock in the morning and I finish at around 8 o'clock in the evening. I'm in the shop only four days a week because I must go to the vocational school once a week.
The work is very interesting and I like having contact with customers. But I don't like my boss very much. He's often in a bad mood and I'm afraid to ask him questions. My colleagues at work are really nice. We often help each other and have a lot of fun.

1. Julia Bachmann is
   - ☐ a) 10 years old.
   - ☐ b) 17 years old.
   - ☐ c) 18 years old.
   - ☐ d) 25 years old.
2. She starts work at
   - ☐ a) 7 o'clock in the morning.
   - ☐ b) 11 o'clock in the morning.
   - ☐ c) 9 a.m.
   - ☐ d) 1 p.m.
3. Why doesn't she like her boss?
   - ☐ a) He's too old.
   - ☐ b) He doesn't look nice.
   - ☐ c) He's often in a bad mood.
   - ☐ d) He's always in a bad mood.
4. What does Julia like about her job? She likes
   - ☐ a) unpacking goods.
   - ☐ b) her colleagues.
   - ☐ c) her teachers.
   - ☐ d) tagging products.

INTERCULTURAL BOX **Berufsbezeichnungen**

Das deutsche System der dualen Ausbildung hat keine direkte Entsprechung in Großbritannien und den USA. Deshalb können viele deutsche Berufsbezeichnungen nicht einfach übersetzt werden.
Zudem gibt es für einige Berufsbezeichnungen in Großbritannien und den USA unterschiedliche Begriffe. So heißt der Verkäufer in Großbritannien z. B. *shop assistant*, während er in den USA oft als *sales assistant, sales clerk* oder *salesperson* bezeichnet wird. Den Einzelhandelskaufmann nennt man in Großbritannien *retailer* oder *shopkeeper*, in den USA ebenfalls *retailer* sowie *retail salesman* oder *storekeeper*. Des Weiteren gibt es auch die Bezeichnungen *management assistant in retail* business und *retail management assistant*.

WORD BANK

to be afraid – Angst haben
to be training to become – in der Ausbildung sein zum / zur
department – Abteilung
department store – Kaufhaus
to have contact with – Kontakt haben mit
management assistant in retail business – Kaufmann/-frau im Einzelhandel
mood – Stimmung
once – einmal
retail management assistant – Kaufmann/-frau im Einzelhandel

P **2** **Your own blog** ● ○ → page 130

Write a blog about yourself and your job. Use your exercise book.

→ **PHRASES:** page 17

3 **Products in a supermarket**

Write the correct English names under the photos.

still water • chocolates • fruit • magazines

1. ______ 2. ______ 3. ______ 4. ______

4 **Goods at your place of work**

Use a dictionary and write down some goods that you sell at your place of work.

______

______

I/P **5** **Talking about jobs**

Ask a partner where he / she works and what he / she sells. Take notes about your partner's job.

→ **PHRASES:** page 17

LANGUAGE BOX **Fragebildung im *simple present***

Fragen stellt man mit *do* oder (bei *he, she* und *it*) mit *does*.
Beispiel: *Where* ***do*** *you work and what* ***do*** *you sell?*
ABER: *Where* ***does*** *he work and what* ***does*** *he sell?*

→ **GRAMMAR:** page 149

Üben interaktiv
Fragebildung im simple present
r2jg2r

SKILLS **Practical dictionary work**

You can look up words in a dictionary or on the internet. But be careful: Many words have more than one meaning.

1 Using a dictionary

Write down the correct German translation for the underlined words.

1. I hope that I can pass the test next month. ______
2. Some customers like jewellery. ______
3. This shop has a good reputation. ______
4. My sister wants to try on new shoes. ______

2 Using the internet

Find the words in an online dictionary and write down the English translation.

1. Internetzugang ______
2. im Internet surfen ______
3. Spielzeugwarengeschäft ______

WORD BANK

meaning – Bedeutung
to take notes – Notizen machen

E | Personal skills of sales staff

R **1** **Listening comprehension: Talking about Roberto's job**

A 1.3 Listen to the dialogue and answer the following questions.

1. What is Roberto's job and where does he work?

2. What is his daily routine?

3. What does he do when a customer asks him questions about products?

4. What does Roberto often do so that customers don't have to wander around in the shop looking for the articles on offer?

5. What does Roberto sometimes have to do when there are a lot of customers in the shop?

R **2** **Reading comprehension**

Now read the dialogue and check your answers in exercise 1.

Talking about Roberto's job

Roberto works for a home entertainment shop in Bristol that belongs to a large chain of stores. This summer he is being visited by Ayshe from Dortmund, who is currently doing her work placement there. It is Ayshe's first day and she wants to know more about Roberto's daily routine.

Ayshe: Hello, Roberto. I'm a bit excited as it's my first day with you here. What exactly do you have to do in your job?

Roberto: Hello Ayshe. Don't worry, I'll explain everything to you. Today is Monday and there is always a special task we have to do in the shop. At the weekend we delivered flyers to customers about new products on offer in the coming week. So on Mondays we have to display the flyers at the shop entrance so that customers can pick one up on their way into the shop.

Ayshe: Why do you do that? I mean, they've already received them in the mail at the weekend.

Roberto: That's true for most of them. But if customers come from further away they probably haven't seen the flyers yet and still

WORD BANK

to belong to – gehören zu
daily routine – Tagesablauf
to deliver – (aus)liefern, zustellen
to display – auslegen, zur Schau stellen
further away – weiter weg
home entertainment shop – Geschäft für Unterhaltungselektronik
on offer – im Angebot
shop entrance – Ladeneingang
skills – Fähigkeiten, Fertigkeiten
staff – Personal, Belegschaft
to worry – sich Sorgen machen

need to be informed about our special offers. Besides, there are customers who have read about our offers but have left the flyers at home. So now they can take a new one to look again at the products they're interested it.

Ayshe: Ah, I see. That's quite clever. And I guess you have to study the flyers, too, to be well prepared if a customer wants to know something about the products mentioned in them.

Roberto: Exactly! Now, do you have any ideas about what we can do to help our customers find the products on offer more easily in the shop?

Ayshe: Well, you could display them in a special sales area. That makes sense as the customers don't have to wander around in the shop. And you could have one or two experts waiting there to give them advice in case they need help or want to buy something.

Roberto: Great ideas, Ayshe! So that's one of the jobs I have to do on Monday mornings before the shop opens.

Ayshe: What else do you have to do in your job?

Roberto: Oh, we have to unpack articles and put them on the shelves. Then, we always have to be ready to answer questions from customers who need special advice. Sometimes we also have to deal with customer complaints and customer refunds. And, of course, we have to look out for shoplifters.

Ayshe: Wow, you need a pair of eyes in the back of your head! But surely your job also includes lots of further training. I mean, your products often change and they're more complicated than products like food, for example.

Roberto: Yes, that's true. We often get products with new functions that have to be explained to customers, especially to elderly ones. But, fortunately, we don't need further training every day.

Ayshe: Is there anything else that you haven't told me about yet?

Roberto: Let me think. Yes, there is. Quite often there are lots of customers in the shop at the same time. Then I also have to help out at the cash desk so that they don't get angry about having to wait in long queues, you know.

Ayshe: I see. And now I think it's time for a short break …

Roberto: Yes, you're right. That's also part of our daily routine. Let's go to our canteen and have breakfast together.

Ayshe: That's a really good idea, Roberto.

WORD BANK

advice – Ratschlag
besides – außerdem
case – Fall
cash desk – Kasse
complaint – Beschwerde
to deal with – umgehen mit, es zu tun haben mit
queue – Warteschlange
elderly – älter
refund – Erstattung, Rückzahlung
shoplifter – Ladendieb/in
to wander around – herumirren

M **3**
Mediation

Lesen Sie den Text auf Seite 12–13 noch einmal und übertragen Sie die folgenden Aussagen ins Englische.

1. Ayshe kommt aus Dortmund und absolviert gerade ein Praktikum in einem Geschäft für Unterhaltungselektronik in Bristol.

____

____

2. Die Kunden erhalten Flyer mit Angeboten aus dem Geschäft.

____

____

3. Es ist wichtig, dass die Kunden nicht im Laden herumirren, sondern die Produkte leicht finden.

____

____

4. Wir stellen die neuen Produkte oft auf speziellen Verkaufsflächen aus.

____

____

5. Man muss immer darauf vorbereitet sein, Fragen von Kunden zu beantworten.

____

____

6. Wir müssen uns auch mit Kundenbeschwerden und Rückvergütungen für Kunden beschäftigen.

____

____

7. Es gibt oft Warteschlangen an den Kassen.

____

____

P **4**
Talking about further training

Look at the information below and ask a partner about the further training he or she gets at work in order to be able to advise customers successfully. Then take turns.

Example:

> What kind of further training do you get at work to help customers?

> I get further training on how to help customers find the products in the shop.

- give advice on special products and services
- handle certain situations
- deal with customers who have special needs

P **5**
Giving a five-minute talk

Prepare and practise a five-minute talk on useful further training at work. Say what kind of training is useful and why you think it is helpful.

WORD BANK

to advise – beraten
to handle sth – mit etw. umgehen, behandeln
service – Service, Dienstleistung
special needs – spezielle Bedürfnisse, Sonderanforderungen

6 Vocabulary work

Underline the right prepositions in the following sentences.

1. I am good **in/at** selling products to customers.
2. Customers should pick a flyer **on/up** before they enter the shop.
3. The flyer can be useful to find and look **after/at** the products you want to buy.
4. We have lots of goods **on/in** offer today.
5. Sometimes sales assistants have to deal **in/with** customer complaints.
6. If products are complicated, you have to explain them **for/to** your customers.

P

7 Project work: Skills that employers look for

Working in sales you have routine work that you should be good at. But there are also special personal skills that are required for the job. What skills are employers looking for?

Step 1: Meet in small groups and search the internet for appropriate answers.

Step 2: List some requirements, and combine them with examples from your daily work.

Example: *an* outgoing *and likeable* personality:
In my job I have to have an outgoing and likeable personality because I want to sell goods. If people like me and I am friendly to them, it is more likely that they will buy something.

List of personal skills that are required

____

____

____

____

____

____

____

____

____

Step 3: Make a poster and present your results to the class.

WORD BANK

appropriate – geeignet, passend
employer – Arbeitgeber
outgoing – kontaktfreudig
personality – Persönlichkeit
required – benötigt
requirement – Bedingung, Voraussetzung
to search – durchsuchen

F | Checking

1 **Sales crossword**

Fill in the right words.

Across:

1. It is sweet and you can eat it.
4. A person who wants to buy something in a shop.
5. You use this book if you want to look up the meaning of a word.

Down:

2. Somebody who works with you at your place of work.
3. You give this person the money when you buy goods in a shop.
6. You pay with it.
7. Another word for apples, bananas, oranges, etc.
8. You can put goods on it.
9. A school where you learn more about your job is a … school.

2 **Odd one out**

Underline the odd word out. Say why it is different from the other words.

In group 1 … is the odd one out because …

1. colleague • trainee • stationery shop • branch manager
2. money • buy • shelf • traineeship
3. shop • supermarket • department store • school
4. England • London • Germany • Turkey

3 **Words with the same meaning**

Find synonyms for these words. (Tip: All of the words are in Unit 1.)

Example: *shop assistant (BE); sales clerk (AE), salesperson (AE), sales assistant (AE)*

1. goods __________
2. hello __________
3. nice to meet you __________
4. retailer __________
5. duty __________

ICH KANN JETZT …

1. mich und andere Personen vorstellen. ○○○
2. sagen, was andere verkaufen und wo sie arbeiten. ○○○
3. sagen, was ich in meinem Job mache. ○○○
4. über meine Verkaufsprodukte Auskunft geben. ○○○
5. mithilfe eines Wörterbuchs richtig übersetzen. ○○○
6. über persönliche Fähigkeiten beim Verkauf von Waren sprechen. ○○○

WORD BANK

odd one out – nicht dazugehören

☺☺☺ = Kann ich schon!
☺☺ = Kann ich ein bisschen!
☺ = Kann ich bald!

G | Phrases: Introducing yourself and others

Meeting people	
Good morning/afternoon/evening, Mrs Smith/Mr Green.	Guten Morgen/Tag/Abend, Frau Smith/Herr Green.
Good morning, Susan/Roberto.	Guten Morgen, Susan/Roberto.
Hi/Hello/Morning, Franziska.	Hallo/Tag/Morgen, Franziska.
I'm Peter./My name is Peter Rex.	Ich heiße Peter./Mein Name ist Peter Rex.
Please call me Tina.	Nennen Sie mich doch Tina.
My surname is Krey, my first name is Silke.	Mein Familienname ist Krey, mein Vorname ist Silke.
How do you do?	Guten Tag.
How are you?/How are you doing?	Wie geht es Ihnen/dir? *(informelle Begrüßung)*
I'm fine, thanks.	Danke, gut.
I'm from Berlin, and I'm 20 years old.	Ich stamme aus Berlin und bin 20 Jahre alt.
I'm British/German.	Ich bin Brite/Britin/Deutsche/r.
May I introduce you to Mrs Rogers?	Darf ich Sie Frau Rogers vorstellen?
May I introduce Mr Stein (to you)?	Darf ich Ihnen Herrn Stein vorstellen?
Pleased/Nice to meet you.	Ich freue mich/Schön Sie kennen zu lernen.
And how are you?	Und (wie geht es) Ihnen/dir?

Talking about your training and your work	
I'm a trainee shop/sales assistant.	Ich mache eine Ausbildung zum Verkäufer/zur Verkäuferin.
I'm training to become a management assistant in retail business/retail management assistant/retailer/shopkeeper/retail salesman/storekeeper.	Ich mache eine Ausbildung zum Einzelhandelskaufmann/zur Einzelhandelskauffrau.
I started my traineeship in August.	Ich begann meine Ausbildung im August.
I work for a retail chain/medium-sized family firm/large supermarket.	Ich arbeite für eine Einzelhandelskette/ein mittelständisches Familienunternehmen/einen großen Supermarkt.
I sell many different goods.	Ich verkaufe viele verschiedene Waren.
I sell fruit/shoes/clothing/DIY products/accessory for mobile phones/household goods/toys/textiles/furniture/stationery/sporting goods/electrical appliances.	Ich verkaufe Obst/Schuhe/Kleidung/Baumarktprodukte/Zubehör für Mobiltelefone/Haushaltswaren/Spielwaren/Textilien/Möbel/Schreibwaren/Sportartikel/Elektroartikel.
Our products are …	Unsere Produkte sind …
I unpack articles and sort them.	Ich packe Artikel aus und sortiere sie.
I must fill up the shelves tomorrow.	Ich muss morgen die Regale auffüllen.
I often tag the products that we sell.	Ich zeichne oft die Produkte aus, die wir verkaufen.
I sometimes serve customers.	Ich bediene manchmal Kunden.

ig54s6

2

NACH DIESER UNIT:

- ✓ kann ich Produkte und ihre Vorteile beschreiben,
- ✓ kann ich Kunden erfolgreich beraten und bedienen,
- ✓ kann ich Redewendungen im Umgang mit Kunden richtig benutzen.

Products and services

A | Describing products

1 Different products

Use adjectives from the box and write a sentence about each product shown in the photos above.

comfortable • delicious • colourful • elegant • healthy • solid • stylish • useful • well-designed

Photo A: ______________________________

Photo B: ______________________________

Photo C: ______________________________

Photo D: ______________________________

R

2 Listening: Visiting a shoe shop ○ → page 130

◎ A 1.4

1. Listen to the text. Which of the following statements are true and which are false?

	true	false
a) Franziska and Susan go to an expensive shoe shop.	☐	☐
b) Susan's friend in Manchester likes to go shopping with her.	☐	☐
c) Susan finds a pair of shoes for Franziska.	☐	☐
d) Franziska finds a pair of shoes that matches her trousers.	☐	☐
e) At the end, Franziska suggests they look for a pair of shoes for Susan.	☐	☐

2. Correct the false statements on an extra sheet of paper.

WORD BANK

colourful – farbenfroh
comfortable – bequem
delicious – köstlich
elegant – elegant
expensive – teuer
healthy – gesund
service – Dienstleistung
solid – stabil
stylish – elegant, stilvoll
trousers – Hose
useful – nützlich
well-designed – gut gestaltet
wheelbarrow – Schubkarre

B | Explaining the benefits of products

R **1** **Reading comprehension**

Read the text and answer the questions in complete sentences.

Visiting a shoe shop

It is 9 o'clock in the morning, and Franziska and Susan are having breakfast. They have just decided to go shopping for shoes. About half an hour later, they are in the city centre.

Franziska: Let's try this shoe shop first. It's more for young people, and the shoes look stylish, too. They're not so expensive, so maybe we can buy two pairs instead of one.

Susan: That sounds good to me! It's great going shopping with you this morning. You know, my friend in Manchester hates going shopping with me. He's only interested in the latest smart phones and tablet computers.

Franziska: Well then, in this case I seem to be a good alternative to him.

Franziska and Susan enter the shop and Susan soon finds a pair of shoes that she likes.

Susan: Look Franziska! These shoes are great, aren't they?

Franziska: Yes, they are. But they look like the wrong size for me, I'm afraid.

Susan: Just try them on and let's see.

Franziska: Hm, you're right, they seem to fit. But do they really suit me?

Susan: They do! And they match your blouse, too.

Franziska: Yes, and they also go well with my trousers. What do you think, will they attract some nice boys at the disco next time?

Susan: Oh come on Franziska! Boys don't look at shoes! But all the girls will hate you!

Franziska: Then I have to have them! Right, now let's look for a pair for you, Susan.

Susan: What about that pair over there?

1. When do Franziska and Susan decide to go shopping?
   9 o'clock
2. What products is Susan's friend in Manchester interested in?
   Latest smartPhone Tablet and Computer
3. Does the pair of shoes fit and suit Franziska?
   Susan say's yes Franziska too
4. Who does Franziska want to attract at the disco?
   nice Boys

WORD BANK

benefit – Nutzen
to change – tauschen, wechseln
to decide – entscheiden
to describe – beschreiben
to enter – betreten
to fit sb – jdm. passen
to go well with – gut passen zu
to guess – (er)raten
latest – neueste/r/s
to match sth – zu etw. passen, zueinanderpassen
size – Größe
to store – (ab)speichern
to suit sb – jdm. stehen

P **2** **Which product is it?**

Make a list of five products and show it to a partner. Then describe a product from your list. Your partner tries to guess which one it is. Then change roles.

→ **PHRASES:** page 29

Example: A: It's small and you can store things from your computer on it.
B: It's a USB stick.

3 What are the people doing?

Write down what the people are doing. Use the present continuous.

1. To tie shoes
2. return card
3. looking at Shoes in the shopwindow
4. Look at Shoes

LANGUAGE BOX **Das *present continuous***

Aussage	**Verneinung**	**Frage**
I am (I'm) helping	I'm not helping	Am I helping?
you are (you're) working	you aren't working	Are you still working here?
he / she / it is (he's / she's / it's) looking	he / she / it isn't looking	Isn't he / she / it looking fantastic?
we are (we're) going	we aren't going	Are we going home now?
you are (you're) working	you aren't working	Are you still working?
they are (they're) sleeping	they aren't sleeping	Are they still sleeping?

Das *present continuous* wird verwendet für

1. Handlungen, die im Moment stattfinden.
   Beispiel: *He **is unpacking** shoes now. They **are starting** their traineeship today.*
2. Handlungen, die zeitlich begrenzt bzw. nicht abgeschlossen sind.
   Beispiel: *She **is living** in England this year. We **are staying** in Bonn this week.*
3. zukünftige Handlungen (mit Zeitbestimmung).
   Beispiel: *I **am serving** customers this afternoon. They **are closing** at 1 p.m.*

Typische Zeitangaben, in Verbindung mit dem *present continuous*, sind: *at the moment* (= im Augenblick), *just* (= gerade), *now* (= jetzt), *still* (= noch immer).

→ **GRAMMAR:** page 150

Üben interaktiv
Present continous
r6vq4g

C | Different ways of serving customers

Distribution channels

There are different ways to sell products to customers. Some companies sell their products online only, others have stationary stores. Some companies have both. In some cases, you can order a product online and collect it in the local stationary store. This is called "click and collect".

A

retail stores (stationary distribution)

B

online stores (online distribution, e-commerce)

C

retail and online stores (multichannel distribution)

WORD BANK

distribution – Vertrieb, Verkauf
channel – Kanal
e-commerce – elektronischer Handel
retail store – Ladengeschäft
to collect – abholen
stationary – stationär, ortsgebunden

1 Reading comprehension: Distribution channels

Read the information on page 20 and the dialogue. Decide which type of distribution channel (A, B or C) it is. Explain your answer.

In a garden centre

Paul from Bristol, England, has just rented a house near Braunschweig and is now in urgent need of a lawnmower to cut the grass in the garden.

Sales assistant:	Good morning, sir, What can I do for you?
Paul:	I am looking for a lawnmower. I just rented a house with a very big garden.
Sales assistant:	I see. First of all you should decide if you prefer a self-propelled lawnmower or a push mower.
Paul:	I'd prefer a self-propelled lawnmower because it takes some time mow my big lawn. Furthermore, it should run on petrol.
Sales assistant:	I would suggest that too. A corded one is not that suitable for a big lawn as it would need a very long cord.
Paul:	Yes, that's right. Please show me a lawnmower with those features.
Sales assistant:	This is our model Time Master 50. The cutting width is 50 cm. It runs on petrol and you can adjust the speed and the cutting height.
Paul:	That sounds perfect. But what does it cost? I can see no price tag on it.
Sales assistant:	If you want to buy it in our shop here you would have to pay 690.
Paul:	Not a real bargain, I must say.
Sales assistant.	Have you got a computer and internet access at home?
Paul:	Yes, I have.
Sales assistant:	To make our online shop better known to the public, we are offering new customers a discount of 10% on an initial order.
Paul:	Now that sounds like a real bargain. But I have a different problem. I work from 8 to 4 and can't receive the delivery personally at home.
Sales assistant:	That is no problem at all. You can order it online and have it delivered to our shop. When your lawnmower arrives we will inform you by phone or e-mail and you can pick it up here.
Paul:	That's really fine. I would appreciate that a lot. Could you give me the address of your online shop then, please?
Sales assistant:	Yes, of course. The online address is: Gartencenterbraunschweig.de. In the search engine on our home page you just key in "Time Master 50" and you will be passed on to the right page automatically. Then, you tick the box of our retail store and the product will be sent to us.
Paul:	OK, I'll do that. Thank you very much for your help.
Sales assistant:	You're welcome. Have a nice day.

2 Partner work

One of you does task a), the other one does task b).

a) Explain the features of the lawnmower, model Time Master 50.

b) Explain what the customer has to do to get the model delivered to the shop.

WORD BANK

garden centre – Gartencenter
to rent – mieten
to be in urgent need – dringend benötigen
lawnmower – Rasenmäher
self-propelled – mit Eigenantrieb
to mow – mähen
to run on sth – betrieben werden mit etw.
cord – Kabel
corded – mit Kabel
features – Eigenschaften
cutting width – Schnittbreite
to adjust – anpassen
cutting height – Schnitthöhe
price tag – Preisschild
bargain – Schnäppchen
discount – Preisnachlass
initial order – Erstauftrag
search engine – Suchmaschine
to key in – eingeben
to be passed on – weitergeleitet werden

D | Serving customers successfully

R **1** **Listening: Serving customers**

◎ A 1.5 Listen to the three conversations. Then match the dialogues to the photos. Write the correct number in the box next to the photo.

A ☐

B ☐

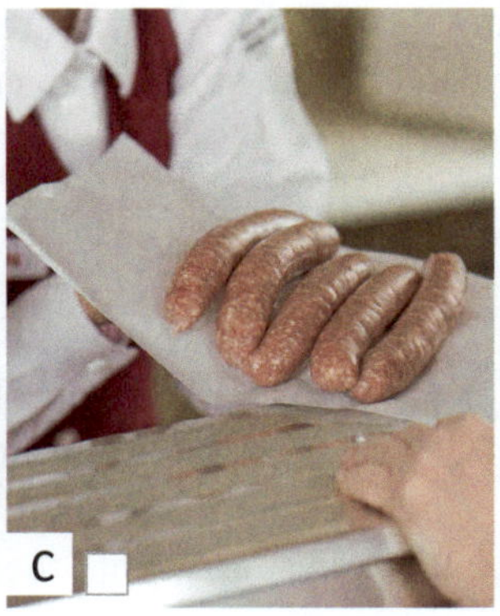
C ☐

WORD BANK

acceptable – akzeptabel
certainly – sicherlich
change – Wechselgeld
drill – Bohrmaschine
to miss – fehlen, vermissen
of course – selbstverständlich
receipt – Quittung, Kassenzettel
sausage – Würstchen
successfully – erfolgreich

2 **Reading comprehension** ○ → page 131

Answer the questions on the following text on a separate piece of paper

1. What product does Dennis want to buy?
2. What must be special about the product he is interested in?
3. Whydoesn‘t he buy the product that the assistant shows him first?
4. What is special about the product he finally buys?

In a home entertainment shop

Dennis: Excuse me. Do you speak English?
Peter: Good morning, sir. Yes, I do. Can I help you?
Dennis: Perhaps. I'm looking for a tablet computer. They seem to be cheaper here than in Britain.
Peter: I don't know about the prices in Britain, but we've got some great tablets on offer, right over there. What exactly are you looking for?
Dennis: One that's not too heavy, runs fast and has lots of connectivity options , like a USB connection and room for a small memory card.
Peter: No problem, Sir. Have a look at this one here. It's on special offer and it has WiFi internet access and 3G.
Dennis: Well, actually I only need WiFi. I don't want a contract with a mobile service provider. I just need the tablet for use at home. I've got my smart phone for when I'm on the move.
Peter: I see. Let me show you this one then. It's a bit smaller but it has a fast processor , so films run without jerking. But it is a bit more expensive, I'm afraid.
Dennis: Actually, that sounds great. It's the quality that counts!
Peter: You're so right. And as you can see it has a camera, a slot for a memory card and a port for a USB cable.
Dennis: Perfect! I'll take it.
Peter: Is there anything else I can do for you?
Dennis: Not right now, sir. Thanks very much for your help.
Peter: You're welcome. You can pay at the cash desk right over there. We hope to see you again soon, sir.
[At the cash desk]
Cashier: That's 250 euros, please.
Dennis: Here you are.
Cashier: Thank you. Here's your change and your receipt.

WORD BANK

actually – eigentlich, tatsächlich
connection – Anschluss
connectivity – Netzwerkfähigkeit
to have room for – Platz haben für
I'm afraid – leider
to make a contract – einen Vertrag abschließen
memory card – Speicherkarte
mobile service provider – Mobilfunkanbieter
on the move – unterwegs
slot – Steckplatz
special offer – Sonderangebot
WiFi internet access – drahtloser Internetzugang
without jerking – ohne Ruckeln
You're welcome. – Bitte schön, gern geschehen.

3 Partner work

Read the intercultural box. Underline the phrases in the text on page 22 that are important for serving a customer. Compare your findings with your partner.

INTERCULTURAL BOX **Kunden bedienen**

Es ist wichtig, Kunden freundlich und höflich anzusprechen. Manche englischen Redewendungen klingen für Deutsche übertrieben höflich oder werden im Deutschen nicht verwendet. Dennoch sollten Sie diese beherrschen.

1. **Begrüßung**
   "Good morning / afternoon / evening, Sir / Madam. / Excuse me, Sir / Madam. Can I help you? / Is there anything I can do for you? / Are you being served, Sir / Madam? / How can I help you?"
2. **Redewendungen im Laufe des Kundengesprächs**
   "Are you interested in ...? / Would you like to ...? / Have a look at ... / Let me show you ... / What about ...? / Anything else, Sir / Madam?"
3. **Verabschiedung des Kunden**
   - Nach einem Verkaufsgespräch: Im Allgemeinen verabschiedet sich der Kunde / die Kundin mit *"Thank you for your help."* Darauf antworten Sie mit *"You're welcome."*. Sollte der Kunde / die Kundin nichts sagen, beenden Sie mit *"We hope to see you again soon, Sir / Madam."* das Gespräch.
   - An der Kasse nach dem Bezahlen: *"Here you are, Sir / Madam. Your* change *and your* receipt. *Thank you very much for shopping with us. Have a nice day."*

WORD BANK

change – Wechselgeld
receipt – Beleg, Kassenzettel

WORD BANK

available – verfügbar
clothing line – Modelinie
conventionally made – herkömmlich gefertigt
ethically made – nach ethischen Maßstäben hergestellt
factory-made – industriell gefertigt
grower – Erzeuger/in, Bauer / Bäuerin
guarantee – Garantie
labour standard – Arbeitsnorm
to launch – einführen, starten
to trade – handeln

I/P

4 Role play: Sales talk

Work with a partner. Partner A is a customer who wants to buy a product (for example, a television or a car). Partner B is a shop assistant. Use the dialogue on page 22 and change it where necessary. Practise the dialogue and then act it out in class.

→ **PHRASES:** page 29

V1 Fairtrade clothing line

BBC Worldwide Learning

Before watching

1. What are Fairtrade products? How are they different from conventionally produced products? Give some examples.
2. Do you buy Fairtrade products? Why, or why not?

While watching

3. Decide whether the following statements are true or false.

	true	false
a) The Fairtrade label is a guarantee that growers in developing countries are getting a fair wage.	☐	☐
b) Fairtrade clothing is now available at Top Shop in Britain.	☐	☐
c) Fairtrade clothes are cheaper than factory-made clothing.	☐	☐
d) Shopper 1 can imagine buying something that is ethically made and traded.	☐	☐
e) Shopper 2 is more interested in the fashion than in the price.	☐	☐

After watching

4. Find out what Fairtrade products are sold at your local supermarket. Make a list of the products and where they come from. Then present your findings in class.

E | Products at a DIY store

P **1** **At a DIY store**

Look at the picture and write down what you can see. Use the words from the box and write complete sentences. Then compare your answer with your partner's. Complete or change your sentences if necessary.

> sales assistant • customer • to paint a wall • paint roller • to demonstrate

____

____

____

____

____

____

P **2** **What do you think?**

Why do people go to a DIY store? Write at least two sentences.

____

____

____

3 **Have you ever been to a DIY store?**

Look at the following two sentences and complete the sentence that applies to you.

1. I have already been to a DIY store because ______________________

   ______________________.

2. I have never been to a DIY store so far because ______________________

   ______________________.

R/P **4** **Internet research: Shopping at a DIY store**

Find ten different products you can buy at a DIY store and write them down. Then explain the usage of five of the products to your partner. Use suitable adjectives. Then take turns.

> A drill is a convenient/comfortable tool to drill a hole in a wall.

____________	____________
____________	____________
____________	____________
____________	____________
____________	____________

→ **PHRASES:** page 29

WORD BANK

convenient – zweckmäßig, praktisch
to demonstrate – zeigen
DIY store – Heimwerkermarkt, Baumarkt
to drill – bohren
hole – Loch
to paint – streichen
paint roller – Farbroller
to take turns – sich abwechseln
tool – Werkzeug
usuage – Gebrauch

R 5 Listening: Shopping at a DIY store

A 1.6

Listen to the conversation. Say whether the following statements are true or false, and correct the false statements.

1. Susan wants to go to a DIY store to buy a bathroom cabinet.

   ____

2. She immediately sees a bathroom cabinet that she likes and buys it.

   ____

3. The assistant tells her that no extra material is supplied with the product.

   ____

4. Susan finally buys a bathroom cabinet and has to pay €118.35.

   ____

R/P 6 Project work: Explaining how to hang up a bathroom cabinet

You are doing a work placement at a DIY store in Bochum. An open day is taking place on Sunday next week and you have been given the job of showing customers how to hang up a bathroom cabinet successfully with all the tools needed. Do the following tasks to prepare yourself for this special job.

Step 1: Go on the internet and enter "How to hang a bathroom cabinet" in a search machine. Look for the "Wickes" entry, which is a British DIY store, and watch the video.

Step 2: Look at the following notes on how to hang up the bathroom cabinet. Use the word bank and a dictionary for help. Then put the notes into the right order.

☐ a) Place the cabinet on the wall so that the cabinet is centred on it.
☐ b) Use a spirit level to make sure that the cabinet is levelled.
☐ c) Mark the position on the wall where you want to hang up the bathroom cabinet with a tape measure.
☐ d) Mark the position on the cabinet with a pencil.
☐ e) Now measure the width of the cabinet and find its centre point.
☐ f) Take a cable detector to make sure that you do not hit any electrical wiring.
☐ g) In order to have the bathroom cabinet centred above the basin, you have to use a tape measure to measure the length of the sink to find the centre point.
☐ h) Then hang up the bathroom cabinet by screwing it on the wall with the help of a screwdriver.
☐ i) Replace the doors on the bathroom cabinet and screw them on.
☐ j) Mark the position on the wall.
☐ k) Now, start drilling the holes into the wall.
☐ l) Take a spirit level and place it against the mark on the wall.
☐ m) Use a pencil to mark the bracket holes on the wall.
☐ n) Then put the wall plugs in by using a hammer.

Step 3: Now explain the whole procedure to your partner without looking at your notes. Take turns and correct one another, if necessary.

Step 4: Check your explanation by watching the video again.

WORD BANK

bracket hole – Loch für die Halterung
to centre – zentrieren
centre point – Mittelpunkt
explanation – Erklärung
levelled – *(hier:)* waagerecht
to measure – messen
open day – Tag der offenen Tür
procedure – Ablauf, Verfahren
to screw – (an)schrauben
screwdriver – Schraubenzieher
spirit level – Wasserwaage
tape measure – Maßband, Metermaß
width – Breite, Weite

WORD BANK

bathroom cabinet – Badezimmerschrank
to brighten up – aufhellen
to get sth done – etwas schaffen
to hang sth up – etwas aufhängen
to replace – ersetzen
plasterboard screw – Rigipsschraube
to be supplied with – ge-/beliefert werden mit
to suppose – annehmen, vermuten
wall plug – Wanddübel
to worry – sich Sorgen machen

F | Shopping for clothes

1 Confusing words

Look at the photos and the Language box below. Then complete the speech bubbles with the right forms of 'fit', 'suit' or 'match'.

What colour ______________ me best? Pink or blue? I guess both pink and blue ______________ me. But will the dresses also ______________? I'll have to try them on.

1

2

This tie ______________ this shirt perfectly, don't you think?

Yes, but I think purple doesn't really ______________ me and it also doesn't ______________ my new brown jacket.

This pair of jeans is quite tight. I'm not sure they ______________ me anymore. What a pity because they really ______________ this white shirt.

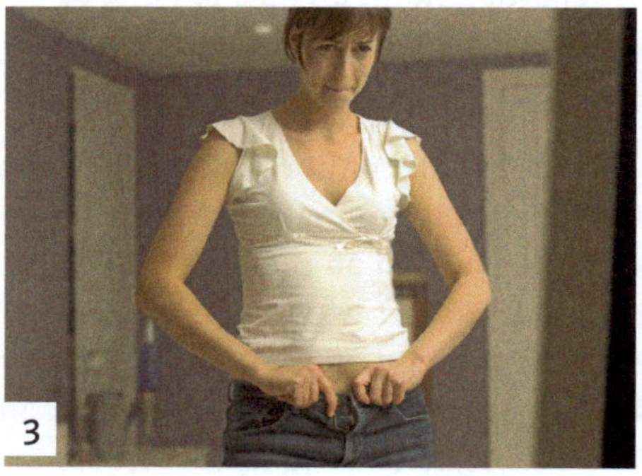
3

LANGUAGE BOX ***Fit, suit* und *match***

Die Verben *fit*, *suit* und *match* werden leicht verwechselt: *fit* benutzt man, wenn es um die passende Größe geht; *suit*, wenn man ausdrücken möchte, ob jemandem etwas steht; *match*, wenn es darum geht, ob etwas zu etwas anderem passt.

Beispiele: *This dress **fits** me best in size 40.*
*I think green and blue **suit** you very well.*
The pink tie *doesn't **match** the green shirt.*

2 Say it in English

Put the following sentences into English.

1. Diese Jeans passt mir nicht sehr gut.

____

2. Ich finde, dass mir diese Bluse nicht gut steht.

____

WORD BANK

tie – Krawatte
tight – eng
what a pity – wie schade

3. Der blaue Rock passt zu den weißen Schuhen, aber nicht zu den schwarzen.

4. Das Kleid mit dem blau-gelben Muster steht dir wirklich gut.

5. Das rote T-Shirt steht ihm und es passt ihm auch.

P/I **3** **Role play: Advising customers**

Look at the following information and take the roles of a shop assistant and a customer. Prepare a dialogue and act it out with your partner. Then change roles and choose another piece of clothing.

→ **PHRASES:** page 29

Partner A: Shop assistant	**Partner B: Customer**
Begrüßen Sie die Kundin und fragen Sie, ob Sie helfen können.	Sagen Sie, dass Sie zu Ihrer blauen Hose eine passende Jacke in Größe 38 suchen.
Zeigen Sie der Kundin passende Jacken in verschiedenen Farben und fragen Sie, welche Farbe die Kundin persönlich bevorzugt.	Nennen Sie eine der Farben, die Ihnen gezeigt wurden und sagen Sie, dass Sie diese Jacke gerne anprobieren möchten.
Sagen Sie, dass sie die Jacke in der Umkleidekabine (*fitting room*) anprobieren kann.	Sagen Sie, dass die Jacke leider nicht passt und Sie sie gerne in Größe 40 anprobieren würden.
Teilen Sie der Kundin mit, dass sie sich einen Moment gedulden soll und geben Sie ihr die neue Größe.	Teilen Sie dem/der Verkäufer/in mit, dass die Jacke jetzt passt und Sie sie gerne kaufen wollen.
Drücken Sie Ihre Freude aus, dass Sie helfen konnten und verabschieden Sie sich.	Bedanken Sie sich und verabschieden Sie sich ebenfalls.

WORD BANK

fitting room – Umkleidekabine

G | Checking

WORD BANK

to draw – zeichnen
to enjoy – genießen

1 Say it in English

Put the sentences into English.

1. Werden Sie schon bedient?
   Are you being served ?
2. Wonach suchen Sie?
   For what are you looking for ?
3. Wie wäre es mit diesem Produkt?
   What about this product ?
4. Ich wünsche Ihnen einen schönen Tag.
   Have a nice day

2 Talking to customers

Match the phrases 1.–5. with the correct answers a)–e). Draw lines.

1. Here you are. e)	a) You're welcome.
2. Good morning, Sir. d)	b) Yes, of course.
3. Could you help me, please? b)	c) A nice blouse for the summer.
4. What product are you interested in? c)	d) Hello.
5. Thank you for your help. a)	e) Thank you.

3 Writing an e-mail

Use the verbs in the box and complete the sentences in the present continuous.

drink • eat • enjoy • go (2x) • have (2x) • sing • sit • take • visit • write

Subject: Hi from Dresden!

Dear David,

How are you? I [1] writing you from my trip to Dresden.
I [2] having a wonderful time here. At the moment I [3] ~~eat~~ am eating breakfast with my cousin Fatima. We [4] have bread with honey and we [5] are drinking tea. The weather is fantastic, so we [6] are sitting in the garden. The birds [7] are singing and we [8] are enjoying ourselves.
Soon we [9] are going to town. In the afternoon my grandmother [10] visiting us. At the moment my uncle [11] is taking her to the doctor.
And in the evening we [12] are going to the cinema.
Hope to hear from you soon.
Love, Ayşe

ICH KANN JETZT …

1. Produkte und ihre Vorteile beschreiben. ○ ○ ○
2. Kunden begrüßen und ihnen Hilfe anbieten. ○ ○ ○
3. den Kunden bei der Auswahl von Produkten helfen. ○ ○ ○
4. die Kunden richtig verabschieden. ☺ ○ ○

☺☺☺ = Kann ich schon!
☺☺ = Kann ich ein bisschen!
☺ = Kann ich bald!

H | Phrases: Serving customers

To greet customers	
Hello.	Hallo.
Good morning/afternoon/evening, Sir/Madam.	Guten Morgen/Tag/Abend.
Nice to see you (again), Sir/Madam.	Schön Sie (wieder) zu sehen.

To offer help	
Excuse me, Sir/Madam.	Entschuldigen Sie.
Are you being served, Sir/Madam?	Werden Sie schon bedient?
Can I help you?	Kann ich Ihnen helfen?
What can I do for you?	Was kann ich für Sie tun?
How can I help you?	Wie kann ich Ihnen helfen?
Is there anything I can do for you?	Kann ich Ihnen behilflich sein?
Would you like to look around first, Sir/Madam?	Möchten Sie sich erst selbst umsehen?
Let me know if you need any help.	Lassen Sie (es) mich wissen, wenn Sie Hilfe benötigen.

To help customers find a product	
What exactly are you looking for?	Wonach suchen Sie genau?
What do you need the product for?	Wofür brauchen Sie das Produkt?
What about this product?	Wie wäre es mit diesem Produkt?
Have a (closer) look at this product.	Sehen Sie sich dieses Produkt mal (genauer) an.
Let me show you how it works.	Lassen Sie mich Ihnen zeigen, wie es funktioniert.
How much money do you want to spend on the product?	Wieviel Geld möchten Sie für das Produkt ausgeben?

To show the benefits of a product	
The product is comfortable/delicious/fashionable/healthy/reliable/portable/stylish/well-designed.	Das Produkt ist bequem/köstlich/modisch/gesund/zuverlässig/tragbar/stilvoll/gut gestaltet.
The product helps you to *(+ infinitive)* …	Das Produkt hilft Ihnen …
It allows you to/enables you to …	Es erlaubt/gestattet Ihnen …
It is made of …	Es ist hergestellt aus …
It was made in …	Es wurde in … hergestellt.
It is/can be used for *(+ -ing-form)* …	Es wird/kann verwendet werden für …

To close a sales talk	
Is there anything else I can do for you?	Gibt es noch etwas, das ich für Sie tun kann?
You're welcome.	Bitte schön, gern geschehen.
We hope to see you again soon, Sir/Madam.	Wir hoffen, Sie bald wiederzusehen.
Here you are, Sir/Madam. Your change and your receipt.	Bitte schön. Ihr Wechselgeld und Ihre Quittung.
Thank you for shopping with us.	Vielen Dank für Ihren Einkauf.
Have a nice day.	Ich wünsche Ihnen noch einen schönen Tag.

3

NACH DIESER UNIT:

- √ kann ich Kundentypen und deren Einkaufsgewohnheiten unterscheiden,
- √ kann ich mich auf verschiedene Kundengruppen einstellen,
- √ kann ich typische Merkmale verschiedener Geschäfte nennen,
- √ kann ich Verbraucherrechte verstehen.

A

B

C

D

Customers

A | Types of customers and their shopping habits

R **1** **Listening: Different types of customers**

A 1.7 Listen to the description of different types of customers. Then look at the photos above and write down what type of customer they show.

1. ☐ customer of habit
2. ☐ green customer
3. ☐ hectic customer
4. ☐ sceptical customer

2 **Identify yourself**

What type of customer are you? Write two sentences about yourself.

Start like this: *I'm a … customer because …*

____

____

____

P **3** **Talk to each other**

Ask a partner what type of customer he / she is. Then present him / her in class.

> Murat is a green customer because …

WORD BANK

habit – Gewohnheit
to identify – identifizieren, erkennen

WORD BANK

behaviour – Verhalten
carefully – sorgfältig
to distinguish – unterscheiden
environmentally friendly – umweltfreundlich
hectic – hektisch
in a hurry – in Eile
to leave – (ver)lassen
packaging – Verpackung
sceptical – skeptisch, kritisch
to take one's time – sich Zeit nehmen

B | Keeping customers satisfied

R **1** **Adapting to different customers**

Decide how you would react in the following situations and tick (✓) the right box. Then read the Intercultural box below and check your answers.

Situation 1

A customer always looks at his watch and runs through the shop. He takes the things he needs and puts them into his trolley. He seems to know what he wants.

I should
- ☐ a) do nothing.
- ☐ b) ask, "Can I help you, Sir/Madam?"
- ☐ c) say, "Nice to see you, Sir/Madam."

Situation 2

A couple looks at different plants. They seem to be discussing what they should buy. They haven't made eye contact with you yet.

I should
- ☐ a) do nothing.
- ☐ b) greet the couple and ask, "Excuse me, is there anything I can do for you?"
- ☐ c) greet the customers.

Situation 3

A customer looks at products made of natural materials. She seems to be comparing different clothes.

I should
- ☐ a) ask, "Are you interested in more information about the products?" Then I should tell her what the products are made of.
- ☐ b) say, "Let me know if you need any help."
- ☐ c) do nothing.

Situation 4

A disabled man in a wheelchair is looking at products that are high up on a shelf.

I should
- ☐ a) ignore the customer.
- ☐ b) ask the customer what products he is interested in, get them for him and then go away.
- ☐ c) ask the customer what products he is interested in, get them for him and stay with him to answer questions and put the products the customer does not want to buy back on the shelf.

INTERCULTURAL BOX **Kundentypen und -gruppen**

Im Alltag müssen wir uns auf unterschiedliches Kundenverhalten einstellen, um im Verkauf erfolgreich zu sein. Einen Eindruck, ob und wie wir Kunden ansprechen sollten, gewinnen wir durch Beobachtung. Dabei können wir die folgenden Kundengruppen mit ihren jeweiligen Besonderheiten voneinander unterscheiden:
- **Ausländische Kunden** sprechen zum Teil kein oder wenig Deutsch und suchen evtl. Produkte, die sie aus ihrer Heimat kennen. Wichtig ist, Verständnis zu zeigen, langsam und in kurzen Sätzen zu sprechen und ggf. den Gebrauch der Ware zu demonstrieren.
- **Kindern** sollte ein positives Einkaufserlebnis vermittelt werden. Wir sollten sie grüßen und uns Zeit für sie nehmen. Oft hilft es auch, sie direkt anzusprechen.
- **Senioren** sind eine Kundengruppe, die zahlenmäßig zunimmt. Sie verfügen oftmals über ein gesichertes Einkommen und erhebliche Ersparnisse. Gelegentlich ist ihr Sehvermögen oder ihre Hörfähigkeit eingeschränkt. Sich mit ihnen zu unterhalten erfordert Einfühlungsvermögen und Geduld.
- Bei **behinderten Kunden** sind Fingerspitzengefühl und ein freundlicher Umgang gefragt. Man sollte stets nachfragen, wenn man den Eindruck hat, dass der Kunde auf Hilfe angewiesen sein könnte, ohne aber aufdringlich zu sein.

WORD BANK

to adapt to – (sich) anpassen an
to compare – vergleichen
couple – Paar, Pärchen
disabled – behindert
to keep sb satisfied – jdn. zufrieden stellen
to make eye contact with sb – Blickkontakt mit jdm. aufnehmen
natural – *(hier:)* naturbelassen
plant – Pflanze
trolley – Einkaufswagen
wheelchair – Rollstuhl

R/I **2** **Listening: Helping customers**
A 1.8 Read and listen to the dialogues between different customers and shop assistants. Then choose one dialogue and practise it with a partner.

→ **PHRASES:** page 41

Dialogue 1: A tourist from Greece

Ifigenia, a foreign customer from Greece, has just entered a sports and leisure shop in Leipzig.

Assistant: Guten Tag, wie kann ich Ihnen behilflich sein?
Customer: Good morning. I'm afraid my German is not very good. I'm from Greece. Do you speak English?
Assistant: No problem, Madam. How can I help you?
Customer: I'm looking for a tracksuit for my sister back home.
Assistant: I see, Madam. Come with me, please. I'll show you some. They're over there.
Customer: That's very kind of you. Thank you.

Ifigenia and the shop assistant have just arrived at the rack with a range of tracksuits.

Assistant: Where will she be wearing the tracksuit most: indoors or outdoors?
Customer: Oh, she loves walking and running outdoors before she starts work in the morning.
Assistant: OK, Madam. Well, we've got a wide variety of different tracksuits, as you can see. Do you know her size?
Customer: Hmm, let me see. I wrote it down. … It's 36.
Assistant: OK, you can choose one from these tracksuits here.
Customer: Oh, I really like these grey ones. I'll take two of them in size 36 – one for me and one for my sister. Thank you very much for your help.
Assistant: You're welcome, Madam. Have a nice day.

Dialogue 2: Shopping with kids

A family is looking for a picture frame in a big photographic shop. The kids are getting on their parents' nerves. The shop assistant hears them talking in English.

Assistant: Sorry to disturb you. Can I help you?
Man: Thank you, but we don't need any help.
Assistant: All right. I'd like to tell you that we have a special kids' zone. We take care of your children there while you're doing your shopping.
Man: Well, that's interesting. Where is it?
Assistant: It's near the entrance, Sir. If you wish, I can take your children there. You can pick them up when you've finished your shopping.
Woman: That's great. Let's do that. Then we'll have time for our shopping.

Dialogue 3: An elderly couple from England

An elderly couple is comparing prices of different packages of butter. They are tourists from an English-speaking country.

Assistant: Good morning. Do you need any help?
Woman: Yes, I'm afraid we do. We can't really read the prices. They're so small.
Assistant: No problem, Madam. I can read them out to you. This package costs 1 euro and this one is 2 euros. Is there anything else I can do for you?
Man: Pardon?
Assistant: Is there anything else I can do for you?
Man: No, thank you. You were very helpful.

WORD BANK

to choose – wählen
to disturb – stören
to finish – beenden
to get on sb's nerves – jdm. auf die Nerven gehen
Greece – Griechenland
kids' zone – Kinderbereich
kind – freundlich
outdoors – draußen, im Freien
over there – dort drüben
to pick sb up – jdn. abholen
picture frame – Bilderrahmen
photographic shop – Fotogeschäft
rack – Regal
a range of – eine Reihe von, zahlreiche
to read out – vorlesen
sports and leisure shop – Sport- und Freizeitgeschäft
to take care of – aufpassen auf
tracksuit – Trainingsanzug
to wear – tragen
wide variety of – große Auswahl/Vielfalt an

C | Different types of shops

R **1** ◎ A 1.9

Listening: Types of shops

Look at the photos and describe what you see. Then listen to the text and put the pictures in the right order. Write the correct number in the box next to the photo.

A ☐

C ☐

B ☐

R **2** ◎ A 1.9

Advantages of different shops ○ → page 131

Listen again. Then put the words in the correct order and add the name of the right type of shop.

Example: a • where • near • live • is • people • ?
→ *A corner* shop *is near where people live.*

1. at • people • old • often • products • buy • a • ?

____

2. can • cheap • you • buy • at • food • a • ?

____

3. designs • has • a • in • products • different • ?

____

4. are • help • you • there • assistants • at • shop • can • who • you • ?

____

P **3**

Which shops do you like?

Ask three people in your class about the type of shop they like best and why they go there. Take notes and present your results in class.

Name	Type of shop	Reasons

WORD BANK

to add – hinzufügen
advantage – Vorteil
corner shop – (kleines) Lebensmittelgeschäft
result – Ergebnis

WORD BANK ◎

to collect – (ein)sammeln
to count – zählen
design – Gestaltung
discounter – Billigsupermarkt
to earn – verdienen
far away – weit weg
owner – Besitzer/in
shop fittings – Ladenausstattung
specialist shop – Fachgeschäft

D | Future plans

R **1** **Your life in ten years**

You are taking part in a survey called "How do you see your life in ten years?"
Read the statements and tick (✓) the right answer.

Statements	Yes, I will.	No, I won't.	I don't know.
1. I will have lots of money.	☐	☐	☐
2. I will have a good job.	☐	☐	☐
3. I will live in another country.	☐	☐	☐
4. I will have a nice car.	☐	☐	☐
5. I will own a house.	☐	☐	☐
6. I will be married.	☐	☐	☐

P **2** **Talking about the future**

Work in groups. Say how you see your life in ten years and why.

I think I will …

I don't think I will …

I don't know …

P **3** **Plans for the weekend**

Talk to a partner about his / her plans for the next weekend.

Example: A: What are you planning to do on Friday?
B: I think I'm going to visit some friends from school.

4 **Future tenses**

Underline the correct answer.

1. I hope that he **will / is going to** buy a new blue-ray disc.
2. We **will / are going to** meet at school every Monday.
3. They think she **will / is going to** sell her old car.
4. I know you **will / are going to** be on holiday next month.

LANGUAGE BOX **Das Futur**

Will-future

Will und *won't* bleiben in allen Personen unverändert.

I will ('ll) visit	I won't visit
he / she / it will ('ll) visit	he / she / it won't visit
we / you / they will ('ll) visit	we / you / they won't visit

Das *will-future* wird verwendet, um Tatsachen, Vorhersagen und Vermutungen zu äußern.

Beispiel: *In 2020 **I'll be** 30 years old. I think **I'll have** a good job then.*

Going to-future

Diese Zeitform wird mit *to be* + *going to* + Verb (im Infinitiv) gebildet. Für Verneinungen benutzt man die Verneinungsformen von *to be*.

I'm going to visit	I'm not going to visit
he / she / it's going to visit	he / she / it isn't going to visit
we / you / they're going to visit	we / you / they aren't going to visit

Mit dem *going-future* spricht man über Pläne und Vorhaben.

Beispiel: *What are you **going to do** next Sunday? **I'm going to visit** a friend.*

→ **GRAMMAR:** page 153

Üben interaktiv
Das Futur
nx3mf6

WORD BANK

married – verheiratet
to own – besitzen
survey – Umfrage, Befragung
to take part – teilnehmen

R **5** **Reading comprehension** ○ → page 132

Read the text and sum up what it says about future shopping. Write in your exercise book.

Future visions

In the future many things will change. People already buy lots of things on the internet today. In the future we will buy even more. Shops will perhaps be only showrooms where we can see things and then order them online later at home. There will be supermarkets in the future, but they will be different. A computer screen on your trolley will show you where things are. You will put an electronic card in the computer on the trolley and it will give you a list of the things which you often buy. The computer will also contact your fridge at home and the fridge will inform you, "You need milk, sugar and eggs." There will not be any shop assistant anymore. Instead we will have electronic sales assistants. You ask a computer a question and it will give you an answer on the computer screen.

WORD BANK

development – Entwicklung
disadvantage – Nachteil
fridge – Kühlschrank
screen – Bildschirm
showroom – Ausstellungsraum
taste – Geschmack
to translate – übersetzen
valuable – wertvoll
word for word – wortwörtlich

WORD BANK ◎

daily requirement – Tagesbedarf
to develop – *(hier:)* ausbilden
to harvest – ernten
organic – organisch, biologisch
pesticide – Pflanzenschutzmittel
skin – *(hier:)* Schale
to treat – behandeln

P **6** **Discussion: Shopping in the future** ●

Discuss the advantages and disadvantages of the developments described in the text above. How do you think shopping will be in the future? Take notes and present your ideas in class.

SKILLS **Mediation**

'Mediation' means that you say in another language what a text is about.
It does not mean that you translate word for word!

Mediation: English → German
Explain in German what the text above says about shopping in the future.
Use your exercise book.

V2 Oranges: Healthy and full of vitamins

As a sales assistant working in the fruit section of a big supermarket, you have been asked by your boss to watch the following video. It contains lots of valuable information you can use to advise customers effectively.

Before watching

1. What sorts of oranges do you know of and how different are they in taste and look?

While watching

2. Watch the video and answer the following questions.
   a) Why is it a good thing to harvest oranges later?
   b) How can you and the customer distinguish between the good and the bad fruit?
   c) Why should juices and health drinks be made with organic oranges?
   d) How many oranges should you eat to meet your daily requirement for vitamin C?

After watching

3. What sorts of oranges and other fruit do you buy? Give reasons for your answer.

E | The importance of different types of customer

R **1** **Listening: Talking about different types of customer**

A 1.10 Listen to the conversation and then complete the sentences correctly.

1. You always have to be friendly to a customer because the customer is …

   ____

   ____.

2. Loyal customers are very important to sales assistants because …

   ____

   ____.

3. Wandering customers are those customers who …

   ____

   ____.

4. They make up the smallest percentage of sales in general. So, the time spent with them …

   ____

   ____.

5. Sales assistants like impulse shoppers very much as they …

   ____

   ____.

R **2** **Checking**

Now compare your answers with your partner. Then read the text and correct your answers, if necessary.

Talking about different types of customers

In the canteen Olivia gets into a conversation with Patrick, an intern from their branch in Bristol. Patrick has a lot of questions about different types of customers and wants to know the different ways sales assistants deal with them and why.

Patrick: It's good to have a short break!

Olivia: You're right. Sometimes, there are customers who really get on my nerves. But the customer is always right, you know. You have to be friendly all the time, even if they're not.

Patrick: Yes, that's true. But there are different types of customers. So, you don't have to give everyone the same attention, right?

Olivia: Yes, regular customers, for example, make up more than 50% of our sales. So they are very important to us and we have to give them special attention. The people I don't like are the wandering customers.

Patrick: "Wandering customers"? What do you mean by that?

Olivia: I mean the ones who have no specific need or desire in mind when they come into the store. They just want to look around and they make up the smallest percentage of sales in general.

Patrick: But they might tell others about your shop.

Olivia: OK, that's true, but the time spent with them needs to be minimized.

WORD BANK

branch – Filiale
desire – Wunsch
give sb attention – jdm. Aufmerksamkeit schenken
importance – Wichtigkeit, Bedeutung
to make up – *(hier:)* ausmachen
need – Bedarf, Bedürfnis

Patrick: And which type of customer do you like most?
Olivia: The impulse shoppers, definitely!
Patrick: And why is that?
Olivia: They often need our help and they like to be served. In the end, you are always happy if you can convince them to buy a special product.
Patrick: They sound interesting. Oh well, our break's over already. Right, I'm going to look for some of those impulse customers now.
Olivia: OK, then, let's go and try to find some.

P **3** **Internet research: The customer's needs and expectations**

In order to increase your sales, you have to identify the customer's needs and expectations. There are several things you can do to be more successful.

Step 1: Work in small groups and write down your ideas.

Example: *Give customers your full attention.*

____

____

____

____

____

Step 2: Discuss your ideas and complete them by searching the internet.

Step 3: Present your results to the class.

R/P **4** **Tips for giving a presentation**

Read the following text about giving presentations and make a list of tips. Use a dictionary if necessary and add your own ideas, too. Write in your exercise book.

How to make a presentation

Structure your presentation
Make sure your presentation has a clear structure: introduction, main body and conclusion.

Include visual aids
Use visual aids (for example, pictures, graphs, flowcharts) to underline what you are saying.

Use note cards
If you're allowed to use notes or an outline, then put the main points on small note cards. Write on each card only one main point and a few supporting points. Don't write complete sentences on the cards because they're hard to read and make you lose eye contact with the audience.

Think of your audience
Always remember your audience. Is the audience a group of students? Your class? Colleagues at work? Think about which aspects your audience might find interesting and include them.

Speak slowly and clearly
Speakers often speak too fast – this happens to most of us when we're nervous. Try to avoid this because it will make your presentation difficult to understand. You should also speak loudly and clearly so that your audience can hear you. Make short pauses, too. Practise your presentation with someone you know and ask them to check this aspect.

Make eye contact
Eye contact helps your audience to listen to you. It also makes you look more confident. If you are speaking to a smaller group, try to make eye contact with each person at least once during your presentation. If you feel nervous about speaking in front of the class, you can look at something just behind the people in the audience (for example, a clock on the wall).

WORD BANK

audience – Publikum, Zuhörer
to avoid – vermeiden
conclusion – Abschluss, Schlussfolgerung
confident – selbstbewusst
to convince – überzeugen
definitely – eindeutig, auf jeden Fall
expectation – Erwartung
graph – Diagramm, Grafik
impulse shopper – Impulskäufer/in
to increase – steigern, erhöhen
introduction – Einleitung
main body – Hauptteil
visual aid – visuelles Hilfsmittel

R/P **5**
Useful phrases for presentations

Look at the phrases and put them in the correct order. Say in which part of a presentation you would use them. Add at least three more phrases and match them to the correct part.

Order	Sentences	Intro-duction	Main body	Con-clusion
☐	Another important aspect is …	☐	☐	☐
☐	First, I would like to …	☐	☐	☐
☐	In conclusion …	☐	☐	☐
☐	Finally, I'd like to say something about …	☐	☐	☐
☐	This brings me to my third point …	☐	☐	☐
☐	I'd like to start/begin by …	☐	☐	☐
☐		☐	☐	☐
☐		☐	☐	☐
☐		☐	☐	☐
☐		☐	☐	☐

P **6**
Project work: Different types of customers

Step 1: Get together in a group with people who are working in the same branch, if possible. Prepare a presentation on different types of customers who come to your shop. Think about the following aspects:

- the characteristics of the different types of customers
- their importance as customers for the shop
- how you can adapt to their needs and expectations

Step 2: Think of visual aids you can use and prepare them.

Step 3: Practise the presentation in your group.

Step 4: Give the presentation to the class and be prepared to answer questions.

WORD BANK

characteristic – Eigenschaft

F | Consumer rights

P **1** **Customer behaviour**

Look at the cartoon and describe what it shows. What does the cartoon say about customer behaviour? And how would you deal with this situation?

"This banana I bought yesterday, when I peeled it, it was empty!"

M **2** **Mediation**

A friend wants to use the online shop of a British retailer of men's clothing. But before he does, he would like to know what rights he has, especially if he is not satisfied with the goods. Read the following information on consumer rights and sum it up in German for your friend.

Our promise

We promise to refund any item that you are not happy with when you return it to us in saleable condition by post within 14 days of receipt. Refunds will be credited to you by the original method of payment.

Please note that, for reasons of hygiene, we cannot offer refunds on underwear and swimwear if the hygiene seal has been removed. Cosmetic products are also excluded from refunds if they have been used or the hygiene seal has been broken. This may not apply if there is a fault with your item.

How to return an item by post: International customers

International customers will not receive a freepost return label and will have to return unwanted goods or faulty products at their own cost.

When returning items, please allow 28 days from the day the parcel is posted for the processing of your refund. We will e-mail you when we receive the returned parcel and when your refund has been processed.

Please ask your local posting office for a proof of posting certificate and keep it carefully. The post office will also give you a tracking reference number which proves that the item has been returned. Without this we will not be able to refund any money if we do not receive the returned items.

WORD BANK

to apply – zutreffen
to credit – gutschreiben
consumer rights – Verbraucherrechte
to exclude – ausschließen
method of payment – Zahlungsform
to peel – schälen
processing – Bearbeitung
promise – Versprechen
proof – Nachweis
receipt – *(hier:)* Erhalt
seal – Siegel
tracking reference number – Nachverfolgungsnummer

G | Checking

1 Different customers

Complete the sentences and add the right type of customers.

compare • environmentally friendly • exactly • help • natural • take their time • usually • well-known

1 ____________ customers like buying 2 ______________________ (*umweltfreundlich*) products. They often buy goods made of 3 __________ (*naturbelassen*) materials. 4 ________ customers ________ (*vergleichen*) products with one another. They also 5 ____________________ (*sich Zeit nehmen*) with shopping. Often they need 6 __________ (*Hilfe*) from a sales assistant. Customers of 7 ________ buy __________ (*bekannt*) products. They know 8 __________ (*genau*) what they want to buy.

2 Plans for tomorrow

Make sentences with 'going to'. Fill in the gaps.

1. "What ______________ do tomorrow?" – "I __________ unpack goods. Peter ______________ help me with it."
2. "______________ be here tomorrow?" – "Yes, our boss __________ meet a colleague from our branch in Toronto."

P **3** **Future plans**

Tina has received a message from a friend. Write back and answer his questions.

Hi Tina,
Great that you have a job now! But what will you do after your traineeship? Will you look for a different job? Will you go to another country? Or will you work for the same company?

Love,
Jack

Hello Jack,

____

____

____

____

____

____

ICH KANN JETZT ...

1. verschiedene Kundentypen und ihre Einkaufsgewohnheiten unterscheiden.	○○○
2. mich auf verschiedene Kundengruppen einstellen.	○○○
3. typische Merkmale verschiedener Geschäfte nennen.	○○○
4. Gründe nennen, weshalb Kunden bestimmte Geschäfte aufsuchen.	○○○
5. eine Präsentation vorbereiten und halten.	○○○
6. Verbraucherrechte verstehen.	○○○

WORD BANK

gap – Lücke

☺☺☺ = Kann ich schon!
☺☺ = Kann ich ein bisschen!
☺ = Kann ich bald!

H | Phrases: Addressing different customers

Questions to open a conversation with a customer	
Sorry to disturb you, can I help you?	Entschuldigen Sie, wenn ich störe, aber kann ich Ihnen in irgendeiner Weise helfen?
Do you need any help?	Kann ich Ihnen behilflich sein?
Please let me know if you need any help.	Bitte lassen Sie mich wissen, wenn Sie Hilfe benötigen.
Excuse me, is there anything I can do for you?	Entschuldigen Sie, kann ich Ihnen irgendwie behilflich sein?

Adapting to different types of customers	
The product is good for the environment.	Das Produkt ist umweltverträglich.
It is biodegradable.	Es ist biologisch abbaubar.
Do you want to know what the product is made of?	Wollen Sie gerne wissen, woraus das Produkt gefertigt ist?
Are you interested in more information about the product?	Sind Sie an weiteren Informationen über das Produkt interessiert?
Would you like to try out another product?	Möchten Sie gerne ein anderes Produkt ausprobieren?
The product comes with a guarantee.	Das Produkt ist mit einer Garantie versehen.
I can speak more slowly if you wish.	Ich kann langsamer sprechen, falls Sie es wünschen.
I can repeat everything again.	Ich kann alles noch einmal wiederholen.
I can say that again.	Ich kann das nochmal wiederholen.
I can show you how the product works.	Ich kann Ihnen zeigen, wie das Produkt funktioniert.
I can explain the difference to you.	Ich kann Ihnen den Unterschied erklären.
We have a special kids' zone.	Wir haben einen speziellen Kinderbereich.
We can take care of your children.	Wir können auf Ihre Kinder aufpassen.
We can look after your children.	Wir können uns um Ihre Kinder kümmern.
Pardon?	Wie bitte?
I can take the products from the shelves if you can't reach them.	Ich kann die Produkte für Sie aus dem Regal nehmen, wenn Sie nicht an sie herankommen.
If you wish, I can read out the text on the label for you.	Wenn Sie möchten, kann ich Ihnen den Text auf dem Etikett vorlesen.
It's our pleasure to help you load your purchases into your car.	Es ist uns eine Freude Ihnen dabei zu helfen, Ihre Einkäufe in den Wagen zu laden.
Please let me know if there is anything else I can do for you.	Bitte geben Sie Bescheid, wenn ich noch etwas für Sie tun kann.

4

NACH DIESER UNIT:

- ✓ kann ich über die Verwendungsmöglichkeiten von Geld sprechen,
- ✓ kann ich über Preise sprechen,
- ✓ kann ich Probleme an der Kasse lösen,
- ✓ kann ich verschiedene Strategien der Preisfestsetzung verstehen.

A

B

C

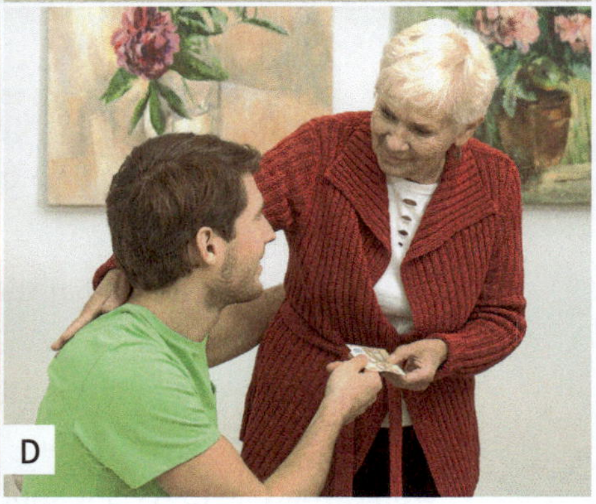
D

Money

A | Talking about money

1 Dealing with money

What are the people doing? Use the words in the box and talk about the photos above.

borrow money from • count money • withdraw money from a cash dispenser • pay money for

P **2 At Harrods** ○ → page 132

Describe the cartoon. (Tip: Harrods in London is one of the world's most famous department stores.)

WORD BANK

to borrow – sich ausleihen
cash dispenser – Geldautomat
to deal (with) – umgehen mit, es zu tun haben mit
to withdraw – abheben

B | Goods and quantities

R **1** **Listening: At the corner shop**

A 1.11 Listen to the dialogue and complete the shopping list for Steven.

1. one ______________ apples	6. two ______________ honey
2. a ______________ tomatoes	7. a ______________ washing powder
3. six ______________	8. ten ______________ toilet paper
4. three ______________ chocolate	9. two ______________ milk
5. five ______________ lemonade	10. a ______________ bread

At the corner shop

Assistant: Guten Morgen, was kann ich für Sie tun?
Steven: Excuse me. Do you speak English?
Assistant: Yes, I do. What can I do for you, Sir?
Steven: First of all, I'd like to buy one kilogram of apples. How much are they?
Assistant: They're €2.50 a kilogram. Anything else?
Steven: Yes, a pound of tomatoes and some bananas, please.
Assistant: How many bananas would you like, Sir?
Steven: Six, please. And I need three bars of chocolate.
Assistant: The expensive ones or the cheap ones?
Steven: Is there a big difference in price?
Assistant: Yes, there is. The expensive ones cost twice as much as the cheap ones, Sir.
Steven: I'll take three bars of the cheaper chocolate, please.
Assistant: OK, Sir. Anything else?
Steven: Yes, five bottles of lemonade and two glasses of honey, please.
Assistant: A bottle of lemonade is €0.95. Honey is on offer this week. You can have two for the price of one for €4.00.
Steven: Excellent. Have you got any pineapples?
Assistant: Sorry, Sir. But we haven't got any left. They're completely sold out.
Steven: Well, I still need a packet of washing powder and ten rolls of toilet paper.
Assistant: No problem, Sir. Here you are. Anything else?
Steven: Yes, two litres of milk and a loaf of bread, please. Thank you. That's all for today. How much is it?
Assistant: That's €28.95, Sir. Have you got exact change? I'm afraid I've got very few coins this morning.
Steven: Let me see. Yes, here you are.
Assistant: That's very kind of you, Sir. Do you need a carrier bag?
Steven: Yes, please.
Assistant: Here you are. Thank you for shopping with us.

WORD BANK

a bar of (chocolate) – eine Tafel (Schokolade)
carrier bag – Tragetasche
completely sold out – vollständig ausverkauft
to cost – kosten
difference – Unterschied
to have exact change – es passend haben
to have sth left – etw. übrig haben
honey – Honig
a loaf of (bread) – ein Laib (Brot)
a packet of – eine Packung
pineapple – Ananas
quantity – Menge
a roll of – eine Rolle
twice as much as – zweimal so viel wie

R **2** **Reading comprehension** ○ → page 133

Read the text on page 43 and answer the questions.

1. What problem does Steven have when the assistant greets him?

2. Does Steven buy the cheap or the expensive bars of chocolate?

3. How much is a bottle of lemonade?

4. Why can't Steven buy any pineapples?

5. Why does the assistant ask Steven if he has the exact change?

6. What does Steven get so that he can take his shopping items home safely?

WORD BANK

safely – sicher

LANGUAGE BOX **Zahlen und Mengenangaben**

Bei **Zahlen** ab 100, die mit einer 1 beginnen steht grundsätzlich *a* oder *one* davor.

1 one	11 eleven	21 twenty-one	40 forty
2 two	12 twelve	22 twenty-two	50 fifty
3 three	13 thirteen	23 twenty-three	60 sixty
4 four	14 fourteen	24 twenty-four	70 seventy
5 five	15 fifteen	25 twenty-five	80 eighty
6 six	16 sixteen	26 twenty-six	90 ninety
7 seven	17 seventeen	27 twenty-seven	100 a / one hundred
8 eight	18 eighteen	28 twenty-eight	101 a / one hundred and one
9 nine	19 nineteen	29 twenty-nine	200 two hundred
10 ten	20 twenty	30 thirty	201 two hundred and one
1000 a / one thousand		5251 five thousand two hundred and fifty-one	

Mengenangaben werden in die Pluralform gesetzt, wenn mehrere Waren gekauft werden (z.B. *two bars of chocolate*). Die danach genannte Ware steht nur dann im Plural, wenn sie zählbar ist (z.B. *a packet of cigarettes*, ABER: *a packet of washing powder*). Weitere Mengenangaben sind z.B. *a bag of, a bottle of, a kilogram of, a litre of, a loaf of, a pound of, a roll of.*

C | Talking about prices

P **1** **Products and their prices**

Look at the photos and talk to a partner about the products and their prices.

→ **PHRASES:** page 53

1

£1.19 a kilo

2

€13.99 each

3

one for £3.50, two for £6.00

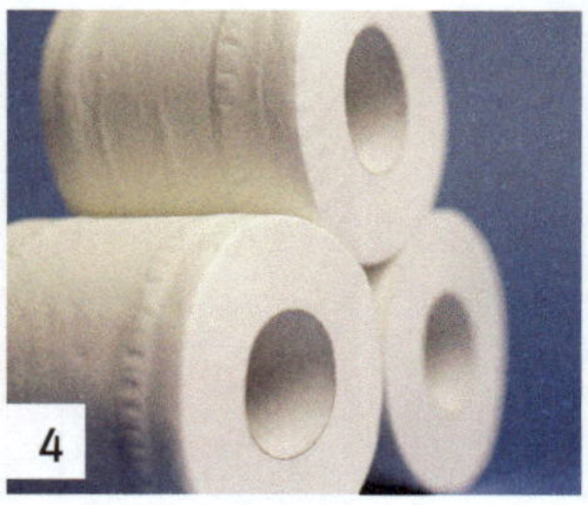

4

ten for €2.75, twenty for €4.99

INTERCULTURAL BOX **Preisauskünfte**

Der Kunde / Die Kundin kann Fragen mit oder ohne *to do* stellen. Er / Sie könnte z.B. sagen: *"How much are the tomatoes?"* oder bei nur einem gewünschten Kilo: *"How much is a kilogram of tomatoes?"* Mögliche Antworten sind: *"The tomatoes are €2.99."* bzw. *"A / One kilogram of tomatoes is €2.99."* Wird die Frage mit *to do* gestellt, muss das Verb *cost* verwendet werden: *"How much do the tomatoes cost?"* oder *"How much does a kilo of tomatoes cost?"* Diese Frage wird mit *"The tomatoes cost €2.99."* bzw. *"A / One kilo of tomatoes costs €2.99."* beantwortet. Wird der Preis einer Ware genannt, muss ggf. eine Pluralform verwendet werden: *"The glass of marmalade is one euro."* ABER: *"A glass of honey is two euros."*

R **2** **Using adverbs and adjectives**

Read the text below. Then complete the sentences with adverbs and adjectives from the text.

1. Dennis needs a birthday present for his little______ brother.
2. The remote-controlled car was ______ overpriced before and now it looks as if it is a ______ bargain.
3. Dennis has found a truck that looks ______ and seems to be ______ his brother's taste.
4. He also read the leaflet ______ and is sure that the price of the truck is ______ a bargain.
5. Dennis and Paul always keep their eyes ______.
6. Dennis thinks that Paul is ______ clever.

In the toys department

Dennis and Paul have just popped into a department store. Dennis wants to buy a new remote-controlled car for his little brother in Bristol, whose birthday is next week.

Paul: Look, this one looks great and it's 35 percent off the regular price. The full price of this car was originally 40 euros, and now it's just 26 euros. You save 14 euros!

Dennis: Well, I think it was heavily overpriced before. Now it only looks like it's a real bargain! Besides, my brother Daniel is more interested in monster trucks, you know. But look over there! That truck looks good and seems to be exactly his taste.

Paul: Is it the one that was in the leaflet this morning?

Dennis: Yes, I read the leaflet carefully and the price of that truck is really a bargain. You get a brand-name product at the price of a no-name one. I think I'll take it.

Paul: Yes, and as we always keep our eyes open we can now take advantage of this price reduction. Perhaps we can even get a further discount if we try to bargain with the sales assistant. OK?

Dennis: I know that you're good at bargaining, Paul. You're incredibly clever. So, let's look for a sales assistant and have a try!

WORD BANK

to bargain – handeln
to be … percent off – … Prozent weniger kosten
brand-name product – Markenprodukt
discount – Nachlass, Rabatt
incredibly – unglaublich, unvorstellbar
to keep one's eyes open – die Augen offen halten
leaflet – Prospekt
no-name product – No-Name-Produkt, kein Markenprodukt
overpriced – überteuert
to pop into – schnell vorbeischauen
reduction – Ermäßigung
remote-controlled – ferngesteuert
to save – sparen
to take advantage of sth – etw. ausnutzen
toys department – Spielwarenabteilung
truck – Laster

3 Adverb or adjective?

Choose the correct word and cross out the wrong one.

1. Merle shops **quick / quickly**.
2. Mr and Mrs Brown look **careful / carefully** at every product before they buy it.
3. Mohammed is a **nice / nicely** shop assistant.
4. Maria is **good / well** at English.
5. The monster truck is a **real / really** bargain.
6. Konstantinos is **particular / particularly** interested in computer games.

WORD BANK

to cancel – (*hier:*) stornieren
to cross out – durchstreichen
particular(ly) – besonders
repayment – Rückzahlung

LANGUAGE BOX **Adjektive und Adverbien**

• Ein Adverb wird gebildet, indem *-ly* an das Adjektiv angehängt wird.	quick	quick**ly**
• Bei Adjektiven mit den Endungen *-y* wird das *-y* zu *-ily*, *-le* wird zu *-ly* und *-ic* wird zu *-ically*.	easy	eas**ily**
	simple	simp**ly**
	automatic	automat**ically**
• Das Adverb von *good* ist *well*.	good	**well**

Adjektive beschreiben Personen und Sachen. Sie stehen meist vor einem Substantiv oder nach *to be*.
Beispiel: *He works in a **big** shop.* *The shop is **big**.*

Adverbien sagen etwas über Verben aus. Sie sagen uns, wie etwas passiert.
Beispiel: *Frank works **quickly**.*

→ **GRAMMAR:** page 157

Üben interaktiv
Adjektive und Adverbien
5v2g5q

D | At the cash desk

R **1** **Right or wrong?**

Look at the dialogues and photos. Then tick (✓) the correct boxes.

Situation 1

Assistant: Sorry, Madam. Have you got 30 cents?
Customer: I've only got a €100 note, I'm afraid.

☐ a) The cashier asks for some change from the customer.
☐ b) The customer has to pay more money for her goods.
☐ c) The customer has got exact change.

1

Situation 2

Customer: Sorry, Sir but there's a mistake on my receipt.
Assistant: Oh, what's wrong with it, Sir?
Customer: I've got two litres of milk on it but I only bought one litre.
Assistant: I'm sorry, Sir. I'll cancel your old receipt. Here's your repayment and your new receipt.

☐ a) The cashier doesn't know what the customer wants.
☐ b) The customer finds a mistake on her receipt.
☐ c) The customer gets a repayment.

2

2 A mistake on the receipt

Complete the conversation and act it out.

→ PHRASES: page 53

Customer	Shop assistant
Sorry, Sir/Madam, but I think … on my receipt.	Oh, …, Sir/Madam.
I've bought … but there are … on the receipt.	I'm …, Sir/Madam. I'll … Here's your …
…, Sir/Madam.	You're … Thank you for …

SKILLS Doing internet research

When you are looking for information you can use a search engine. It is important to put in good key words in order to find the right information.

1 Using a search engine
Put the word 'Harrods' into a search engine. Find the homepage of Harrods and search for more information about its history. Then complete the following sentences.

Harrods was started in 1 ______________ in London's 2 ______________. Charles Harrod set up there as a 3 ______________ grocer. In 1849 Harrod took over a small shop in the new district of 4 ______________. Today Harrods is known all over the 5 ______________.

2 Using an online dictionary
Check your spelling and any unknown words with an online dictionary.

WORD BANK

crowds – Menschenmassen
to descend upon sth – *(hier:)* etw. stürmen
economic crisis – Wirtschaftskrise
to fulfill – erfüllen
to get a glimpse of sth – einen Blick auf etw. erhaschen
to indicate sth – auf etw. hindeuten
to kick off – beginnen
to outbid – überbieten
outlook – Perspektive, Aussicht
pastime – Zeitvertreib
to rake – einstreichen, erzielen
rush – *(hier:)* Andrang
season – Saison, Jahreszeit
to take place – stattfinden
takings – Einnahmen
Thanksgiving – Erntedankfest in den USA

V3 Black Friday

ZDF.enterprises

You will watch a video about "Black Friday sales". These are the sales that take place on the Friday after Thanksgiving and that kick off the Christmas shopping season in the USA.

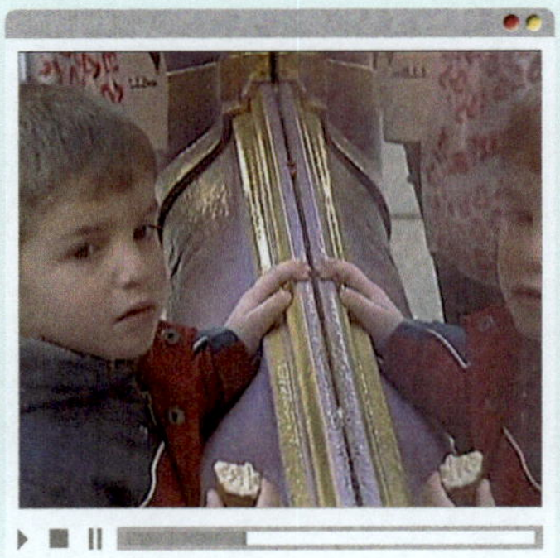

Before watching

1. What time of the year do you like going shopping best? What do you buy then?

While watching

2. What is special about Black Friday that attracts lots of shoppers?
3. Why have many shoppers got time to visit the stores on that day?
4. Why do most children like Black Friday, too?

Before watching

5. Do you think it is useful to have special days for shopping? Say why, or why not.

E | Dealing with customers professionally

R **1** ◎ A 1.12

Listening: An irritated customer

Listen to a sales assistant's blog entry about her work at the cash desk today. Sum up what she says in three sentences. Use the word bank on page 49 for help.

P/R **2**

Project work: Professional behaviour

Get together in small groups and read Sue's blog entry on page 49. Then do the following tasks and take notes of your results.

Step 1: How would you have reacted in the situation Sue describes? Explain why.

Step 2: Think of similar situations with customers from your own experience and say how you dealt with them.

Situations	How we dealt with them

Step 3: Brainstorm possible 'bad behaviour' of shop assistants towards the customer. Discuss professional ways of dealing with such situations.

Step 4: Get together with some of the other groups and share your ideas.

Step 5: Use your notes to present your results in class.

WORD BANK

irritated – verärgert
similar – ähnlich

So, today, I was serving customers at one of the cash desks, and I had a rather unpleasant experience.

As you know, I work at a supermarket, and of course it has a whole row of cash desks with up to six or seven operators working alongside each other at any one time. The supervisor doesn't like any of us standing around doing nothing, so she keeps the number of open desks to a minimum, and sends us off to do other things like putting goods in the shelves and so on.

So there are always queues of customers at the open cash desks. The queues have to get pretty long before the supervisor will open another one or two. Of course, customers often get irritated when the queues are long, but that's not our fault! It's supermarket policy!

Anyway, I had just finished serving a customer, and, in my usual friendly way, I said, "Next, please!"

Now, I might have said it in a bit of a monotone way – I mean, I'd been on that cash desk for hours and I was a bit tired, but what happened next really took me by surprise!

The next customer was a woman in her early 50s. She walks up to me with a very angry look on her face and says in a really sharp tone, "Really! I have to say that was so arrogant, the way you asked for the next customer!"

So I say to her, "Oh, I'm terribly sorry about that. I certainly didn't want to sound arrogant!"

Then she lifts her nose in the air and replies, "That's because most arrogant people aren't aware of how they come across."

Well, you can imagine what was going on in my head at that point. And what I felt like saying to her!

But I managed not to laugh out loud or get angry and simply said, in the friendliest possible way, "Oh well, thank you for letting me know how I sounded. I'll try and work on that in the future."

And then she says, "That's an even more arrogant thing to say!"

Well, I gave up trying at that point. I quietly finished scanning her items, completed the transaction, and then, with the biggest smile I could manage to give, I turned away from her to the queue.

I raised my arms and called out merrily, "I'm ready to serve the next of our honoured and respected customers – with all the joy and attention that they so well deserve!"

And that was my day at work today!

Sue McNeil

WORD BANK

alongside – nebeneinander
attention – Aufmerksamkeit
to be aware of sth – sich etw. bewusst sein
to come across – wirken, rüberkommen
to complete a transaction – einen Kaufvorgang abschließen
to deserve – verdienen
fault – Fehler
honoured – verehrt, geschätzt
to lift – hochhalten
look on sb's face – Gesichtsausdruck von jdm.
merrily – fröhlich, vergnügt
operator – Kassierer/in
policy – Strategie, Grundsatz, Politik
to raise – erheben
to reply – antworten, reagieren
row – Reihe
to scan – einscannen
supervisor – Vorgesetzte/r
to take sb by surprise – jdn. überraschen
unpleasant – unangenehm

F | Product pricing

R/P **1** **Internet research: Different pricing strategies**

You have to do a presentation about the importance of retail pricing. Search the internet and find more information about the following pricing strategies that are often used to increase profits in retailing. Take notes on their main characteristics and practical uses.

Pricing strategy 1

Competitive pricing

Main characteristics:

____

____

Practical uses:

____

____

Pricing strategy 2

Pricing below the competition

Main characteristics:

____

____

Practical uses:

____

____

WORD BANK

competition – Konkurrenz
competitive – konkurrierend
practical use – praktische Anwendung
pricing strategy – Preisstrategie
product pricing – Preisfestsetzung

Pricing strategy 3

Pricing above the competition

Main characteristics:

____

____

Practical uses:

____

____

Pricing strategy 4

Psychological pricing

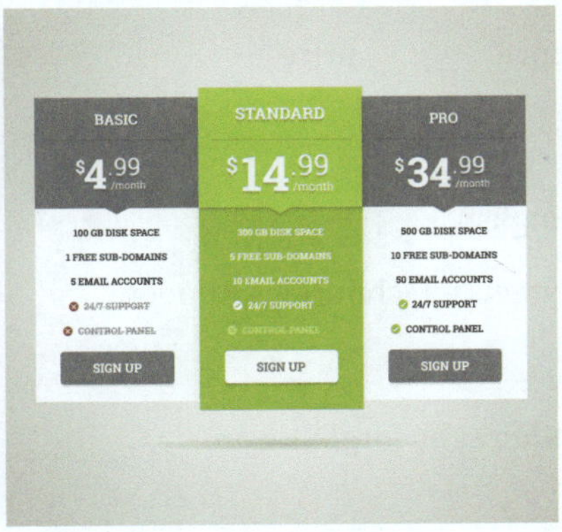

Main characteristics:

____

____

Practical uses:

____

____

P **2** **Pricing strategies at your workplace**

Ask a partner about examples for different pricing strategies that are used in his or her place of work. Then take turns.

→ **PHRASES:** page 53

G | Checking

R **1** **Listening: Pricing products**

A 1.13 Listen to the announcements in a supermarket. Write down what each product costs.

1. 1,20
2. 1.50
3. 2,99
4. 1.99/kg

2 **Prepositions**

Put in the missing prepositions.

for · in · of · off · on · out · of

1. Frank buys three packets for the price of one.
2. The bananas are completely sold out.
3. Two glasses of marmalade are on offer this week.
4. Some electrical appliances are 40 percent off the regular price.
5. There is a big difference in price.

3 **Say it in English**

Put the sentences into English.

1. Ich bediene normalerweise nachmittags Kunden.
2. Ich sehe mir die Kunden sehr sorgfältig an.
3. Mein Chef ist nett und er spricht gut Englisch.
4. Natasha packt Ware sehr schnell aus.

ICH KANN JETZT ...

1. über Verwendungsmöglichkeiten von Geld sprechen. ○○○
2. Mengenangaben für Produkte richtig anwenden. ○○○
3. Preise nennen und Preisverhandlungen führen. ○○○
4. Probleme mit Kunden an der Kasse lösen. ○○○
5. Strategien der Preisfestsetzung verstehen und erklären. ○○○

WORD BANK

announcement – Durchsage

☺☺☺ = Kann ich schon!
☺☺ = Kann ich ein bisschen!
☺ = Kann ich bald!

H | Phrases: Dealing with money

Talking about goods and quantities	
Would you like to buy a/one kilogram of/a pound of/ a bar of/a bottle of/a litre of/a loaf of/a packet of/ a roll of ...?	Hätten Sie gern ein Kilogramm/ein Pfund/eine Tafel/ eine Flasche/einen Liter/einen Laib/eine Packung/ eine Rolle ...?
I'm very sorry, but the product is completely sold out.	Es tut mir sehr leid, aber das Produkt ist vollständig ausverkauft.
We haven't got any ... left, I'm afraid.	Wir haben leider keine/n ... mehr da.

Talking about prices	
The apples are/cost €2.00 a kilogram.	Die Äpfel kosten 2,00 € das Kilo.
The product is excellent value for money.	Das Produkt ist sein Geld wert.
The goods are on offer this week.	Die Waren sind diese Woche im Angebot.
It's a real bargain.	Es ist ein wirkliches Schnäppchen.
You can save a lot of money.	Sie können eine Menge Geld sparen.
You can get a good deal on it.	Sie können dafür ein gutes Angebot bekommen.
You can even get a further discount.	Sie können sogar einen weiteren Rabatt erhalten.
The article is 30 percent off the regular price.	Der Artikel ist 30 Prozent günstiger als sonst.
We can give you big reductions.	Wir können Ihnen große Nachlässe gewähren.
I can't go down with the price any further.	Ich kann mit dem Preis nicht weiter heruntergehen.
You can buy two products for the price of one.	Sie können zwei Produkte für den Preis von einem kaufen.
There's a big difference in price.	Der Preisunterschied ist groß.
You can get one for free.	Sie bekommen eine/s umsonst.

Problems at the cash desk	
Have you got exact change?	Haben Sie es passend?
Have you got 30 cents?	Haben Sie 30 Cent?
Sorry, Sir/Madam, but I don't have any change this morning.	Es tut mir leid, aber ich habe heute morgen kein Wechselgeld.
What's wrong with your receipt, Sir/Madam?	Was stimmt auf Ihrem Kassenzettel nicht?
Have you got your old receipt?	Haben Sie Ihren alten Kassenzettel noch?
Sorry for overcharging you.	Es tut mir leid, dass wir Ihnen zuviel berechnet haben.
I'll cancel your old receipt.	Ich werde Ihren alten Kassenzettel stornieren.
Here's your repayment and your new receipt.	Hier ist Ihre Rückerstattung und Ihr neuer Kassen-zettel.

Das Produkt ist sein Geld wert – The product is excel
Diese Waren sind im Angebot – These Goods are on offer.

5

NACH DIESER UNIT:

- ✓ kann ich Kunden mitteilen, wo sie die gewünschten Produkte finden,
- ✓ kann ich den Weg in verschiedene Abteilungen weisen,
- ✓ kann ich Personen und Sachen miteinander vergleichen,
- ✓ kann ich Produkte detailliert beschreiben.

At the department store

A | Different floors

1 Where are the departments?

Look at the photos and say on which floor the departments are.

children's wear · cosmetics · food · restaurant

Start like this: *The ... department is on the ... floor / in the basement.*

1. Ground floor: ______
2. Top floor: ______
3. Basement: ______
4. First floor: ______

R **2 Listening: A new department store**

A 1.14 Listen to a radio programme. Write down on which floor certain products will be. Then listen again and take notes about the reasons why they are on different floors.

	Food	Cosmetics	Children's wear
1. Where?			
2. Why?			

WORD BANK

basement – Untergeschoss
children's wear – Kinderbekleidung
cosmetics – Kosmetik
floor – Stock(werk)
ground floor – Erdgeschoss
top floor – Obergeschoss

WORD BANK

to look forward to – sich freuen auf
news – Nachricht(en)

B | Finding products

R **1** **Reading comprehension**

Read the dialogue between Lucy from the USA and a shop assistant. Then write down the products that can be found according to the shop assistant's instructions.

In the cosmetics department

Lucy:	Excuse me, could you help me, please? I'm looking for the cosmetics department.
Assistant:	Certainly. Just follow me. I work in the cosmetics department and I'm just coming back from my lunch break. It's on the ground floor and I suggest we take the lift. It's a lot faster.
Lucy:	Yes, OK,
Assistant:	So here we are. This is our cosmetics department. What exactly are you looking for?
Lucy:	I need a new lipstick. It should be a bright colour.
Assistant:	No problem. Let's go into the first aisle here. We have to go up to the end. Now, here they are, on the left: lipsticks in lots of different colours.
Lucy:	Thank you very much. Wow, I like this lipstick. I'll definitely take it.
Assistant:	Fine. Is there anything else I can do for you?
Lucy:	Yes, please. I also need some eye make-up.
Assistant:	It's right here in the second aisle round the corner and opposite the body lotion.
Lucy:	OK. What I'm looking for is something to make my eyes look more attractive, especially after a long night at the disco. You know what I mean?
Assistant:	Oh, I know that problem all too well. This eye make-up is good for hiding the tiredness round your eyes in the mornings.
Lucy:	Excellent. That's a real must-have. Oh, and one more thing. I need some styling gel.
Assistant:	That's easy. It's at the beginning of the third aisle on the right next to the hairspray.
Lucy:	Thank you very much for your help.
Assistant:	You're welcome.

1. They are at the end of the first aisle on the left:

____

2. It's round the corner across from the body lotion in the second aisle:

____

3. It's in the third aisle, right at the beginning where the hairspray is:

____

I/P **2** **Role play: Saying where the products are**

Read the dialogue above with a partner. Then ask each other questions about where the products are.

Start like this: A: Excuse me, where can I find …?
B: The … are …

WORD BANK

a must-have – ein Muss
according to – entsprechend, gemäß
across from – gegenüber von
aisle – Gang
bright – hell
colour – Farbe
to follow sb – jdm. folgen
Here we are. – Hier wären wir.
to hide – verbergen, verstecken
instruction – Anweisung
lipstick – Lippenstift
lift – Aufzug
lunch break – Mittagspause
next to – neben
on the left – auf der linken Seite
round – um … herum
to suggest – vorschlagen

→ **PHRASES:** page 65

LANGUAGE BOX **Ordnungszahlen**

1st	first	6th	sixth	11th	eleventh	16th	sixteenth
2nd	second	7th	seventh	12th	twelfth	17th	seventeenth
3rd	third	8th	eighth	13th	thirteenth	19th	nineteenth
4th	fourth	9th	ninth	14th	fourteenth	18th	eighteenth
5th	fifth	10th	tenth	15th	fifteenth	20th	twentieth

C | Finding different departments

R **1** **At the information desk**

A 1.15 Look at the questions 1.–4. and match them to the correct answers a)–d). Draw lines. Then listen to the conversations and check your answers.

Customers	Assistant
1. Excuse me. Could you tell me where I can buy a doll?	a) Please go downstairs to the supermarket in the basement.
2. Hello. Could you help me, please? We're having a barbecue this weekend. Where can I buy some sausages?	b) Yes, of course. You just have to go to the toys department, Sir. You can take the lift round the corner up to the third floor, if you want.
3. Sorry to disturb you. I'd like to buy some perfume but I can see only leather goods around me.	c) You need to go to the children's wear department. Please take the escalator up to the second floor. The lift is out of order and must be repaired.
4. Excuse me. My son needs a new jacket. Where do I have to go?	d) I can help you, Madam. Just stay on the ground floor. Please go straight on and you'll find the cosmetics behind the leather goods department.

WORD BANK

barbecue – Grillparty
doll – Puppe
downstairs – (nach) unten
escalator – Rolltreppe
information desk – Informationsschalter
out of order – außer Betrieb
to repair – reparieren
to stay – bleiben
straight on – geradeaus

R **2** **Listening: Finding the way** ○ → page 134
A 1.15 Listen again and complete the following sentences.

1. Please ______________________ (*nach unten gehen*) to the supermarket ______________________ (*im Untergeschoss*).
2. The ______________________ (*Spielzeugabteilung*) is on the third floor. You can take the ______________________ (*Fahrstuhl*) if you want.
3. You have to take the ______________________ (*Rolltreppe*) to go to the children's wear department. The lift is ______________________ (*außer Betrieb*).
4. The cosmetics department is ______________________ (*hinter*) this one. Just go ______________________ (*geradeaus*).

D | Making comparisons

1 **New shoes for a friend back home**
Susan has received an SMS from her friend Lilly in Swinton near Manchester.
Read the text and write down the meaning of the abbreviations Lilly uses.

Hi Susan,
I miss u a lot and hope ur fine.
Please do me a favour, as ur my best friend, Susan. Ino that they have some really fashionable shoes with high heels in Germany that look prettier and more stylish than those in the shops around here. As u know, they're also more expensive here in Britain than in Germany. If u find some cheaper ones which look at least as stylish as the ones I always wear, then please BUY them. I'll give u the money when ur back. Promise!
TXS
CU, Lilly

Abbreviations	Meaning
1. u	
2. ur (*two meanings*)	
3. ino	
4. TXS	
5. CU	

P **2** **Writing an SMS** ○ → page 134
Now write Susan's answer to her friend Lilly in your exercise book. Use the words in the box and the abbreviations in exercise 1.

best • cheaper • less stylish • more beautiful • more expensive • prettiest

WORD BANK

abbreviation – Abkürzung
favour – Gefallen
heel – (Schuh-)Absatz

GRAMMAR BOX **Steigerung von Adjektiven**

Einsilbige Adjektive werden im Englischen mit *-er* und *-est* gesteigert, zweisilbige Adjektive, die auf *-y* enden mit *-ier* und *-iest*. Bei Vergleichen benutzt man *than* (= als).
Beispiele: *He is **older than** Frank. He is **the oldest**. Susan is **prettier than** Tina. Dana is **the prettiest**.*

Die meisten anderen zweisilbigen Adjektive und alle mehrsilbigen Adjektive, werden mit *more* und *most* gesteigert.
Beispiele: *The house is **more modern** than Paul's. Jackie's house is **the most modern** one in Brighton. My car is **more expensive** than Melanie's. Bob's car is **the most expensive**.*

Bei Vergleichen von Personen und Sachen verwendet man *as ... as* oder *not as ... as*.
Beispiele: *Conny's trolley is **as big as** Frank's. Sean's stereo is **not as good as** Naomi's.*

Einige Adjektive haben unregelmäßige Steigerungsformen:

good	**better**	**best**	bad	**worse**	**worst**
much / many	**more**	**most**	little	**less**	**least**

Beispiel: *This jam is **the least expensive**.*

→ **GRAMMAR:** page 157

Üben interaktiv
Steigerung von Adjectiven
5v2g5q

P **3** **Comparing products at Marks & Spencer**

First write down three adjectives for each bag. Then work with a partner and describe the bags. Compare the bags and decide which one you would like to buy and say why.

Start like this: The bag on the left is ...

1. ____________________

2. ____________________

3. ____________________

INTERCULTURAL BOX **Warenhäuser in Großbritannien**

Das berühmteste und exklusivste britische Kaufhaus **Harrods** befindet sich im Südwesten Londons. Es zählt keineswegs zu den preisgünstigsten Einkaufsmöglichkeiten, dennoch steht es allen Menschen offen und wird von vielen Touristen besucht.
Marks & Spencer ist als Warenhauskonzern in Großbritannien sehr bekannt und mit ca. 300 Geschäften vertreten. Er gilt als das profitabelste Einzelhandelsunternehmen Europas. Anders als viele deutsche Warenhäuser bietet Marks & Spencer kein umfassendes Sortiment an, sondern beschränkt sich auf Bekleidung, Nahrungsmittel und Haushaltswaren. Ca. 16 Millionen Kunden kaufen dort jede Woche ein.

4 Explaining things in different words

Sometimes you may not remember certain words in English. Then you should use other words to say the same thing. Use the verbs in brackets and rewrite the sentences in simple language.

Example: Can I borrow some money from you? **(to give)**
→ Can you give me some money?

1. How much does a pound of tomatoes cost? **(to be)**

____

2. This remote-controlled car is heavily overpriced. **(to cost)**

____

3. Could you tell me where I can buy some toilet paper? **(to know)**

____

4. Can you do me a favour, please? **(to help)**

____

SKILLS

British and American English

Certain words are different in British English and American English. Sometimes just the spelling is different, but some words are completely different. In your dictionary British and American English words are usually marked as BrE or Brit and as AmE or Am.

1 Different spelling
Write the sentences in American English. Use a dictionary, if necessary.

1. My dad is a sales assistant.

____

2. Our house is near the city centre.

____

3. Can you do me a favour, please?

____

2 Different words
Fill in the missing words and complete the list. Then check your answers with the help of a dictionary.

British English	American English	German
shop assistant		*Verkäufer/in*
	vacation	
biscuit		*Keks*
	elevator	*Aufzug*
	fall	*Herbst*
flat		*Wohnung*

WORD BANK

bracket – Klammer
to remember – sich erinnern (an)
spelling – Rechtschreibung

E | Department stores and product information

P **1** **Different product and departments**

Look at the photos and describe what they show. Write down in which department you can find these products in a department store.

1

2

3

4

P **2** **Harrods in London**

Look at the photo of Harrods on page 61 and write two sentences about what you think you might find inside.

R **3** **Listening: Shopping at Harrods**

A 1.16

Listen to the dialogue between Susan and Franziska during the coffee break at the stationery shop in Rostock. Then answer the questions in complete sentences.

1. How many different departments are there at Harrods?
2. How can you easily identify Harrods' customers when you walk through London?
3. What is the central escalator at Harrods decorated with?
4. What is special about the toys department?
5. What does Susan say about Harrods' dress code policy?

WORD BANK

amazing – toll, unglaublich
Are you kidding? – Machst du Witze?
curious – neugierig
to decorate – dekorieren
dress code – Kleidervorschriften
Egyptian – ägyptisch
exhausting – anstrengend, ermüdend
to forget – vergessen
huge – riesig
impressive – beeindruckend
to keep in mind – im Hinterkopf behalten
luckily – glücklicherweise
motive – Motiv
to offer – anbieten
selection – Auswahl
selling space – Verkaufsraum, Verkaufsfläche
soft toy – Plüschtier
square foot, (pl.) square feet – Quadratfuß *(Fuß = 0,3048 Meter)*
to turn sb away – jdn. abweisen
worn out – verschlissen

R/P **4**

Internet research: Researching products

Find the official website of Harrods in London and choose a department you find particularly interesting. Write down at least five different items they offer in this department. Then describe three of the products with suitable adjectives and make a note of the prices. Use the following form and a dictionary.

Name of the department

____

Products that can be bought in the department

____

____

____

Product details

Product 1

Description: ______________________________

Price: ______________________________

Product 2

Description: ______________________________

Price: ______________________________

Product 3

Description: ______________________________

Price: ______________________________

Product 4

Description: ______________________________

Price: ______________________________

WORD BANK

detail – Detail, Einzelheit

P **5** **Comparing products**

Talk to a partner and tell him / her about your department and products. Compare the products and their prices. Take notes on your partner's department and the three of his / her products that you find most interesting.

→ **PHRASES:** page 53 and 65

I looked at the … department. They sell … there.

Name of the department

____

Products that can be bought in the department

____

____

____

Product details

Product 1

Description: ______________________________

____

____

____

Price: ______________________________

Product 2

Description: ______________________________

____

____

____

Price: ______________________________

Product 3

Description: ______________________________

____

____

____

Price: ______________________________

P **6** **Product presentation**

Decide on one product you would like to buy and think about why you want to buy it. Prepare a short presentation of the product and include some photos. Then present the product in class.

F | Selling special products

R/P **1** **Project work: Selling jewellery**

You are doing a work placement at a department store in Glasgow, Scotland, which is part of a large German chain. You have been working in the jewellery department for one week now. In order to be better prepared to sell jewellery in the future, your supervisor has asked you to think about what makes selling jewellery a "special business" compared with selling other products.

Step 1: Think about the following aspects and make a list.

- sales process
- product information
- product value
- customer expectations

Special aspects of selling jewellery

Step 2: Compare your list with a partner's and exchange ideas.

Step 3: Read the following article about selling jewellery successfully and add at least one more aspect to your list.

Are you ready to sell jewellery?

Many jewellery purchases are made by consumers who are strongly and emotionally involved in the sales process. So you need to give them a lot of information to meet their needs. You have to know your products very well and you have to be able to answer any questions about them. In order to sell jewellery successfully you need to have a detailed knowledge of the jewellery you are selling. You also have to know what makes it unique, what the benefits for the buyer are, the exact prices and so on. In other words, you must be the expert your customers expect you to be, appearing professional, confident, and knowledgeable about every detail of your products.
The best way to achieve good jewellery sales is to fulfill your customers' needs and desires with what you have to sell. This ability comes from good preparation and product knowledge and experience in providing excellent customer service.

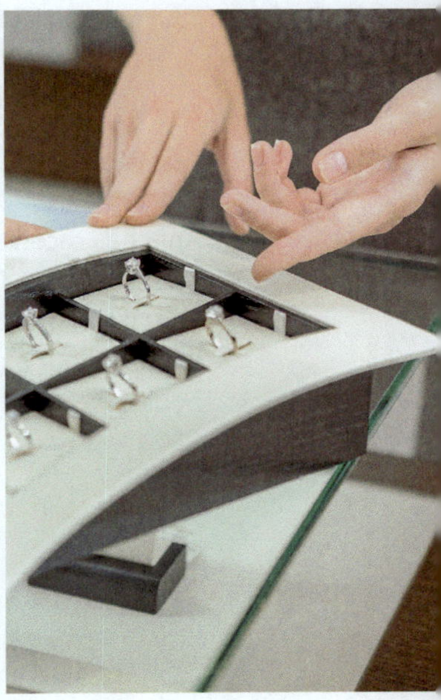

Step 4: Think about when you bought some jewellery and explain the sales process to your partner.

P **2** **Discussion: Special products**

The sale of what other products could be seen as a "special business"? Think about your experiences as a sales assistant and as a customer and exchange your ideas. Then present the results of your discussion in class.

WORD BANK

ability – Fähigkeit
to achieve – erreichen, erzielen
to appear – auftreten
customer service – Kundenbetreuung
to expect – erwarten
to involve – beinhalten, umfassen
jewellery (BE), jewelry (AE) – Schmuck
knowledgeable – sachkundig
to provide – liefern, bereitstellen
purchase – (Ein-)Kauf, Ware
to be ready to do sth – bereit sein, etw. zu tun
unique – einzigartig
value – Wert

G | Checking

1 Retail crossword

Find the right words and fill in the crossword.

Across:

1. It moves up and down between different floors.
3. You walk through the … between rows of shelves in a shop.
5. It is a stair and it moves.
10. In most department stores the food department is in the …
11. Another word for lipsticks, body lotions, etc.

Down:

2. I usually withdraw money from the cash …
4. Please go upstairs, don't go …
6. The … floor is below the first floor.
7. The highest floor in a building is the … floor.
8. When you work hard, you have to take a … sometimes.
9. On the other side.

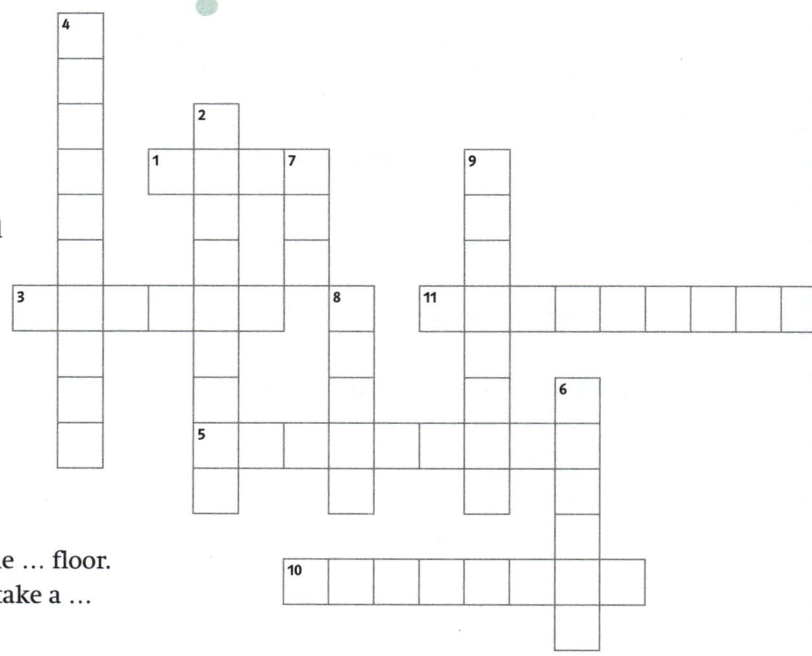

2 Comparisons

Find the correct words in each sentence and underline them.

1. The eye make-up is **expensive / more expensive** than the lipstick.
2. The new department store is **more modern / most modern** than the old one.
3. Franziska's English is **the worst / worse** than Verena's.
4. This is the **biggest / bigger** supermarket in our town.
5. Ulrike is **as nice as / as nice than** Julia.

M 3 Mediation

Anja has received a message from Tom. Sum it up in German. Write in your exercise book.

Hi Anja,
How are you?
You know, I've just come back from a weekend in Paris. It was fantastic. What I liked best was going shopping there. It was much more interesting than here in Manchester. I went to the biggest department store in Paris and bought myself some cool CDs. Then I went up to the top floor and had lunch in the restaurant. The food was much better and less expensive than English food.
What about you? What did you do last weekend?
Love, Tom

ICH KANN JETZT …

1. die Stockwerke eines Warenhauses benennen. ○○○
2. Kunden sagen, wo sie Produkte finden können und den Weg in verschiedene Abteilungen weisen. ○○○
3. Personen und Sachen miteinander vergleichen. ○○○
4. Produkte detailliert beschreiben. ○○○

WORD BANK

to move – bewegen

☺☺☺ = Kann ich schon!
☺☺ = Kann ich ein bisschen!
☺ = Kann ich bald!

H | Phrases: At a department store

Asking for products	
Excuse me, could you tell me where I can find …?	Entschuldigen Sie, könnten Sie mir sagen, wo ich … finden kann?
Sorry to disturb you, but could you show me where … is/are?	Es tut mir leid Sie zu stören, aber könnten Sie mir zeigen, wo … ist/sind?
Excuse me, Sir/Madam but I need your help to find …	Entschuldigen Sie, aber ich benötige Ihre Hilfe, um … zu finden.
Excuse me, where is/are …?	Entschuldigen Sie, wo ist/sind …?

Showing the way to different departments	
The product you are looking for is in the basement/on the ground/first/second/third/top floor.	Das Produkt nach dem Sie suchen befindet sich im Untergeschoss/Erdgeschoss/ersten/zweiten/dritten/obersten Stock.
Please take the lift to the … floor.	Bitte nehmen Sie den Aufzug in den … Stock.
You can also take the stairs up/down to the … floor.	Sie können auch die Treppe hoch/runter in den … Stock nehmen.
Just go downstairs/upstairs to the … department.	Gehen Sie einfach die Treppe nach unten/oben in die … Abteilung.
The toys/sports/bakery/… department is …	Die Spielzeug-/Sport-/Backwaren-/…abteilung ist …
Turn right/left and then go straight on.	Gehen Sie nach rechts/links und dann geradeaus.
The department you are looking for is between the jewellery shop and the fashion shop.	Die Abteilung nach der sie suchen ist zwischen dem Juwelierladen und dem Modegeschäft.

Describing and comparing products	
The product offers lots of advantages.	Das Produkt bietet viele Vorteile.
One of the product's major benefits is …	Einer der Hauptvorteile des Produktes ist …
Another point to mention is …	Außerdem sollte erwähnt werden, dass…
The product is unique/trendy/stylish/lightweight/safe/convenient.	Das Produkt ist einzigartig/modisch/stilvoll/leicht (im Gewicht)/sicher/nützlich.
It offers very good value for money.	Es bietet ein sehr gutes Preis-/Leistungsverhältnis.
It is easy to handle.	Es ist einfach in der Handhabung.
The product is bigger/cheaper/prettier than …	Das Produkt ist größer/günstiger/hübscher als …
It is less stylish/more expensive than …	Es ist weniger elegant/teurer als …
It is just as convenient as the other article.	Es ist genauso praktisch wie der andere Artikel.
It is not so trendy as …	Es ist nicht so modisch wie …
He is the best/worst shop assistant in our department store.	Er ist der beste/schlechteste Verkäufer in unserem Kaufhaus.
The big handbag is not as trendy as the smaller one.	Die große Handtasche ist nicht so modisch wie die kleinere.

6

NACH DIESER UNIT:

- √ kann ich Werbematerialien verstehen und entwerfen,
- √ kann ich auf Interesse an Produkten richtig reagieren und produktbezogene Fragen beantworten,
- √ kann ich Maßnahmen zur Verkaufsförderung verstehen.

A

B

C

D

Sales promotion

A | Promoting products online and offline

1 Product planning and promotion

Look at the pictures above and match them to the correct captions.

1. ☐ Attracting customers and promoting sales with free product trials and tastings
2. ☐ Discussing new products at a product meeting
3. ☐ Flyers advertising goods and offering discounts
4. ☐ Planning the sale of products online

P 2 Sales promotion at your company

What does your company do to make customers buy your products online and offline? Write down at least three different measures. Be prepared to present them in class.

____

____

____

____

____

____

____

WORD BANK

to advertise – Werbung machen für
caption – Bildunterschrift
measure – Maßnahme
to promote – fördern
sales promotion – Verkaufsförderung
tasting – Kostprobe, Verköstigung
trial – Probe, Versuch

B | Planning a product promotion

WORD BANK

bio-degradable – biologisch abbaubar
challenge – Herausforderung
chance – Möglichkeit, Gelegenheit
eco-friendly – umweltfreundlich
environment – Umwelt
harmful – schädlich
impact – Auswirkung, Einfluss
to introduce – einführen
to reduce – reduzieren
solution – Lösung
toxic – giftig

R **1** **Reading comprehension** ○ → page 135

Your boss has given you the flyer for eco-friendly cleaning products that you are going to offer to customers in a promotion week. A British company plans to introduce the new cleaning products in Germany. Read the flyer and answer the questions below.

ECO FRIENDLY

BUY NOW!
Eco-friendly cleaning products

THE FACTS:
Household cleaning is hard work. It is not important whether it is the table in the living room or the bathroom floor you have to deal with – the challenge is to get the job done in the most effective way.
But many of the cleaning products we buy today contain chemicals which have toxic side effects and are harmful to the environment.

THE SOLUTION:
Eco-friendly cleaners help you not only to clean your household efficiently but also to reduce the toxic substances in your home and in our environment. Eco-friendly cleaning products contain natural substances that are non-toxic and bio-degradable. So their impact on the environment, and on our bodies, is minimal.

Don't miss this chance to do something good for yourself and your environment!

1. What is the problem with conventional cleaning products?

___

2. What are two main characteristics of eco-friendly cleaners?

___

___

3. What is the effect of eco-friendly cleaners on your household and the environment?

___

P **2** **Designing a poster for a new product**
Find partners who work in the same or a similar branch as you. Together design a poster for a new product that you are planning to sell soon. Present your poster in class and say what is special about the product.

→ **PHRASES:** page 77

C | Promoting online and offline sales

R **1** **Reading comprehension**

You are currently working in Manchester for the department store Northern Pride for a couple of weeks during your apprenticeship. The manager of Northern Pride tells you that they are about to open an online shop with all the products you can buy in the department store. Read the following flyer that informs customers about the plan. Then answer the questions on the next page in your exercise book

NORTHERN PRIDE **GOES ONLINE ON 3 NOVEMBER!**

Imagine:
- It's Friday evening. Northern Pride have already closed and you suddenly remember something you forgot to buy this morning.
- You always like to shop at Northern Pride, but the nearest store is an hour away. It's too far to go there often, and you need to save time.

From now on you can shop at Northern Pride 24/7!

Do you need help making an online order? Here is how it works:
1. Start your browser and key in our address: BuyersParadise.co.uk
2. When you buy online for the first time, you need to fill in a form with your personal details, decide on how you want to pay and give your payment details. Then with your next orders, you just log in with your email address and password.
3. Choose the right category (e.g. Shoes, Clothing, etc.) and scroll through the products on offer. Alternatively, you can use the search function and key in what you are looking for.
4. When you have decided to buy a product, click on the SHOPPING TROLLEY symbol below the product.
5. After you have finished shopping, click on the BASKET OF ALL GOODS at the top of the page.
6. Check the goods in your shopping trolley. Delete products or change them, if you wish.
7. When you are sure that you want to buy all the products in the list, click on the button CHECKOUT.
8. Finally, check all your entries again and place your order by clicking on the ORDER button.
9. A confirmation of your order will be automatically sent to your email address or alternatively you can print it out from the webpage.

You need more help?

Just click on our red CHAT button you can find at the bottom of each page and one of our shop assistants will assist you. Just key in your questions and we are there for you – personally!

WORD BANK

to assist – helfen
basket of all goods – gesamter Warenkorb
category – Kategorie
chat button – Chat-Schaltfläche
confirmation – Bestätigung
to delete – löschen
entry – Eingabe
to place an order – eine Bestellung aufgeben
search function – Suchfunktion

1. What does Northern Pride plan to do?
2. When does the new online department store go online?
3. What are some of the advantages of online shopping?
4. You know the exact product you want to buy. What can you do on the home page in order to save time?
5. What can you still do when you look at the BASKET OF ALL GOODS before placing your online order?
6. What does the online department store offer in case the customer still has some questions?

P **2** **Attracting customers to buy offline**

Today, more and more customers buy their products online and local shops have started to think about what they can do to make more customers go to their shops again. Do the following tasks.

a) What do your local shops do so that more customers shop there?

b) Do some internet research. Find some suggestions from experts about how local shops can become more attractive to customers. List at least three ideas. Present your results to the class.

P **3** **How to get elderly customers to shop online**

Do the tasks in groups of four. Then present your results to the class.

a) Why are elderly customers an interesting target group for online stores? List reasons.

b) Make suggestions how to persuade them to shop online.

WORD BANK

in case – im Falle, dass

P **4** **Assessing the attractiveness of an online store** ○ → page 135

Do some internet research with a partner. Look at an online store of your choice and answer the following questions in your exercise book. Present your findings to the class.

a) How does the online store try to attract attention?
b) What are the advantages and disadvantages of the store?

R **5** **Promotions in the store**

Read the dialogues. What does the shop assistant suggest that customers can do before they buy a product?

Dialogue 1: ______________________________

Dialogue 2: ______________________________

Dialogue 3: ______________________________

Dialogue 1

Assistant: Good morning. Can I help you?
Customer: Yes, you can. I listened to the advert about your new mobile phone on a social networking site. What new features does the mobile phone have?
Assistant: Well, first of all, it's more stylish than the old one and easy to use. Besides, it has got a 4k video camera. For more information, you can simply watch our promotion video here on your right in which all the new features are explained and presented.
Customer: Yeah, that's a very good idea.

Dialogue 2

Assistant: Good morning, sir. You seem to be interested in our treadmill which is currently on special offer.
Customer: That's right. I clicked on a link in your email newsletter to get some more information about it. I need to watch my figure, you see!
Assistant: Would you like to try out the treadmill here in the shop?
Customer: Can I? That's great. Thanks a lot!

Dialogue 3

Assistant: Excuse me, sir. Are you interested in more information about our cameras?
Customer: Well, I can't really decide, and I am in rather a hurry.
Assistant: No problem, sir. I can give you a leaflet about the cameras we have got on offer right now and you can look at it at home. If you have got any questions, please feel free to contact us again.
Customer: Thanks. Maybe I'll come back tomorrow.

WORD BANK

besides –darüberhinaus
promotion video –Werbevideo
social networking site – Seite in den sozialen Netzwerken
treadmill – Laufband

LANGUAGE BOX **Das *simple past***

Das *simple past* wird verwendet, um Ereignisse in der Vergangenheit zu schildern, die jetzt abgeschlossen sind. Regelmäßige Verben bilden das *simple past* mit *-ed*. Unregelmäßige Verben haben Sonderformen. Verneinungen bildet man mit *didn't*, Fragen mit *did*. Nach *did* und *didn't* steht immer die Grundform.

	I / He / She / It / We / You / They	start**ed**	**went**
	I / He / She / It / We / You / They	**didn't** start	**didn't** go
Did	I / he / she / it / we / you / they	**start**?	**go**?

Das Verb *to be* hat zwei Formen im *simple past*. Fragen und Verneinungen werden in diesem Fall ohne *did / didn't* gebildet.

I / He / She / It	**was / wasn't**
We / You / They	**were / weren't**

Beispiel: *When **was** your birthday? Where **were** you last week?*

Typische Zeitangaben in Verbindung mit dem *simple past* sind: *ago, in 1990, last week, then.*

→ **GRAMMAR:** page 151

Üben interaktiv
Das simple past
44c65k

R **6** **An e-mail from a customer**

Look at the sentences and put the verbs into the simple past form. Then put the sentences into the correct order and write the numbers 1–8 in the boxes.

☐ When I ________________ (**get**) home, I ________________ (**call**) my wife in Manchester and ________________ (**have**) a long conversation with her.

☐ Last week I ________________ (**visit**) your shop and ________________ (**buy**) the new mobile phone that you ________________ (**offer**) in your campaign.

☐ Simon Berry

☐ Yours faithfully

☐ I hope you will advertise more products in the future.

☐ Your shop assistant ________________ (**be**) very nice and ________________ (**inform**) me about all the details.

☐ Yesterday I even ________________ (**send**) her an e-mail from my mobile.

☐ Dear Sir or Madam

I/P **7** **Role play: Product promotion**

Form groups and make dialogues between shop assistants and customers. You can choose ideas from the box or think of a promotion in your own shop.

diet drinks • eco-friendly cleaning products • outdoor jackets • styling gel

- Agree on a product that you want to promote.
- Collect benefits of the product that make it special for the customers.
- Identify the target group (teenagers / elderly people / …).
- Practise dialogues between customers and shop assistants.
- Present your role plays in class.

WORD BANK

to agree – sich einigen
target group – Zielgruppe

D | The history of shopping habits

M **1** **Mediation**

You have to do a class project on how shopping habits have changed in the course of time. You have just found the following article about the history of shopping habits on the internet. Sum up the main information for your group in German.

Over the last 50 years there have been tremendous changes in the way people shop. In the 60s people went to their local newsagent, butcher's, grocer, etc. Later, more and more supermarkets and big department stores opened and traditional small shops had to close because the variety of goods they could offer was only small and their prices were no longer competitive. The opening hours of the shops were limited by law. Outside those opening hours, it was only possible to shop at railway stations, petrol stations, motorway services or small corner shops, usually for higher prices.
In Germany, regulations on opening hours have existed until today. It is the job of the individual federal states to fix the opening hours. But shops today are allowed to stay open much longer. Nowadays also, more and more people are buying goods online.
This is currently a major problem for local shops, who must look for new ways to attract customers.

WORD BANK

competitive – wettbewerbsfähig
federal state – Bundesland
to fix - festlegen
limited – begrenzt, eingeschränkt
motorway service – Autobahnraststätte
tremendous – gewaltig, enorm

E | Promoting and advertising products

R **1** **Listening: Launching an advertising campaign**

◎ A 2.1 Listen to the telephone conversation between Frank Wesemann, the product manager of a German tablet pc producer and Lilly Winter, who works in the advertising department of their British partner and who is planning an advertising campaign to launch the product on the British market. Decide if the following sentences are true or false. Correct the false sentences.

	true	false
1. The new tablet pc to be launched on the British market is called "Challenge 2.0".	☐	☐
2. This tablet pc allows consumers to read tiny texts on websites without problems.	☐	☐
3. The tablet is very heavy.	☐	☐
4. It has only got a front-facing camera.	☐	☐
5. The lowest possible storage is 16 GB and it cannot be expanded by the users.	☐	☐

Corrected sentences

____

____

____

____

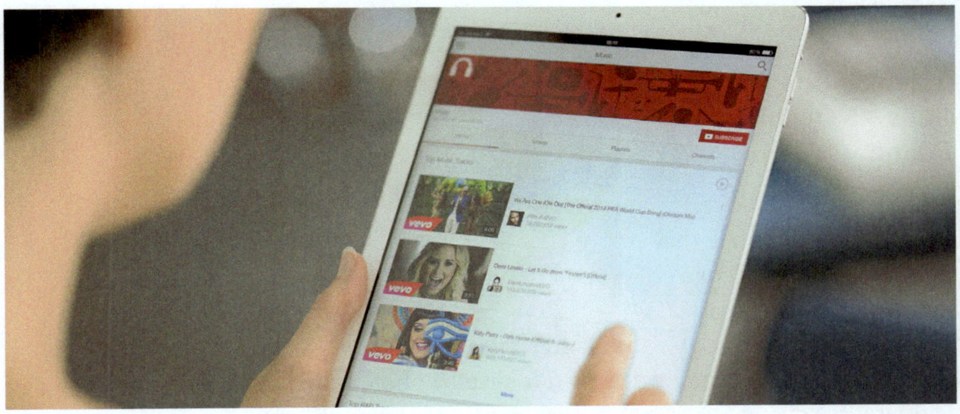

R **2** **Filling in a memo**

◎ A 2.1 Listen to the telephone conversation again and fill in the memo.

MEMO

Caller: ______________________________

Call taken by: ______________________________

Subject: ______________________________

____

____

____

____

WORD BANK

subject – Betreff, Thema

WORD BANK ◎

additional – zusätzlich
back-facing – nach hinten zeigend
capable – fähig
to expand – erweitern
extraordinary – außergewöhnlich
front-facing – nach vorne zeigend
furthermore – außerdem
Go ahead, please. – Fahren Sie bitte fort.
lightweight – Leichtgewicht
on-board – *(hier:)* auf der Platine
operating system – Betriebssystem
storage space – Speicherplatz
tiny – winzig
unique selling point (USP) – Alleinstellungsmerkmal

R **3**

Taking notes ●

⊙ A 2.1

Listen to the dialogue once more and take notes on the product details.

Name of the product

____

Technical details

Display: ______________________________

Weight: ______________________________

Camera: ______________________________

Storage space: ______________________________

Operating system: ______________________________

R/P **4**

Project work: Product descriptions

You are currently spending some time in the marketing department of your company to find out how to advertise a product. Your supervisor has given you the task to write a product description for a product of your choice.

Step 1: Read the following example of a product description and the tips on how to write a successful one.

Product description: "Grandkids – 5 Opening" Photo Frame

They will bring a smile to your grandparents' faces every time they see them. If you are looking for a timeless present for a grandparent, this is the frame you should buy!
Our "Grandkids" frame is lovingly designed to display photographs of your grandparents' loved ones. If you have favourite photographs of your kids you want to show them, this frame will display up to five of them perfectly.
This frame is the ideal gift for the loving grandparent. Simply choose five favourite photographs and frame them. It's sure to be enjoyed and remembered for many, many years! The rear-side of the frame has a sturdy flap and is suitable for desk display, so it's ideal for showing off the grandkids in any room you wish. Give your grandparents one of the best presents in their life with a "Grandkids" frame that is sure to warm their hearts forever!

Tips: How to be successful when writing a product description

- ✓ Start by imagining your ideal buyer and address him/her directly and personally. Ask and answer questions as if you're having a conversation with them. Then choose the words your ideal buyer would use. Use the word 'you' and think of a suitable heading, too.
- ✓ Highlight the main features of your product.
- ✓ Prove why your product is, for example, the best or the easiest. In order to do this you will sometimes need to use superlatives.

WORD BANK

to address sb – jdn. ansprechen
choice – Wahl
favourite – Lieblings-
flap – Klappe
to frame – (ein)rahmen
gift – Geschenk
heading – Überschrift
to highlight – hervorheben
to imagine – sich vorstellen
to prove – beweisen
rear-side – Rückseite
sturdy – stabil
superlative – Übertreibung, Superlativ
timeless – zeitlos

Step 2: Choose a product that is sold at your company and write a product description. Your description should not have more than 100 words.

→ **PHRASES:** page 77

Heading

____

Product description

____

Step 3: Present your product description in the class.

R/P **5**

Internet research: Sales promotion in stores

Shop owners use sales promotions in order to make more money, and many of the products that consumers buy are indeed from sales promotions in stores. Search the internet for a video about sales promotions in stores. Watch the video and fill in the following form. Then explain your findings to your partner.

Product: _______________

Type of promotion: _______________

Possible effects: _______________

P **6**

Presentation: Your company

Think about your own workplace and prepare a presentation about how sales are or could be promoted there.
If possible, take pictures of different types of sales promotion and include them in your presentation. Then present it in class.

WORD BANK

effect – Wirkung
workplace – Arbeitsplatz

F | Checking

1 Prepositions

Put in the correct preposition. Use the words from the box.

after • for • to • with • for

We have prepared a flyer **1** ______________ promote an energy drink that helps you to cope **2** ______________ your daily challenges. It is **3** ______________ people who want to stay fit. Customers can ask **4** ______________ a glass of the drink. **5** ______________ a few minutes they will feel great.

P

2 Asking questions

Make questions and ask for the underlined parts of the sentences.

1. Anita worked <u>at a DIY store</u> in Gera last month.

____

2. We opened a branch in Bristol <u>in spring</u>.

____

3. My brother bought <u>two batteries</u> at a home entertainment shop.

____

4. I made a lot of phone calls to Britain <u>because members of my family still live there</u>.

____

3 Word order

Find the right order and put the verbs in the simple past.

1. want • Mr Winter • week • the sales promotion • to open • on Monday

____

2. in contact • stay • home • family • We • back • with • our

____

3. Paris • last year • win • We • trip • to • a

____

4. drink • They • the • other • country • sell • no • in

____

ICH KANN JETZT ...

1. Werbematerialien verstehen und erstellen. ○○○
2. auf Interesse an Produkten richtig reagieren und produktbezogene Fragen beantworten. ○○○
3. eine Firmengeschichte nachvollziehen. ○○○
4. verschiedene Maßnahmen zur Verkaufsförderung beurteilen. ○○○

☺☺☺ = Kann ich schon!
☺☺ = Kann ich ein bisschen!
☺ = Kann ich bald!

G | Phrases: Product promotion

Planning a product promotion	
Mrs Kugler is opening a sales promotion week.	Frau Kugler eröffnet gerade eine Verkaufsförderungswoche.
We are planning a product promotion/new campaign.	Wir planen eine Produktwerbung/neue Kampagne.
I will do some promotion for the product.	Ich werde Werbung für das Produkt machen.
We can advertise our product on the radio.	Wir können im Radio für unser Produkt Werbung machen.
We ask assistants from the public relations department to help us.	Wir bitten Mitarbeiter, aus der Abteilung für Öffentlichkeitsarbeit uns zu helfen.
We will design a poster for a new product.	Wir werden ein Plakat für ein neues Produkt entwerfen.
We want to celebrate the launch of the product.	Wir möchten den Verkaufsstart des Produktes feiern.
I can give you some background information about the product.	Ich kann Ihnen einige Hintergrundinformationen zum Produkt geben.
You can take part in a competition.	Sie können an einem Preisausschreiben/Wettbewerb teilnehmen.
You can win a prize.	Sie können einen Preis gewinnen.
You can try our products.	Sie können unsere Produkte ausprobieren.
Here's our flyer for the new energy drink.	Hier ist unser Flyer für den neuen Energiedrink.

Explaining products	
Excuse me, are you interested in more information about our new product?	Entschuldigung, sind Sie an weiteren Informationen über unser neues Produkt interessiert?
You can try our mobile phone, if you want.	Sie können unser Mobiltelefon gerne ausprobieren, wenn Sie möchten.
If you have any questions, please feel free to contact us again.	Falls Sie Fragen haben, können Sie sich mit uns jederzeit wieder in Verbindung setzen.
The product is stylish and easy to use.	Das Produkt ist modisch und leicht zu bedienen.
Would you like to have a closer look at the product?	Möchten Sie sich gern das Produkt näher ansehen?
We have an attractive offer for you.	Wir haben ein attraktives Angebot für Sie.
May I give you a leaflet about the products?	Darf ich Ihnen einen Prospekt über die Produkte mitgeben?
We have a range of products on offer right now.	Wir haben gerade verschiedene Produkte im Angebot.

ig54s6

7

NACH DIESER UNIT:

- √ kann ich Kunden den richtigen Umgang mit Produkten erläutern,
- √ kann ich auf Einwände reagieren,
- √ kann ich Regeln und Vorschriften erläutern,
- √ kann ich verärgerte Kunden beruhigen,
- √ kann ich mit Diebstahl umgehen.

A

B

C

D

Special sales situations

A | Handling goods

1 **Touching products**

Look at the photos above and decide whether customers are allowed to touch the products shown (✓) or not (✗). Then write down what the photos show.

Photo A: ☐ ______________________

Photo B: ☐ ______________________

Photo C: ☐ ______________________

Photo D: ☐ ______________________

2 **Customers handling goods**

Look at the photos again and match them to the following sentences.

☐ 1. Customers are allowed to take it out of the box and study the label.

☐ 2. If there is a sample bottle, you can try it out and find out how it smells.

☐ 3. You are not allowed to touch it because it is fragile.

☐ 4. The customer can try them on and see if they fit.

☐ 5. In some shops you are allowed to taste it before you buy it.

☐ 6. You are allowed to touch it and feel the material.

P **3** **Products at your company**

Name three products you sell at your company which need special handling.

____

____

WORD BANK

to be allowed to – dürfen
fragile – zerbrechlich
sample – Muster
to smell – riechen
to touch – anfassen

B | Giving instructions

1 Dos and don'ts

Look at the list of dos and don'ts in different shops. Use the words in the box to correct the statements. Look at the Language box on page 80 for help.

isn't allowed to • must • mustn't • don't have to

Example: Shop assistants **mustn't price** the goods they want to sell.
→ *Shop assistants must price the goods they want to sell.*

1. Customers **are allowed** to unpack goods in a supermarket to check the content.

2. Children **mustn't climb** onto furniture that is for sale.

3. Shop assistants **don't have to be** friendly to difficult customers.

4. At the cash desk customers **must pay** in cash.

2 Dealing with difficult situations

What would you say to customers in these situations? Use the words in brackets.

→ **PHRASES:** page 89

Example: A customer is pressing buttons on a TV. (**aren't allowed**/**go** wrong)
→ "Excuse me, Sir, but you aren't allowed to do that. It could go wrong. But I can show you how it works if you want."

1. A woman is touching soft fruit. (**aren't allowed to touch**/**go** off)

2. A customer is touching a carpet. (**are allowed to touch**/**feel the material**)

3. A man is reading a travel guide in a book store. (**may look**/**show more guides**)

P

3 Rules at school

Think about the rules at your school and talk to a partner about them.

4 Explaining care instructions

Match the symbols to the instructions and draw lines.

1.		a) You can wash the clothes in the washing machine at 60°.
2.		b) You should wash this piece of clothing by hand.
3.		c) You mustn't bleach this product.
4.	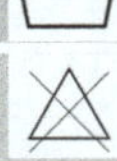	d) You are allowed to iron this piece of clothing with low heat.
5.	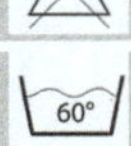	e) You must protect this product against humidity.
6.	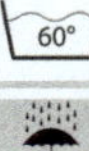	f) Extremely flammable! You must protect it from sunlight.

WORD BANK

to bleach – bleichen
button – Knopf
care instructions – Pflegehinweise
carpet – Teppichboden
to climb (onto) – hinaufklettern
content – Inhalt
flammable – entflammbar
furniture – Möbel
to go off – schlecht werden
to go wrong – schiefgehen
heat – Hitze
humidity – Feuchtigkeit
to iron – bügeln
to press – drücken
to price sth – etw. auszeichnen
to protect – schützen
rule – Regel
travel guide – Reiseführer

LANGUAGE BOX **Modale Hilfsverben**

Mit *must/have to, mustn't* und *don't/doesn't have to* wird ausgedrückt, was man tun muss, nicht tun darf und nicht zu tun braucht.

I	**must**	**mustn't**
he/she/it	**must**	**mustn't**
we/you/they	**must**	**mustn't**
I	**have to**	**don't have to**
he/she/it	**has to**	**doesn't have to**
we/you/they	**have to**	**don't have to**

must/have to = müssen — *I* ***must/have to*** *go to school five days a week.*
mustn't = nicht dürfen — *I* ***mustn't*** *smoke in this room.*
don't have to = nicht brauchen — *I* ***don't have to*** *go to school on Sundays.*

WORD BANK

condition – Zustand
credit card – Kreditkarte
dirty – dreckig
to keep (to) – sich halten (an)
polite(ly) – höflich
regulation – Vorschrift
smoking area – Raucherzone
unfortunately – leider

→ **GRAMMAR:** page 154

Üben interaktiv
Modale Hilfsverben
6en92c

C | Explaining rules and regulations

P/I **1** **Role play: Explaining rules to customers**

Sometimes customers do not keep to the rules in your shop. Work with a partner and match the rules to the situations. Then explain the rules politely to each other. Use the phrases in the box.

→ **PHRASES:** page 89

I'm really sorry, Sir/Madam, but … • Excuse me, but … • Unfortunately I have to tell you that … • Sorry Sir/Madam, but you aren't allowed to … • You mustn't … • You must/have to … • You don't have to …

1. Two boys want to buy alcohol and cigarettes. They are too young to buy these products.
2. A couple enters a home entertainment shop with their bags.
3. A customer enters a fashion shop with an ice cream.
4. A customer smokes in the non-smoking area of a restaurant.
5. An old lady touches clothes with dirty fingers.
6. A customer walks with his dog through the aisles of a supermarket.
7. A customer wants to pay for some sweets by credit card.

- Customers under the age of 17 are not allowed to buy cigarettes and alcohol.
- Customers must leave their bags at the information desk. You can pick them up after shopping.
- Customers mustn't bring any food into the shop.
- Customers are allowed to smoke in special smoking areas.
- You have to keep the products in good condition.
- You are not allowed to bring pets inside. Ask our assistants and they will look after your pet while you go shopping.
- Purchases under €15 mustn't be paid by credit card.

P **2** **Regulations at your place of work**

Which rules do you have in your shop? Work in groups and explain them to each other.

→ **PHRASES:** page 89

D | Dealing with customer complaints

R **1** **Customers complaining**

Read the description of two situations in which customers are complaining.
Complete the sentences with the words given in the box.

> accepts • appreciates • button • exception • exchange • gardening • information desk • point • purchase • receipt • replacement • returns • ruined • suggestion • voucher

Situation 1: At the DIY-shop

A customer bought a pair of gloves for **1** ________________. He is very upset because they were **2** ________________ after two hours of work in the garden. The shop assistant makes a **3** ________________. He offers to **4** ________________ the gloves and gives him a **5** ________________ for €10. The customer **6** ________________ the offer and **7** ________________ the service.

Situation 2: At the toys and games department

A woman enters a shop with a doll and a **1** ________________. She has just come from the **2** ________________ and wants to exchange the doll. She is angry because the doll doesn't speak when you press the **3** ________________. The shop assistant sees her **4** ________________ and wants to know when she bought the doll. The shop accepts **5** ________________ within two weeks after the **6** ________________. He wants to give a **7** ________________ for it but it is now three weeks after the purchase. However, the shop assistant makes an **8** ________________.

I/P **2** **Role play: Talking to a dissatisfied customer** ○ → page 136

Work with a partner. One of you is a shop assistant, the other is a customer.
Use the situations in exercise 1 and the phrases below. Then change roles.

→ **PHRASES:** page 89

Shop assistant	Customer
How can I help you?	I have a complaint to make.
What exactly happened?	I'm very upset.
The problem is easy to solve.	I want to report a problem.
I can offer you a replacement.	I'll accept your offer.
Let me make you a suggestion.	That's very kind of you.
I can see your point.	Thanks a lot.
That can happen sometimes, but …	I really appreciate your excellent service.

WORD BANK

to appreciate – (wert)schätzen
dissatisfied – unzufrieden
exception – Ausnahme
to exchange – (um)tauschen
glove – Handschuh
replacement – Ersatz
return – Rückgabe
ruined – ruiniert
to see a point – einen Standpunkt verstehen
to solve – lösen
suggestion – Vorschlag
upset – aufgebracht, verärgert
voucher – Gutschein

R **3**

Reading comprehension

Read the dialogue and complete the sentences with the correct ending.

Shop assistant: Good morning, madam. What can I do for you?

Customer: Good morning. I have a complaint to make. Last month, I bought myself a treadmill in your online fitness shop. Unfortunately, it was delivered without any detailed operating instructions, but only with a quick start guide.

Shop assistant: I see. I can understand that you feel annoyed. But I think I can help you. When you bought the product you may have seen a link to the website of the maker of the treadmill. On the website you can download a detailed instruction manual about how to use your treadmill. There are also videos which show how to use the treadmill.

Customer: That's exactly what I am looking for! To see how the treadmill works in practice. I am an absolute beginner, you know. I want to keep fit because I sit all day at work. But the problem is that I am not very good at searching for additional information on different websites.

Shop assistant: Right. Well, what I can do for you is to go to the website of the manufacturer here in the shop, and download the videos as well as the detailed instruction manual onto a USB stick. Then you will have access to all the information you need.

Customer: That would be really great. Luckily, USB sticks are so small nowadays that I always have one with my keys. Just a moment, please. Here you are!

Shop assistant: Thank you very much, madam. It will only take five minutes. The internet is fast here. Would you like to look around in our shop while I do it? I'll find you when I've finished.

Customer: That's a good idea. Thank you.

1. The customer has a complaint to make because she
   - ☐ a) didn't receive the right treadmill.
   - ☐ b) can't use the treadmill.
   - ☐ c) didn't receive detailed operating instructions for the treadmill.

2. The shop assistant told her she could look at the producer's website in order to
   - ☐ a) find information about other treadmills.
   - ☐ b) to find out how to contact the producer.
   - ☐ c) download the detailed information as well as videos.

3. The customer
   - ☐ a) is pleased that the shop assistant downloads the information for her.
   - ☐ b) asks the shop assistant to get all the information she is interested in.
   - ☐ c) asks the shop assistant for a USB stick with the information.

4. The shop assistant
   - ☐ a) asks the customer to pay for the service.
   - ☐ b) asks the customer to come back in five minutes.
   - ☐ c) suggests that she can look around in the shop while she is downloading the information.

WORD BANK

operating instructions – Bedienungsanleitung
quick start guide – Schnellstartanleitung
to feel annoyed – sich verärgert fühlen
to do sb a favour – jemandem einen Gefallen tun

WORD BANK ⊙

to calm down – beruhigen
inconvenience – Unannehmlichkeit

E | Convincing upset customers

R **1** **Listening: Dealing with an upset customer** ○ → page 136

◎ A 2.2 A customer is making a complaint. Listen to the dialogue and complete the sentences.

1. The customer is upset because ______________________________.
2. In the future the customer thinks she is going to ______________________.
3. The manager tries ______________________________.

WORD BANK

expiry date – Verfallsdatum, Ablaufdatum

2 **Say it in English**

1. Der Prospekt, der heute morgen aus England kam, war sehr interessant.

   ____

2. Sie sind ein treuer Kunde, den wir nicht verlieren wollen.

   ____

3. Die Cafeteria ist ein Ort, an dem man Essen und Getränke kaufen kann.

   ____

LANGUAGE BOX **Relativsätze**

Wir verwenden *who* für Personen, *which* für Sachen und *where* für Orte.
Beispiele: *A shop assistant is a person/someone* ***who*** *… A computer is a machine* ***which*** *… A supermarket is a place* ***where*** *…*

WORD BANK ◎

caution – Vorsicht
dairy product – Milchprodukt
to estimate – schätzen
flavour – Geschmack
heat-treated – wärmebehandelt, pasteurisiert
to judge – beurteilen, bewerten
legible – lesbar
minced meat – Hackfleisch
to pose a health risk – ein Gesundheitsrisiko darstellen
to retain – bewahren
to spoil – verderben

→ **GRAMMAR:** page 157

Üben interaktiv
Relativsätze
45m3s3

V 4 Food expiry dates

Before watching

1. Can you eat dairy products and minced meat safely some days after the expiry date? Why, or why not?

While watching

2. Now watch the video and check your answers in exercise 1.
3. Watch the video again and answer the following questions.
   a) What is the difference between a best before date and a use by date?
   b) What is the official food tasters' job?
   c) What should you do if food tastes funny?

After watching

4. Do a short quiz and ask each other questions about different food and how important the expiry date is for them.

F | Dealing with dissatisfied customers

R **1** **Listening: A complaint on the phone**

⊚ A 2.3 Listen to a telephone conversation between Ebru Bulat, an upset customer who visited a sportswear shop last week, and the shop manager Justine Baumeister. Then answer the questions.

1. What is the reason for Ms Bulat's call?

____

____

2. How does Justine Baumeister react to the complaint at first?

____

____

3. What does Justine finally suggest to Ms Bulat?

____

____

4. What is Ms Bulat's reply to that?

____

____

R **2** **Telephone phrases**

⊚ A 2.3 Listen to the conversation again and write down the phrases Justine Baumeister uses to reply to the upset customer.

Offering help	Apologizing	Calming down

I/P **3** **Role play: Dissatisfied customers**

Use the following role cards and act out the telephone conversations with a partner.

→ **PHRASES:** page 89

Partner A

Telephone call 1: You are the customer

- You live in Munich and you bought some blue-ray disks when you visited your grandmother in Rostock last week.
- You are annoyed because you can't play the disks on your old DVD player.
- In your view the sales assistant should have informed you about this before you bought the disks.

Telephone call 2: You are the sales assistant

- Inform the customer that he/she could have returned the googles within 14 days of purchase but after three months this is not possible.
- The customer can't send back the used goggles and get a replacement.
- Be friendly and offer the customer a low-value gift voucher.

WORD BANK

low-value – von geringem Wert
sportswear – Sportbekleidung

WORD BANK ⊚

annoying – ärgerlich
at sb's expense – auf jdns. Kosten
by mail – per Post
Hold the line, please. – Bleiben Sie bitte am Apparat.
in stock – vorrätig
in the meantime – zwischenzeitlich
scratch – Kratzer
spot – Fleck

Partner B

Telephone call 1: You are the sales assistant

- Tell the customer that he/she can send the disks back within 14 days of purchase but only if they are still in the original packaging.
- Apologize for the inconvenience caused.
- Find a reason why the customer was not informed about the playability of the blue-ray disks.

Telephone call 2: You are the customer

- You live in Magdeburg and bought some diving goggles in Braunschweig three months ago.
- You used them for the first time last week and noticed that the googles are too small.
- Ask for a full replacement of the googles.

R **4** **Reading comprehension**

Read the e-mail to the owner of an online shop home entertainment. Then answer the questions on page 86.

From: Richard Johnson@supermail.com
To: info@bigstore.co.uk
Sent: May 17, 201.. at 12:15
Subject: My online complaint of 10 May, 20..

Dear Sir or Madam,

I have been a loyal customer of your online shop for many years. Today I would like to praise the reaction of your customer service agent in an online chat to a complaint I had last week.

I am a fan of Heavy Metal music and I bought myself a new CD of my favourite group in your shop about a week ago. Unfortunately, the CD that was delivered had scratches when I looked at it closely. I immediately clicked on the chat symbol in your online shop and explained the situation to one of your customer service agents. He offered to exchange the CD without asking any more questions. Then he asked for my e-mail address to send me a prepaid address label. I only had to stick it on an envelope, enclose the CD and send it back to you. Additionally, he gave me a voucher for a 10% discount on any products that I buy in your online shop within the next six months.

I would like to thank you for your excellent service. I will certainly recommend your online shop to friends of mine.

Please inform your friendly shop assistants about this letter, too.

Your loyal customer,

Richard Johnson

WORD BANK

customer service agent – Kundenbetreuer
diving goggles – Taucherbrille
original packaging – Originalverpackung
playability – Abspielbarkeit
to praise – loben
prepaid address label – frankierte Adressenaufkleber
to recommend – empfehlen

1. Why did Richard Johnson write an e-mail to the owner of the online shop?

2. What did Richard Johnson buy?

3. When did he buy the CD and what did he see when it was delivered??

4. How did the customer service agent react to Richard Johnson's complaint?

5. What did Richard Johnson ask the online shop owner to do at the end of the e-mail?

R/P **5**

Project work: Coping with dissatisfied customers

Read the following guideline about how to behave correctly in a situation with dissatisfied customers. Think about at least three situations in which you had to deal with upset customers and describe how you coped with them. Discuss your behaviour and critically reflect on it. Make suggestions of what you could have done better.

Working in sales and retailing means that you sometimes have to deal with upset or even angry customers. This can be a real challenge, especially if the customer puts all the blame on you even though you are not responsible for what happened.

Here is some advice on how to cope with such situations in a professional way:

1. When a customer starts yelling, never yell back, just stay calm in order not to escalate the situation.
2. Do not feel personally attacked. Remember that the customer is not angry with you as a person but with the quality of the product or the service offered.
3. Listen carefully and do not interrupt the customer. Let her or him let off steam first. Maintain eye contact and keep your arms uncrossed so that the customer can be sure that you are taking an interest in his or her problems.

4. Give the customer personal feedback. Show genuine understanding for what has happened and take it seriously. Apologize for something even if you are sure that it was not your fault.
5. Always try to find a suitable solution to the customer's problem which is acceptable to the customer.

WORD BANK

genuine – echt, ehrlich
to escalate – eskalieren
to interrupt – unterbrechen
to let off steam – Dampf ablassen
to put the blame on sb – jdm. die Schuld geben
to reflect on sth – über etw. nachdenken
uncrossed – nicht gekreuzt
to yell at sb – jdn. anschreien

G | Handling shoplifters

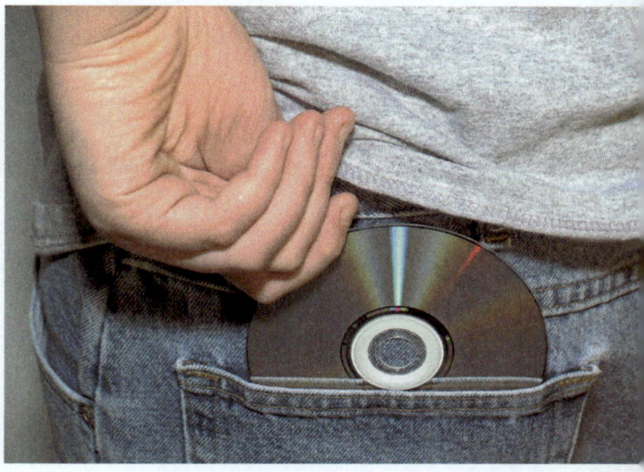

P **1** **Talking about shoplifting**

Work with a partner and describe what you can see in the picture on the right. Then talk about your experiences with shoplifters. Say what happened and how you dealt with them.

R **2** **How to deal with shoplifters**

Read the article about the problem of shoplifting for retailers. Use a dictionary if necessary. Then use the information given in the text and make notes on how retailers can handle this problem. Write in your exercise book.

Shoplifting – a problem for retailers

The statistics are truly shocking: According to a US business journal, the value of goods stolen from stores all over America each year amounts to 37 billion dollars! This means there are more than half a million successful thefts every day.

But experts warn retailers to be careful about reacting too aggressively to the problem. There is a chance that the shoplifter will react violently when confronted. Retailers should always put their own safety and the safety of their staff and customers first.

An indiscriminate hard line on shoplifters can also get retailers into trouble. For example, a DIY chain store was recently sued for damages by a customer they accused of shoplifting a $4 item. The customer had purchased almost $1,500 worth of goods at the store that same day.

Experts also advise retailers not to overreact. A young mother shopping with small children may forget about something she (or possibly they) put under her cart. In such cases it is best to just remind her in a friendly way to go to the register and pay for the extra items.

Furthermore, retailers need to remember that shoplifting may be someone's way of coping with a difficult financial situation. So if someone is caught shoplifting, they still have the right to be treated fairly and with respect.

Finally, retailers should think more about active strategies. If sales staff communicate more often with customers, there are fewer opportunities for them to shoplift. Watching customers can also help to identify potential shoplifters.

Last but not least retailers should make use of modern technology. Electronic tags on articles and sensors at the doors, and of course cameras, are all very effective. Nevertheless, according to current statistics, the average shoplifter will only be caught once for every 50 times they steal something.

R/P **3** **Internet research: Tips for dealing with shoplifting**

Step 1: Search the internet for more tips about how to deal with shoplifting.

Step 2: Use the information you found on the internet and your notes in exercise 2 to write a guideline. Look at the text on page 86 to see how a guideline is structured and give at least five tips.

Step 3: Present your guideline to the class and have a discussion about your proposals.

WORD BANK

to accuse sb of sth – jdn. wegen etw. beschuldigen
average – durchschnittlich
cart – Einkaufswagen
to confront sb – jdm. entgegentreten
indiscriminate – wahllos
nevertheless – trotzdem, dennoch
proposal – Vorschlag
shoplifting – Ladendiebstahl
to sue sb for damages – jdn. auf Schadenersatz verklagen
theft – Diebstahl
violently – gewalttätig

H | Checking

1 Retail crossword

Find the right words and fill in the crossword.

Across:

1. Information that tells you how to do or use something.
4. It tells you what you are allowed or not allowed to do.
6. If something burns easily it is …
9. Something that you can win in a competition.

Down:

2. When you give something and get something similar back.
3. If you don't have to pay for something, then you get it for …
5. A product which breaks easily is …
7. Someone who makes medicines in a shop or hospital.
8. A man who works in business.

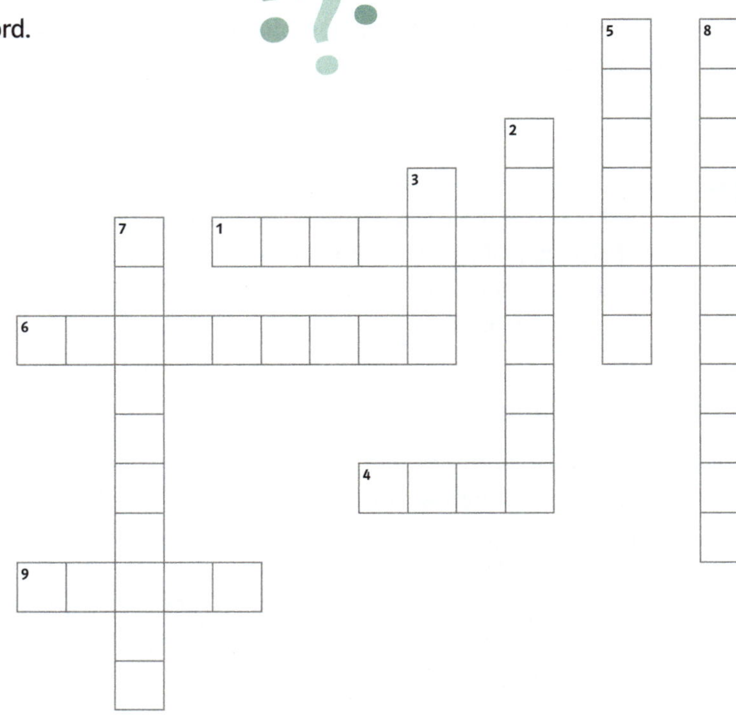

2 Rules and regulations

Underline the correct word(s) in each sentence.

1. You **don't have to/must** save the document before you turn off the computer.
2. In Germany people **must/mustn't** be 18 before they are allowed to drive a car alone.
3. You **mustn't/don't have to** forget to lock the door when you close the shop.
4. A shop assistant **is allowed to/must** serve customers in a shop.

3 Paraphrasing

Give definitions of the following words and use relative clauses.

Example: *computer: A computer is a machine which stores documents.*

1. shop owner: ______________________________
2. high-resolution camera: ______________________________
____
3. shop assistant: ______________________________
4. smoking area: ______________________________

ICH KANN JETZT …

1. Kunden auf den richtigen Umgang mit Waren hinweisen. ○○○
2. den Kunden Pflegehinweise zu Produkten geben. ○○○
3. Regeln und Vorschriften erläutern. ○○○
4. angemessen auf Kundeneinwände reagieren. ○○○
5. verärgerte Kunden beruhigen und ihnen Lösungen anbieten. ○○○
6. mit Ladendiebstahl professionell umgehen. ○○○

WORD BANK

to burn – (ver)brennen
to lock – abschließen

☺☺☺ = Kann ich schon!
☺☺ = Kann ich ein bisschen!
☺ = Kann ich bald!

I | Phrases: Special sales situations

Handling goods	
You are allowed to touch the goods.	Es ist Ihnen gestattet, die Ware anzufassen.
Please look at the label for more information about the product.	Sehen Sie sich bitte das Etikett an, um mehr Informationen über das Produkt zu erhalten.
I'm sorry, but you mustn't touch the goods.	Es tut mir leid, aber Sie dürfen die Ware nicht berühren.
You can try out the product if you want.	Sie können das Produkt ausprobieren, falls Sie es wünschen.
You must wash these clothes by hand.	Sie müssen diese Kleidung von Hand waschen.
Don't iron this product with high heat.	Bügeln Sie dieses Produkt nicht bei hoher Hitze.
This material is extremely flammable.	Dieses Material ist sehr leicht entflammbar.

Explaining rules and regulations	
I must tell you that you are not allowed to buy these products.	Ich muss Ihnen sagen, dass es Ihnen nicht erlaubt ist, diese Produkte zu kaufen.
You mustn't bring food/ice cream/pets into this shop.	Sie dürfen kein Essen/Eis/Haustier mit in diesen Laden nehmen.
You mustn't smoke here.	Sie dürfen hier nicht rauchen.

Dealing with customer complaints	
What exactly happened?	Was ist genau passiert?
I can see your point.	Ich verstehe Ihren Standpunkt.
That's really annoying, Sir/Madam.	Das ist wirklich ärgerlich.
Let me make a suggestion.	Lassen Sie mich Ihnen einen Vorschlag unterbreiten.
We can give you a replacement.	Wir können Ihnen einen Ersatz anbieten.
We accept returns within two weeks after the purchase.	Wir akzeptieren Rückgaben innerhalb von zwei Wochen nach dem Kauf.
The problem is easy to solve.	Das Problem ist leicht zu lösen.
I can show you how it works.	Ich kann Ihnen zeigen, wie es funktioniert.
I can understand what you're saying.	Ich kann nachvollziehen, was Sie sagen.
That can easily be adjusted. Let me show you …	Das kann leicht eingestellt werden. Lassen Sie es mich Ihnen zeigen …

Convincing upset customers	
I will serve you personally.	Ich werde Sie persönlich bedienen.
We are sorry for the inconvenience caused.	Es tut uns leid, Ihnen Unannehmlichkeiten bereitet zu haben.
I can make you an offer.	Ich kann Ihnen ein Angebot machen.
We don't want to lose loyal customers.	Wir möchten keine treuen Kunden verlieren.

ig54s6

8

NACH DIESER UNIT:

- √ kann ich Gründe für eine Rückrufaktion bei Produkten nennen,
- √ kann ich angemessen auf Kundeneinwände reagieren,
- √ kann ich Garantie- und Sicherheitshinweise verstehen,
- √ kann ich eine Befragung zur Kundenzufriedenheit durchführen.

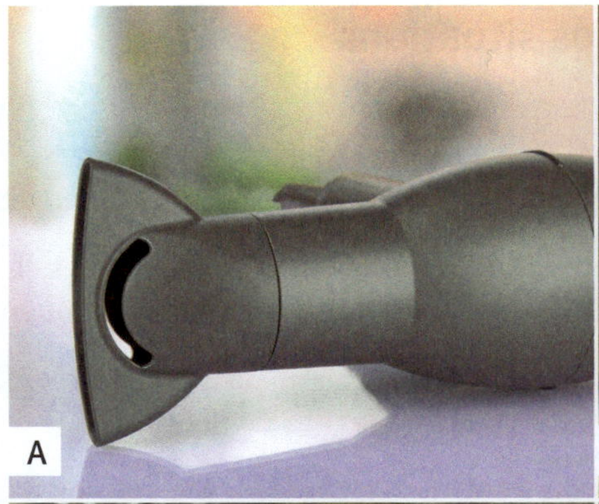

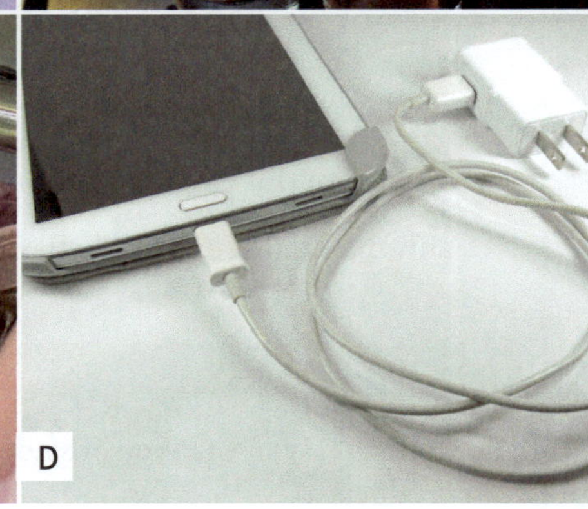

After-sales services

A | Product recall

1 Reasons for a recall

There can be different reasons for a product recall. Look at the photos and match them to possible reasons 1.–4.

Picture	Reasons for a product recall
☐	1. It may get too hot and burn your hair.
☐	2. The material can damage your health in the long run.
☐	3. It could easily break down because of a construction fault.
☐	4. If you use it in the sun it can get extremely hot and damage your mobile phone.

P

2 Problems with product recalls

A product recall is the last thing producers want to do. Write down at least two reasons.

to damage the company's reputation • to lose trust in • to unsettle customers

____

____

____

WORD BANK

construction fault – Konstruktionsfehler
to damage – beschädigen
in the long run – auf lange Sicht
to lose trust in – Vertrauen verlieren in
product recall – Produktrückrufaktion
reputation – Ruf, Ansehen
to unsettle – beunruhigen

B | Dealing with product recalls

R **1** **Reading comprehension**

Read the text and answer the questions.

Product recall for bathroom scale, item no 2011
Customer helpline: +49-531-202020

Press release

Dear Users,

We are very sorry to inform you that because of a construction fault, our bathroom scale, item no 2011, shows the wrong weight.

Therefore, we kindly ask all customers who have this item to bring your bathroom scale back to the shop where you bought it. The assistants will give you a full refund or you can have the bathroom scale replaced by a different one.

We apologize for the inconvenience and have asked the shops to give you a voucher for €20 as a compensation. You can spend the voucher in the shop where you bought the product.

We hope for your further trust in our products and will do our best to meet your needs in the future. If you have any questions, please call our 24-hour helpline.

Ulf Martens
Vice president
Bathroom Equipment and More Ltd

1. Why does the producer have to recall the bathroom scales?

   ____

2. What should the customers do?

   ____

3. What does the producer offer for the inconvenience?

   ____

4. What should customers do if they have any further questions?

   ____

R **2** **Vocabulary work** ◯ → page 136

Read the press release again and find the right words for these explanations.

1. You use it to weigh yourself: ______________________________
2. It is like money and you get goods or services for it: ______________________________
3. The money that you get when you give back a product: ______________________________
4. Another word for ‘hotline’: ______________________________

WORD BANK

to apologize – sich entschuldigen
bathroom scale – Gewichtswaage
compensation – Schadensersatz
helpline – telefonischer Beratungsdienst
to meet sb's needs – die Bedürfnisse von jdm. erfüllen
press release – Pressemitteilung
to replace – ersetzen
weight – Gewicht

C | Customer feedback

R **1** ⦾ A 2.4

Listening: Talking to a friend

Listen to the conversation between Paul, the satisfied customer of a furniture shop, and his friend, Frank.
Then complete the sentences.

1. Frank finds Paul's new furniture ______________________ ______________________.
2. Paul has bought his furniture at Meyer's for ______________________.
3. The furniture shop has always offered the best ______________________.
4. Two years ago Paul wasn't satisfied because ______________________.
5. But Paul is still a loyal customer because ______________________.

WORD BANK

past – vorbei
to push – schieben

WORD BANK ⦾

to share – teilen
on time – pünktlich

R **2**

Customer suggestions

Work with a partner and match the sentence parts. Draw lines.

1. If the aisles in the supermarket are wider,	a) it will be easier to push the trolley past the shelves.
2. If the restaurant offers more meals,	b) I'll go shopping with my whole family.
3. If you clean the bathroom,	c) I won't have to count my money at the cash desk.
4. If you accept credit cards,	d) we will have a better choice.
5. If you open on Sundays,	e) I will use it.

I/P **3**

Role play: Reacting to customer complaints

Work with a partner. One of you is a shop manager, the other one is a shop assistant. Discuss how you should deal with the following complaints. Then change roles.

→ **PHRASES:** page 101

Example: Elderly customers need help after they make their purchase.
Assistant: If we help elderly customers after their shopping, we'll need more shop assistants.
Manager: Yes, somebody should take their shopping to the car.

1. A customer has tried to buy a product in your online shop but the website is currently not available.
2. Many customers want to have a shopping bag for free.
3. Some customers want to take the lift up to the fourth floor but it is often out of order.
4. A customer wants to buy a product that is sold out.

LANGUAGE BOX ***If*-Sätze (Bedingungssätze) Typ 1**

Ein Bedingungssatz besteht aus einem *if*-Satz und einem Hauptsatz. Der *if*-Satz des Typs 1 beschreibt, was unter bestimmten Bedingungen in der Zukunft geschehen wird oder nicht geschehen wird.

Bildung:	*if + simple present*	*will + verb*
Beispiel:	*If you **help** your colleague, she **will be** very happy.*	

→ **GRAMMAR:** page 155

Üben interaktiv
If-Sätze Typ 1
295vu9

D | Apologizing to customers

R **1** **Listening: Asking for a refund** ○ → page 137
◎ A 2.5 Listen to the dialogue between a dissatisfied English-speaking customer and the customer service of a department store. Then answer the questions.

1. What did Mr Lindsay buy in the leather goods department?

   ____

   ____

2. Why did he call the customer service?

   ____

   ____

3. What did the customer service offer Mr Lindsay first?

   ____

   ____

4. But what did Mr Lindsay want to have?

   ____

   ____

"I've got your letter in front of me now, sir."

5. How did the customer service react?

   ____

M **2** **Mediation**
◎ A 2.5 A colleague wants to know why Mr Lindsay called and how the customer service reacted. Listen to the dialogue again and sum it up in German. Write in your exercise book.

3 **Countable and uncountable nouns**
Look at the following sentences and cross out the wrong words.

1. Paul has bought **some furniture / some furnitures**.
2. The careers advisor gave me **good advice / good advices** about work placements.
3. We can give you **some important informations / some important information** about the product.
4. Please don't forget to buy **two pounds of salt / two pound of salts**, **two loaves of bread / two breads** and **some wine / a wine** at the supermarket.
5. You're not allowed to take more than five **clothings / pieces of clothing** into the changing cubicle.

LANGUAGE BOX **Zählbare und unzählbare Nomen**

Es gibt im Englischen genau wie im Deutschen zählbare und unzählbare Nomen. Unzählbaren Nomen im Englischen wird kein *a* oder *an, one, two* usw. vorangestellt und in der Pluralform wird kein *s* am Ende angehängt.

Beispiele: *two kilograms of sugar, four litres of milk, some / any lemonade, a lot of time*

WORD BANK

careers advisor – Berufsberater/in
changing cubicle – Umkleidekabine
countable – zählbar
uncountable – unzählbar

WORD BANK ◎

to rely on – sich verlassen auf
suitcase – Koffer

R **4** **Letter to a customer**

Mr Wienzek has written to Ms Rodriquez about a complaint she made. Read the letter and then match the points 1.–10. to its parts. Write the numbers in the boxes.

1. customer's name and address
2. stating the problem
3. offering compensation
4. the date
5. signature block
6. apologizing
7. the company's name and address
8. salutation
9. subject line (what the letter is about)
10. reference line

☐ Schönfelder Warenhäuser
Alexanderplatz 5
39104 Magdeburg

☐ Your ref/Ihr Zeichen: LW05L ☐ Our ref/unser Zeichen: FW/nm

☐ Ms Rodriquez
Magdeburger Straße 21
39175 Biederitz ☐ 12 May 20...

☐ Yours sincerely,

☐ I have been informed that you called our customer service to make a complaint about a pair of eco-friendly jeans you bought at our store two weeks ago. I understand that you have recently seen a documentary about the inhumane conditions under which jeans are produced in some factories in Bangladesh.

☐ **Your complaint about our eco-friendly jeans produced in Bangladesh**

☐ *Frank Wienzek*

☐ I must admit that the content of the film is generally correct. However, in contrast to the factories shown in the film I can assure you that our eco-friendly jeans are produced under acceptable working conditions that are in keeping with international health and safety standards. Furthermore, the workers who produce our products receive a fair pay above the national average. This is also the reason why our eco-friendly products are more expensive than other products.

☐ Dear Ms Rodriguez,

☐ For your information I enclose a brochure that illustrates the conditions and standards of our eco-friendly products. If you have any more questions, please don't hesitate to contact us again.

☐ We apologize for any inconvenience caused and hope to welcome you again in our stores soon.

P **5** **Writing a letter** ●

Write a letter to a customer who complained about the bad quality of a product with the customer service two weeks ago. Use your exercise book.

→ **PHRASES:** page 101

INTERCULTURAL BOX **Geschäftsbriefe**

Unterschiede zwischen einem englischen und deutschen Geschäftsbrief sind:

1. Nach der Anrede ist der erste Buchstabe des ersten Satzes ein Großbuchstabe.
   Beispiel: *Dear Sir or Madam, We would like ...*
2. Wenn nach der Anrede ein Komma folgt, muss nach der Grußformel ebenfalls eines gesetzt werden. Es kann auch in beiden Fällen entfallen.
   Beispiele: *Dear Sir or Madam ... Yours faithfully*
   Dear Mr Black, ... Yours sincerely,
3. *Yours faithfully* bzw. *Yours sincerely* entspricht im Deutschen „Mit freundlichen Grüßen". *Yours faithfully* wird bei einer allgemeinen Anrede, *Yours sincerely* bei einer personenbezogenen Anrede (*Dear Mr .../Mrs ...*) verwendet.
4. Die Betreffzeile (z.B. *Your invoice from ...*) kommt nach der Anrede.
5. Beim Datum wird der Monat ausgeschrieben.

WORD BANK

to admit – zugeben
to assure sb of sth – jdm. etw. zusichern
documentary – Dokumentarfilm
factory – Fabrik
health and safety standards – Arbeitsschutzstandards
to hesitate – zögern
in keeping with – in Einklang mit
national average – Landesdurchschnitt
recently – kürzlich
reference line – Bezugszeichenzeile
salutation – Anrede
signature – Unterschrift
subject line – Betreffzeile

LANGUAGE BOX ***Present perfect*** **und** ***simple past***

Das ***simple past*** wird für vergangene Ereignisse verwendet, die abgeschlossen sind und keinen Bezug mehr zur Gegenwart haben. Häufige Signalwörter sind: *last, yesterday, ago.*

Das ***present perfect*** wird verwendet

1. für Ereignisse, die in der Vergangenheit begonnen haben und die noch nicht abgeschlossen sind bzw. deren Ergebnisse für die Gegenwart noch wichtig sind. Häufige Signalwörter sind: *(not) yet, this year / month, never, ever, for, since.*
   since = seit (für Zeitpunkt) *for* = seit (für Zeitraum)
   Beispiel: *I haven't been to school* ***for two days****. I have been at home* ***since Monday****.*
2. für Ereignisse, die gerade abgeschlossen wurden.
   Beispiel: *I* ***have*** *just* ***done*** *my homework.*

→ **GRAMMAR:** page 151 – 152

Üben interaktiv
Present perfect und simple past
44c65k

6 Present perfect or simple past?

Underline the correct verb forms in the following sentences.

1. I **have not been to / was not** in Spain during the past two years.
2. Elvira **bought / has bought** a new washing machine yesterday.
3. I **have started / started** my traineeship at the department store one year ago.
4. René **hasn't seen / didn't see** his boss since Monday.
5. We **had / have had** a new colleague at work for two weeks.

SKILLS **Interpreting diagrams**

Statistics and diagrams often illustrate or explain something. When you compare countable things (for example, people) you should use *more, the most, fewer, the fewest.* When you compare uncountable things (for example, time) you should use *more, the most, less, the least* (see also the Language boxes on page 58 and 93).

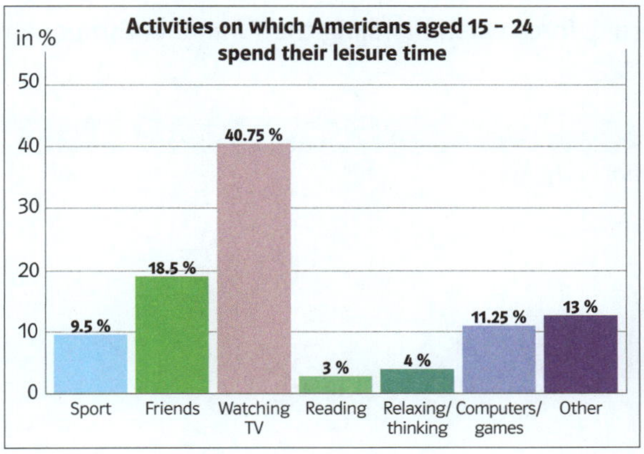

1 Analysing a bar chart

Use the information in the bar chart and answer the questions.

1. What percentage of young Americans spend their leisure time on sport?

   ____

2. What percentage of their time do they spend on computers and games?

   ____

2 What is right?

Complete the sentences with *more, the most, less* or *the least.*

Young Americans spend **1** ______________ time on sport than with their friends. But they spend **2** ______________ time relaxing or thinking than reading. The activity on which they spend **3** ______________ time is watching TV. The activity on which they spend **4** ______________ time is reading.

WORD BANK

bar chart – Balkendiagramm
percentage – Prozentsatz

E | Understanding safety instructions

R **1**
Reading comprehension

People who buy goods often do not read the safety instructions in the user manual before they use a new product. This can lead to problems or even damage to the products and it is usually the customer service that then has to deal with it. Read the following safety instructions for a TV. Use a dictionary if necessary. Then fill in the table below.

Safety instructions

⚠ Choose the location for your TV very carefully. Place it on a stand that has an adequate size and strength to prevent the TV from tipping over.

⚠ Don't put the TV in a place where sunlight or room lighting will be directed towards the screen.

⚠ Use soft or indirect lightning in the room you want to use the TV in.

⚠ Never block ventilation holes on any of the components. Arrange the components in such a way that air can circulate freely.

⚠ Don't stack components.

⚠ Turn off the TV or any other components before you connect or disconnect cables.

⚠ Insert each cable firmly into its designated port.

⚠ Do not use any force when handling the TV and its components.

Potential dangers	Safety instructions
1. Power surges or short-circuits	
2. Overheating	
3. Instability	
4. Bad lighting	

R/P **2**
Internet research: Safety instructions

Step 1: Search the internet for the safety instructions of three more products. Take notes on the recommended safety precautions with the help of a dictionary.

Step 2: Take turns and present the safety instructions to your partner but don't say what product it is. Your partner tries to guess what the product might be.

WORD BANK

to arrange – anordnen
to connect – verbinden
designated – vorgesehen
to direct towards – ausrichten auf
to disconnect – trennen
to insert – hineinstecken, einfügen
instability – Instabilität
overheating – Überhitzung
port – *(hier:)* Anschluss, Schnittstelle
power surge – Überspannung
safety instructions – Sicherheitshinweise
short-circuit – Kurzschluss
to stack – übereinanderstellen
to tip over – umkippen
to use force – Kraft anwenden
user manual – Bedienungsanleitung

F | Giving guarantees

R/M **1** **Listening: A message on the answering machine**

A 2.6 Listen to the message a customer has left on the company's answering machine and write a memo in German for your boss, Martin Schreiber.

TELEFONNOTIZ

Nachricht für: ____________________

angenommen von: ____________________

am (*heutiges Datum*): ____________________

Anrufer: ____________________

Telefonnummer: ____________________

Betreff: ____________________

____

____

____

R **2** **Reading comprehension**

Read the following guarantee information. Correct the statements on page 98 and cross out the wrong information.

OUR GUARANTEE TO YOU

✓ We have been outdoor specialists for backpacking and expedition tents since 1959. Our mission has always been to provide you with the finest quality products and to offer you the best possible customer service. We will only be satisfied when you are satisfied with us.

✓ For this reason, we offer you special guarantee conditions that exceed legal regulations. For every purchase you make, we guarantee a full refund or an immediate replacement within three months of purchase.

✓ We trust that our customers will appreciate the way we treat them. With every order you place you will receive the best quality at a favourable price including best service.

GUARANTEED!

WORD BANK

backpacking – Wandern
to exceed – hinausgehen über
favourable – günstig
legal regulation – gesetzliche Vorschrift
tent – Zelt

WORD BANK

to dispatch – versenden
loudspeaker – Lautsprecher
opening hours – Öffnungszeiten
portable – tragbar
sleep timer – Schlaffunktion, (automatische) Abschaltfunktion
to turn on – anschalten, einschalten
trendy – modisch, schick

1. The company specializes in **all kinds of outdoor equipment/backpacking and tents.**
2. Their guarantee offers **more than/exactly what** legal regulations demand.
3. Customers can rely on a **partial/full** refund within **one month/120 days** of purchase.
4. If a product needs to be replaced this will be done **straight away/within three months.**
5. The outdoor specialist wants to treat its customers in **the best possible way/ a suitable way.**

WORD BANK

beverage – Getränk
graded – abgestuft
interviewee – Befragte/r
satisfaction – Zufriedenheit

P **3** **Product guarantees**

Think of at least three products that you sell at your workplace and the guarantee that is offered on them. Take turns to explain the guarantee conditions to your partner. Use a dictionary if necessary.

G | Customer satisfaction

P **1** **Researching customer satisfaction**

How can you find out how satisfied customers are with your service? Brainstorm different ways to find this out and present your results in class.

2 **Different types of questions**

Look at the examples of four types of question that you can ask in a survey. Write down the correct headings for the different types of questions.

Graded questions • Multiple-choice questions • Open-ended questions • Yes-/No-questions

1. ______________________

Questions that can be answered with 'Yes' or 'No'.

Example:
Have you every complained to our customer service?

☐ yes ☐ no

2. ______________________

The interviewee chooses from given answers.

Example:
Which products do you regularly buy at Superstore?

☐ fruit and vegetables ☐ beverages
☐ dairy products ☐ cleaning products
☐ meat and fish ☐ clothing

3. ______________________________

The interviewee has to choose to what extent they agree/disagree with or like/don't like something.

Example:
How satisfied are you with the customer service at Superstore?

☐ fully satisfied ☐ 50% satisfied ☐ not at all satisfied

4. ______________________________

Questions to which the interviewee must give his/her own answer. The questions usually begin with a question word (for example, who, what, when, where, why).

Example:
How, in your opinion, could our customer service be improved?

____

R/P/I **3** **Project work: Conducting a survey** ●

Work in groups and do a survey on how satisfied customers are with the after-sales service of a company of your own choice.

Step 1: Decide on the products of a certain branch (for example, electrical goods or clothing). Then develop a questionnaire with ten questions suitable for that range of products. Look at the different types of questions in exercise 2 again for help.

Step 2: Make copies of your questionnaire and ask the other people in your class to fill it in. Then look at the completed questionnaires and take notes on the main findings.

Step 3: Prepare a short presentation of the results of your survey and present it to the class.

Customers were most/least satisfied with …

As a result, it can be said that …

P **4** **Your experiences with after-sales service**

Think of a negative experience that you or your friends have had with after-sales service. Write down what happened and what, in your view, could have been done better to achieve customer satisfaction. Then exchange your experience and suggestions with a partner.

What happened	Suggestions for a better service

WORD BANK

to conduct – durchführen
to develop – entwickeln
to disagree – nicht zustimmen
to improve – verbessern
questionnaire – Fragebogen

H | Checking

1 Simple past or present perfect?

Complete the sentences with the verbs in the simple past or present prefect.

agree • be • campaign • have • not start • not think • not offer • spend • talk

My boss and I [1] ______________ two weeks in our branch in Eisenach last month. It [2] ______________ really interesting and we [3] ______________ a great time there. For example, they [4] ______________ for Fairtrade products for a month now. Our store [5] ______________ any Fairtrade products yet. Why [6] ______________ we ______________ such a campaign last month? I think it's because we [7] ______________ ever ______________ about it. So yesterday I [8] ______________ to my boss and he [9] ______________ that we will start a campaign next month. I think that's great!

2 'Since' or 'for'?

Read the sentences and put in 'since' or 'for'.

1. I have known my teacher ______________ several months.
2. Our shop has been closed ______________ Christmas.
3. Karim has been very happy ______________ he started his traineeship last year.
4. Ella has been responsible for unpacking the goods ______________ six weeks.
5. She has had a job there ______________ she finished school last year.

3 False friends

Cross out the wrong words.

I will **get/become** more money if I work harder. Look, this is a photo **from/of** Mr Wienzek. He always **cooks/makes** coffee for us. Yesterday we even **went/have gone** to the cinema together. I think our **chef/boss** is a really nice person.

4 Reacting in the right way

Use the sentence parts and form at least six sentences.

If a product is	broken incomplete damaged the wrong size not working properly of bad quality	you should	exchange it. repair it. replace it. offer a voucher. reduce the price. give a refund.

ICH KANN JETZT ...

1. Gründe für eine Produktrückrufaktion nennen. ○ ○ ○
2. angemessen auf Kundeneinwände reagieren. ○ ○ ○
3. Entschuldigungsbriefe an Kunden verfassen. ○ ○ ○
4. Garantie- und Sicherheitshinweise verstehen. ○ ○ ○
5. eine Befragung zur Kundenzufriedenheit durchführen. ○ ○ ○

☺☺☺ = Kann ich schon!
☺☺ = Kann ich ein bisschen!
☺ = Kann ich bald!

I | Phrases: After-sales talk

Making a product recall	
We are sorry to inform you that we have to recall the product because of a construction fault.	Es tut uns leid, Sie darüber informieren zu müssen, dass wir wegen eines Konstruktionsfehlers das Produkt zurückrufen müssen.
We apologize for the inconvenience.	Wir entschuldigen uns für die Unannehmlichkeiten, die wir Ihnen bereitet haben.
We hope for your trust in our products.	Wir hoffen auf Ihr Vertrauen in unsere Produkte.
We will do our best to meet your needs in the future.	Wir werden unser Bestes tun, um Ihre Bedürfnisse in Zukunft zu befriedigen.
If you have any more questions, please call our 24-hour hotline.	Sollten Sie weitere Fragen haben, rufen Sie bitte unsere 24-Stunden-Hotline an.

Dealing with complaints and apologizing	
Our shop offers the best service and prices possible.	Unser Geschäft bietet Ihnen den besten Service und die bestmöglichen Preise.
We will give you a refund if you aren't satisfied at all.	Wir werden Ihnen eine Rückzahlung/Kostenerstattung geben, falls Sie überhaupt nicht zufrieden sind.
Thank you for informing us about the problem.	Vielen Dank, dass Sie uns über das Problem in Kenntnis gesetzt haben.
I can see why you are so upset.	Ich kann nachvollziehen, warum Sie so aufgebracht sind.
We have been informed by our producer that it was his fault.	Wir sind von unserem Hersteller informiert worden, dass es sein Fehler war.
We don't want to lose you as a loyal customer.	Wir möchten Sie als loyalen Kunden nicht verlieren.
We enclose a small gift/a voucher as compensation.	Wir legen ein kleines Geschenk/einen Gutschein als Wiedergutmachung bei.

Experiences with after-sales service	
I'm fully satisfied with the way they solved the problem.	Ich bin rundum zufrieden mit der Art und Weise, wie man das Problem gelöst hat.
I disagree completely/partly with the proposal made by the after-sales service.	Ich bin überhaupt/teilweise nicht mit dem Vorschlag des Kundendienstes einverstanden.
The reason for my complaint/dissatisfaction is/was …	Der Grund für meine Beschwerde/Unzufriedenheit ist/war …
The after-sales service didn't react to my complaint at all.	Der Kundendienst hat sich überhaupt nicht um meine Beschwerde gekümmert.

9

NACH DIESER UNIT:

- ✓ kann ich ein Telefongespräch inhaltlich richtig wiedergeben,
- ✓ kann ich die Bestandteile englischer Geschäftsbriefe nennen,
- ✓ kann ich Geschäftskorrespondenz verstehen und verfassen,
- ✓ kann ich Lieferungs- und Zahlungsbedingungen nennen und begründen.

Getting goods delivered

A | Making an enquiry

1 Enquiring about products
Look at the photos and describe what they show.

____

____

____

____

____

R **2 Listening: Calling a potential supplier**
◎ A 2.7 Listen to the telephone conversation and sum it up with the help of the photos.

Picture A: ____

____

Picture B: ____

____

Picture C: ____

____

Picture D: ____

____

WORD BANK

enquiry – Anfrage
potential – potenziell
supplier – Lieferant

WORD BANK ◎

wristwatch – Armbanduhr

B | A business letter

R **1** **Reading comprehension**

Read the enquiry that was sent to British Jewellery. Then use a dictionary and translate the following words and phrases into German.

1. with reference to = ______________________
2. as requested = ______________________
3. to extend the range of products = ______________________
4. trade discounts = ______________________
5. terms of delivery and payment = ______________________
6. to look forward to = ______________________
7. Yours sincerely = ______________________

Schrader Schmuck
Königsallee 2100 • 40200 Düsseldorf • Germany
Telefon: 0211-6034808 • Fax: 0211-6034809 • E-Mail: schschmuck@aol...de

British Jewellery Ltd
35 Manchester Road
Bristol
AC5 6BA
Great Britain

Our ref: RS/nm
23 March 20...

Dear Mrs Winter,

Enquiry

With reference to our telephone conversation of 22 March 20... we send you a written enquiry as requested.

We have studied your latest catalogue for wristwatches that was enclosed with the *Jewellery Journal*. We would be interested in offering some of your wristwatches to our customers.

We are a German jewellery shop with three branches in and around Düsseldorf. We have often been asked by our customers to offer wristwatches and therefore want to extend our range of products. We expect to sell watches of high quality in a growing market.

Please be so kind and make us an offer for 50 each of the following watches:
- model Valuable, order no AFD 2005, price per item: €350,–
- model Stylish, order no BAC 2010, price per item: €400,–
- model Uncompromising, order no EDF 2009, price per item €800,–

We would appreciate if you sent us photos of the products for our advertising campaign.

Please also inform us about trade discounts and your usual terms of delivery and payment.

Thank you in advance for your reply. We look forward to hearing from you soon.

Yours sincerely,

Nadia Meier

Purchasing assistant

WORD BANK

in advance – im Voraus
to request – bitten

INTERCULTURAL BOX **Geschäftsbriefe**

Die folgenden Schreibweisen für ein Briefdatum sind üblich:
- in Großbritannien: *5 October 20…* oder *5th October 20…*
- in den USA: *October 5, 20…* oder *October 5th, 20…*

Adressen in Großbritannien und den USA haben die folgende Form:

Mr John Black	*Mrs Betty Jones*
15 Crown Street	*121 Santa Barbara Boulevard*
Manchester	*Portland, OR 87662*
WL4 2DA	*USA*
Great Britain	

Je nachdem, ob der Adressat namentlich genannt wird oder nicht, unterscheiden sich Anrede und Briefabschluss in britischen und amerikanischen Geschäftsbriefen:

Anrede	**Briefabschluss**
Dear Sir(s) or Madam(s)	*Yours faithfully (BE)*
Dear Ladies and Gentlemen: (AE)	*Yours truly/Very truly yours*
Dear Mr Knockwood	*Yours sincerely (BE)*
Dear Ms Saunders	*Sincerely yours (AE)*

P **2** **Paraphrasing**

Choose a part of the letter from the box and explain it to a partner. She / He tries to guess which part it is.

customer's name and address • date • reference line • salutation • signature block • subject line • supplier's name and address

Example: A: In this part of the letter you say when it was written.
B: It's the date.

3 **The date**

How should you write the dates in a letter? Write them down and read them.

24.03.61 ______________ 07.11.15 ______________

4 **British and American addresses**

Use the information in the boxes and write down the addresses.

CA 95621 • 55 Rubio Street • USA • Mrs Rosa Johnson • Los Angeles

Eastbourne • Great Britain • Fashion Design • NR2 2 PA • 27 Beach Street

1. ______________

2. ______________

5 **Salutation and complimentary close**

Match the salutations to the right complimentary close. Draw lines.

1. Dear Sir or Madam	Yours sincerely,
2. Ladies and Gentlemen:	Sincerely yours
3. Dear Mr Brown,	Yours faithfully
4. Dear Ms Johnson	Yours truly/Very truly yours

WORD BANK

complimemtary close – Grußformel
to paraphrase – umschreiben, paraphrasieren

P **6** **Writing an enquiry** ○ → page 138

You are working in the toys department of a department store and you need a supplier of high-quality dolls. Write an enquiry and ask for the catalogue, price list, trade discounts and the terms of delivery and payment. Write in your exercise book.

→ **PHRASES:** page 113

C | Receiving an offer

1 **An offer from British Jewellery**

Mrs Winter has sent an offer. Unfortunately, the text is in the wrong order. Put the different parts into the right order and write the numbers 1–10 in the boxes.

☐ Susan Winter
☐ Your enquiry of 23 March 20…
[1] Dear Ms Meier
☐ Encs: 3 photos, terms of delivery and payment
☐ Sales department
☐ Yours sincerely
☐ The total price for all three items (50 each) is €77,500. We are willing to offer you a discount of 10% off the total price on this order and a further cash discount of 2.5% for settlement within 15 days of delivery.
☐ Thank you for your enquiry about wristwatches. We are pleased to inform you that we have the goods desired in stock (see attached pictures).
☐ We are looking forward to receiving your order.
☐ Payment should be made according to our terms of delivery and payment, which we enclose with this letter. We will dispatch the goods free of charge by air mail within 4 days after receipt of order.

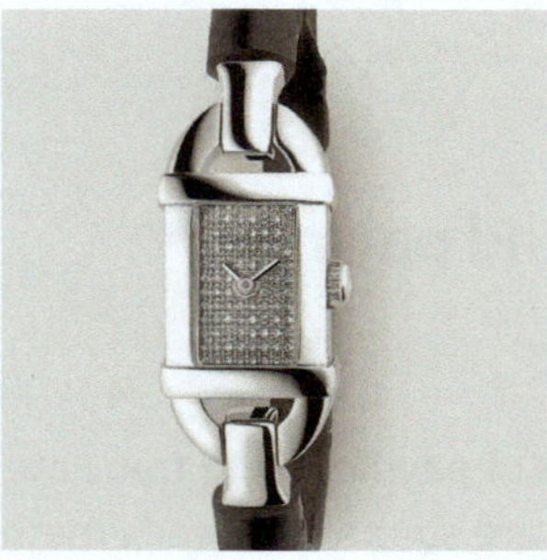

2 **Simple past or past perfect?**

Underline the right tense.

1. After I **had received/received** your telephone call, I **had sent/sent** you an offer.
2. Mr Green **read/had read** the enquiry which his assistant **had written/wrote**.
3. Before the shop owner **sent/had sent** out the enquiry he **called/had called** the supplier.
4. We **had started/started** selling the product before we **made/had made** a recall.

LANGUAGE BOX ***Simple past* und *past perfect***

Das ***simple past*** wird für vergangene Ereignisse verwendet, die abgeschlossen sind und keinen Bezug zur Gegenwart haben. Häufige Signalwörter sind *last, yesterday, ago.*

Das ***past perfect*** wird für Ereignisse verwendet, die vor einem bestimmten Zeitpunkt in der Vergangenheit stattgefunden haben, oft in Verbindung mit Wörtern wie *after* oder *before.*

Beispiele: ***Before** I **went** to school, I **had packed** my schoolbag.*
ABER: ***After** I **had packed** my schoolbag I **went** to school.*

WORD BANK

air mail – Luftpost
cash discount – Barzahlungsrabatt, Skonto
delivery – Lieferung
to desire – wünschen
enc (enclosure) – Anhang
order – Bestellung
receipt of order – Auftragseingang
settlement – Bezahlung
total price – Gesamtpreis
willing – bereit

→ **GRAMMAR:** page 151–152

Üben interaktiv
Simple past und past perfect
44c65k

D | Placing an order

P **1** **Writing an order**

Frau Meier will nun die Armbanduhren bei British Jewellery bestellen. Verwenden Sie dazu das Angebot auf Seite 105 und die folgenden Angaben.

→ PHRASES: page 113

- Bedanken Sie sich für das Angebot und die Fotos.
- Bestellen Sie jeweils 50 Armbanduhren der Marken Stylish, Uncompromising und Valuable im Gesamtwert von 77.500 €.
- Sagen Sie, dass Sie mit den Liefer- und Zahlungsbedingungen einverstanden sind.
- Teilen Sie mit, dass die Ware nach Auftragseingang sofort verschickt werden soll.
- Sagen Sie, dass Sie sich auf den Erhalt der Ware freuen.
- Schließen Sie den Brief formgerecht ab.

M **2** **Confirming an order** → page 138

British Jewellery confirms the order. Sum up the e-mail in German. Write in your exercise book.

Subject: Your order of 4 April 20...

Dear Ms Meier,
Many thanks for your order for wristwatches of 4 April 20....
We are pleased to confirm your order in every detail.
Please note that the goods will be delivered to you on 10 April 20... by air mail free of charge.
We would kindly like to remind you that we can offer you a further discount of 2.5 % for settlement within 15 days of delivery. We would appreciate a payment by credit card or bank transfer. We are certain you will be fully satisfied with our products.
Yours sincerely,
Anoop Nayak
Sales department

E | Delivery and payment

P **1** **Paying for goods**

Look at the means of payment and translate them into German. Then find at least two products that are suitable for each method. Give reasons for your answers.

Means of payment	German translation	Products
1. bank transfer		
2. credit card		
3. EC card		
4. in advance		
5. cash		
6. in instalments		
7. on receipt of goods		
8. on receipt of invoice		

P **2** **Methods of delivery**

Think of four methods of delivery and write them down. Use a dictionary if necessary.

WORD BANK

bank transfer – Banküberweisung
to confirm – bestätigen
in instalments – in Raten
invoice – Rechnung
means of payment – Zahlungsmittel, Bezahlungsverfahren
to place an order – eine Bestellung aufgeben
on receipt – bei Erhalt
to remind – erinnern

P **3** **Using indirect speech**

Complete the sentences with indirect speech. Look at the Language box for help.

1. Mrs Winter: "We've enclosed the latest brochure."

   Mrs Winter says ______________________________.

2. Susan: "Can you tell me where I have to pay?"

   Susan asked the shop assistant where ______________________________.

3. Shop assistant: "The make-up is on special offer today."

   The shop assistant told us that ______________________________.

4. Customer: "I'll call back again later."

   The customer promised that ______________________________.

5. Shop manager: "I can't help you in this case."

   The shop manager said that ______________________________.

LANGUAGE BOX **Indirekte Rede**

Die indirekte Rede wird verwendet, um zu berichten, was jemand sagt oder sagte. Steht das einleitende Verb im *simple present*, dann ändert sich die Zeitform in der indirekten Rede nicht. Steht das einleitende Verb im *simple past*, dann ändern sich die Zeitformen wie folgt: *simple present* wird zu *simple past*, *simple past* und *present perfect* werden zu *past perfect*, *will* wird zu *would*. Pronomen sowie Ort- und Zeitangaben werden angepasst.

Beispiele: *"We can send you the goods tomorrow."*

*They **say** they **can send** us the goods tomorrow.*

ABER: *They **said** they **could send** us the goods on the next day.*

→ **GRAMMAR:** page 158

Üben interaktiv
Indirekte Rede
e3tp8y

SKILLS **Commercial correspondence**

A business letter has to be formal. You have to be polite and should use long forms.

Practising business language

Replace the crossed out words with phrases from the box and improve the letter.

Ms • on 3 March 20… • our best • to meet your needs • Please inform us about • some • Thank you very much for your interest. • With reference to • We look forward to hearing from you. • We will • would like • Yours sincerely,

Dear ~~Miss~~ **1** ______________ Bricks,

~~Thinking about~~ **2** ______________________ our telephone conversation ~~two days ago~~ **3** ______________________, we ~~want~~ **4** ______________ to send you ~~lots of~~ **5** ______________ samples. ~~Let us have~~ **6** ______________________ your special wishes. ~~We'll~~ **7** ______________ do ~~everything we can to make you happy~~ **8** ______________________. ~~Thanks for the trouble.~~

9 ______________________________________

~~Hope to hear from you.~~ **10** ______________________________

~~All the best.~~ **11** ______________________________

Paul Walters

F | Ordering goods

R **1** **Listening: Placing an order by telephone**

⊙ A 2.8 Mara wants to buy some clothing on the internet and finds a British online shop based in Bristol which offers good quality at favourable prices. As she is unsure about the correct sizes, she decides to call them and order by telephone. Listen to the conversation and complete the sentences below with the correct option.

1. Mara is calling a British shop in
   - ☐ a) Manchester.
   - ☐ b) Bristol.
   - ☐ c) Aberdeen.
   - ☐ d) London.
2. She is interested in buying
   - ☐ a) a blue long skirt.
   - ☐ b) a green miniskirt.
   - ☐ c) a white straight skirt.
   - ☐ d) a red and white skirt.
3. Mara needs the skirt
   - ☐ a) in size 32 which is British size 6.
   - ☐ b) in size 36 which is British size 8.
   - ☐ c) in size 34 which is British size 8.
   - ☐ d) in size 38 which is British size 10.
4. Mara orders the skirt in
   - ☐ a) red.
   - ☐ b) red and white.
   - ☐ c) white.
   - ☐ d) blue.
5. She also orders
   - ☐ a) two pairs of blue jeans.
   - ☐ b) two pairs of grey jeans.
   - ☐ c) one pair of blue jeans and one pair of grey jeans.
   - ☐ d) three pairs of jeans.
6. If the clothes do not fit, Mara
   - ☐ a) must keep them.
   - ☐ b) can send them back and get a partial refund.
   - ☐ c) has to exchange them for the suitable sizes.
   - ☐ d) can return them and get a full refund or replacement.
7. Mara pays for her purchase
   - ☐ a) in cash.
   - ☐ b) in advance.
   - ☐ c) on receipt of invoice.
   - ☐ d) by credit card.

WORD BANK

based in – mit Sitz in
to keep sth – etw. behalten

WORD BANK ⊙

conversion chart – Umrechnungstabelle
to cover – bedecken
cut – Schnitt
foot (pl.) feet – Fuß *(= 0,3048 m)*
inch – Zoll *(= 2,54 cm)*
pattern – Muster
plain – einfach, nur
to read sth back – etw. nochmal vorlesen
skirt – Rock
slim – schlank
straight – gerade
valid until – gültig bis
verification code – Sicherheitsziffer(n), Bestätigungscode

R **2** **Filling in an order form**
A 2.8 Listen again and fill in the order form for Laura.

Order taken by: ______________________

Date *(today's date)*: ______________________

Customer name: ______________________

Address: ______________________
____
____

Quantity	Item	Sizes	Unit price

Payment details: ______________________

Delivery date: ______________________

M **3** **Mediation**
A 2.8 Look at the conversion table on page 174 of your book. Then listen to the conversation once more and sum it up in German.

____
____
____
____
____
____
____

G | Making a complaint

P **1** **Writing a complaint**
One week later the goods from TopWear arrive and Mara unpacks them. Unfortunately, the pair of jeans are brown instead of blue and the wrong size. The grey jeans have a small hole and the skirt has a stain. Write Mara's complaint by e-mail and use the following information.

- send the complaint to onlineshopping@internet.co…uk
- think of a suitable subject line, salutation and opening
- ask for a full replacement of the two pairs of jeans
- insist on a 20% price reduction for the skirt
- ask them to send the goods straight away
- say that you are disappointed by the way they carried out your order
- close the letter appropriately

WORD BANK

to carry out – ausführen
to close – *(hier:)* beenden, abschließen
delivery date – Lieferdatum
to insist on sth – auf etw. bestehen

I/P **2** Role play: Handling a customer complaint

Eine Kundin hat in einem Supermarkt eingekauft und kehrt am nächsten Tag verärgert mit drei Joghurtbechern zurück, um sich zu beschweren. Führen Sie das Gespräch mithilfe der Rollenkarten. Tauschen Sie anschließend die Rollen.

→ **PHRASES:** page 29, 89 and 101

Partner A: Verkäufer/-in

- Begrüßen Sie die Kundin und fragen Sie sie, wie Sie ihr helfen können.
- Beruhigen Sie die Kundin und bitten Sie sie, ihre Beschwerde vorzubringen.
- Drücken Sie Ihr Bedauern aus und sagen Sie, dass vermutlich die Kühlkette (*cold chain*) unterbrochen wurde und die Joghurtbecher deshalb vor Ablauf des Verfallsdatums schlecht geworden sind (*to spoil*). Sie werden sie selbstverständlich ersetzen.
- Bitten Sie um den Kassenbon, um den Umtausch durchzuführen.
- Sagen Sie, dass Sie aus Kulanzgründen (*as a gesture of goodwill*) die Joghurtbecher trotzdem umtauschen werden.
- Händigen Sie der Kundin die neuen Produkte aus und entschuldigen Sie sich für die Unannehmlichkeiten (*inconvenience caused*).
- Verabschieden Sie sich angemessen.

Partner B: Kundin

- Teilen Sie dem/der Verkäufer/in mit, dass Sie gestern drei Joghurtbecher erworben haben, die Anlass zur Reklamation bieten und sie deshalb verärgert sind.
- Sagen Sie, dass Sie fünf Joghurtbecher (*yoghurt tubs*) erworben haben, deren Verfallsdatum noch nicht abgelaufen ist, Sie aber in drei Bechern Schimmel (*mould*) entdeckt haben.
- Sagen Sie, dass Sie mit dem Vorschlag einverstanden sind.
- Bedauern Sie, dass Sie in der Eile den Kassenbon zu Hause liegengelassen haben.
- Bedanken Sie sich für das Entgegenkommen (*obligingness*).
- Nehmen Sie die umgetauschten Produkte entgegen, bedanken Sie sich und verabschieden sie sich.

R/P **3** Internet research: Consumer rights

As a sales assistant it is important to know your customers' rights and your own duties. Look at the following cases and find a solution for them according to legal regulations. Use the internet to search for further information. Write in your exercise book.

Case 1

You work for a sportswear shop and someone has just bought a fan T-shirt for his favourite football club. Two weeks later the club is relegated and the customer comes back into the shop to exchange his T-shirt for another one.

Case 2

A customer bought a remote-controlled car as a Christmas present for his grandson. A few days after Christmas he comes to your shop again and asks for a full refund because the remote-control does not work.

WORD BANK

duty – Verpflichtung
relegated – absteigen (in eine niedrigere Liga)

H | Evaluating different methods of delivery

P

Project work: Delivering goods ●

Step 1: Look at the photos and discuss the advantages and disadvantages of the different methods of delivery they show. Think about the following aspects and make a list of pros and cons.

- costs
- packaging
- safety
- speed
- the environment

1

2

3

4

Method of delivery	Pros	Cons

Step 2: Compare your list with another group and complete your list.

Step 3: Different products have different requirements for their delivery. Give examples of various types of goods and explain which methods of delivery are suitable for them. Create a poster or a slide presentation including short texts and some photos.

Step 4: Present your results in class and be prepared to answer questions.

WORD BANK

to evaluate – bewerten
pros and cons – Für und Wider, Pro und Kontra
slide presentation – Folienpräsentation
speed – Geschwindigkeit

I | Checking

1 Word puzzle

Find ten words that you can use for writing an enquiry and write them down.

A	G	T	H	R	E	N	C	L	O	S	E	O	A	Y
P	U	I	N	E	E	E	A	E	F	C	A	C	P	I
F	R	D	A	F	A	R	T	R	C	O	T	O	A	L
A	R	U	K	E	C	M	A	R	K	E	T	N	W	Q
E	R	M	Q	R	N	S	L	T	I	S	W	D	Y	B
M	K	C	D	E	T	M	O	E	N	Q	U	I	R	Y
E	X	T	E	N	D	I	G	R	F	U	N	T	E	S
E	X	P	E	C	T	R	U	M	O	O	N	I	T	A
O	F	A	K	E	B	D	E	S	R	L	B	O	E	C
W	A	S	C	B	G	F	D	E	M	R	A	N	G	E

____

____

____

____

____

____

____

____

____

2 Finding the mistakes

There is one mistake in each address. Find it and rewrite the addresses correctly.

```
Mrs Wilson Betty
London
WE2 BD4
12 Malhound Drive
```

```
Sunshine Fashion
13 Green Street
BX5 TA3
Liverpool
```

```
Mr John Peak
131 Delta Avenue
CA 93332
San Francisco,
```

1. ______________________

____

____

____

2. ______________________

____

____

____

3. ______________________

____

____

____

3 Simple past or past perfect?

Use the correct tense.

1. After I ______________ **(call)** the company in Cambridge, I ______
   ______ **(tell)** my boss about it.
2. Before I ____________ **(place)** the order, I ____________ **(ask)** the supplier to make an offer.
3. I ______________ **(have)** problems with English before I ________
   _____ **(start)** learning with this book.
4. After I ______________ **(help)** Tina to sort the goods, she ________ **(be)** much nicer to me.

ICH KANN JETZT …

1. ein Telefongespräch wiedergeben. ○○○
2. die Bestandteile von Geschäftsbriefen benennen. ○○○
3. englische Geschäftsbriefe verfassen und verstehen. ○○○
4. Lieferungs- und Zahlungsbedingungen benennen und begründen. ○○○

☺☺☺ = Kann ich schon!
☺☺ = Kann ich ein bisschen!
☺ = Kann ich bald!

J | Phrases: Business correspondence

Making an enquiry	
We can see from your advertisement/catalogue that …	Wir können aus Ihrer Anzeige/Ihrem Katalog entnehmen, dass …
We intend/want to extend our range of products.	Wir beabsichtigen/möchten unsere Produktpalette erweitern.
Please (be so kind and) send us your latest catalogue and price list.	Bitte (seien Sie so freundlich und) übersenden Sie uns Ihren neuesten Katalog mit Preisliste.
Please also inform us about trade discounts and your terms of delivery and payment/terms and conditions of business.	Bitte informieren Sie uns auch über Handelsnachlässe sowie Ihre Lieferungs- und Zahlungsbedingungen/Geschäftsbedingungen.
We look forward to hearing from you.	Wir freuen uns darauf, von Ihnen zu hören.

Writing an offer	
Thank you for your enquiry of …	Vielen Dank für Ihre Anfrage vom …
We are pleased to send you the following offer.	Wir freuen uns, Ihnen folgendes Angebot machen/schicken zu können.
We will dispatch the goods immediately after receipt of order.	Wir werden die Waren sofort nach Auftragseingang verschicken.
We are willing to offer you a discount of … % off the total price of this order.	Wir sind bereit, Ihnen einen Nachlass von … Prozent auf den Gesamtpreis dieses Auftrags anzubieten.
Additionally we can offer you a cash discount of … % for settlement within … days of delivery.	Zusätzlich können wir Ihnen einen Barzahlungsrabatt/Skonto in Höhe von … Prozent für das Begleichen der Rechnung innerhalb von … Tagen anbieten.
We would be pleased to receive your order.	Wir würden uns freuen, Ihren Auftrag zu erhalten.

Placing an order	
Thank you very much for your offer of …	Vielen Dank für Ihr Angebot vom …
We would like to place the following order.	Wir möchten gerne den folgenden Auftrag erteilen.
We agree on/accept your terms and conditions of business.	Wir sind mit Ihren Geschäftsbedingungen einverstanden.
We look forward to receiving your goods.	Wir freuen uns darauf, Ihre Waren zu erhalten.

Delivery and payment	
Payment should be made by credit card/bank transfer/on receipt of goods/on receipt of invoice.	Die Bezahlung sollte mit Kreditkarte/Banküberweisung/bei Erhalt der Ware/bei Erhalt der Rechnung erfolgen.
We also accept payment in advance/in instalments/in cash.	Wir akzeptieren auch Zahlungen im Voraus/in Raten/in bar.
We will dispatch the goods by air freight/road/air mail/train/ship.	Wir werden die Ware per Luftfracht/Straßentransport/Luftpost/Zug/Schiff verschicken.

ig54s6

10

NACH DIESER UNIT:

- ✓ kann ich über meine und die Jobvorstellungen anderer reden,
- ✓ kann ich einen Bewerbungsbrief und meinen Lebenslauf schreiben,
- ✓ kann ich mich in einem Vorstellungsgespräch richtig verhalten.

A

B

C

D

Job hunting

A | Which job?

P **1 Different jobs** ○ → page 139

Look at the photos above. Where do you think the people work? Describe the people and their jobs.

R **2 Listening: The right person for the job**

⊙ A 2.9

Listen to five people talking about themselves and how they got their jobs. First match the people to the photos above. (One person is not shown in the photos.) Then write down which job each person wanted to do and which job they are now doing.

fashion shop • home entertainment shop • perfumery • shop for mobile phones • shoe shop • supermarket • tattoo studio

Photo	Name	Job wanted	Job now
☐	Jens		
☐	Kristina		
☐	Petra		
☐	Erkan		
☐	Susanne		

P **3 Your plans**

Which job would you like to do after your traineeship? Discuss your plans.

WORD BANK

to hunt – *(hier:)* suchen

WORD BANK ⊙

career – Karriere
to fire – entlassen
to give up – aufgeben
job centre – Arbeitsamt
letter of application – Bewerbungsschreiben
rejection – Absage, Ablehnung

B | Looking at job adverts

R **1** **Reading comprehension**

Read the information about Marco and the two job adverts. Then translate the German words and phrases into English.

Hi. My name's Marco. I'm a trainee at Schneider's shoe shop. I've almost finished my traineeship. My marks are fine and I'm very good at English. Next month I'll be a fully qualified shop assistant for shoes. I'd like to stay at Schneider's but they can't employ me. So I'm looking for a new job. Yesterday I saw some job adverts at my vocational school. Perhaps I'll apply for one of them.

1. gesucht = ______
2. Teilzeit = ______
3. Vollzeit = ______
4. wir suchen = ______
5. ist geeignet für = ______
6. voll qualifiziert = ______
7. zur Zeit = ______
8. weitere Informationen = ______
9. mindestens zwei Jahre Berufserfahrung = ______
10. Bewerber/in = ______

For You Shoe Shop
We are looking for a fully qualified

ENGLISH-SPEAKING SHOP ASSISTANT

to work full-time in our shop. Applicants must have a very good knowledge of English. The shop currently has five shop assistants and is open from 9 a.m. to 10 p.m. Mo–Fri.

For further information, please contact:
Ms Christiane Gerlich, tel.: 020 33 60 55

WANTED for Best Prices Shoe Shop: Part-time assistant for six months

We are looking for a shop assistant for our busy Best Prices Shoe Shop in the centre of Berlin. Applicants must have at least two years' experience and speak English well. The job is suitable for a person who is looking for a temporary job only.
Please contact: Mr Seebach, tel.: 0172 346879

2 **Different job offers**

Marco is thinking about the adverts. Match the sentences and draw lines.

1. If I worked at Best Prices,	a) I would work part-time.
2. If I worked at For You,	b) I would work there only for six months.
3. If I worked at Best Prices,	c) the job would be full-time.

P **3** **If I were Marco ...**

If you were Marco, which job would you apply for? Talk to a partner and give reasons.

Start like this: If I were Marco, I would apply for the job at the … shoe shop because …

LANGUAGE BOX ***If*-Sätze (Bedingungssätze) Typ 2**

Bedingungssätze des Typs 2 werden benutzt, um über eventuelle Situationen zu sprechen. Sie werden mit *if + simple past* und *would* gebildet.
Beispiele: *If I **got** the job, I **would be** very happy.*
*I **would be** very happy if I **got** the job.*

WORD BANK

to apply – sich bewerben
to employ – beschäftigen, einstellen
job advert – Stellenanzeige
mark – Note
temporary job – befristete Stelle

→ **GRAMMAR:** page 155

Üben interaktiv
If-Sätze Typ 2
295vu9

INTERCULTURAL BOX **Jobsuche im Ausland**

Bei Anzeigen für Stellen im Ausland sollte man auf zusätzliche Angaben achten. So ist es z.B. in den USA nicht üblich, dass der Arbeitgeber die Hälfte der Kosten für die Krankenversicherung oder eine spätere Rentenversicherung bezahlt. Diese Zahlungen kann der Arbeitgeber verweigern oder nach einiger Zeit einfach einstellen. In Stellenanzeigen ist in diesem Zusammenhang z.B. von *medical and dental benefits* die Rede.

WORD BANK

to advertise – *(hier:)* inserieren
to attend – teilnehmen, besuchen
CV (= curriculum vitae) – Lebenslauf
to invite – einladen
job interview – Bewerbungsgespräch
personnel manager – Personalchef/in

C | Writing a letter of application

R **1** **A letter of application**

Read the following advert and complete Francesca's letter of application with words from the box.

apply • as advertised • attended • communication • enjoy • hearing • improved • lessons • position • qualified

LATEST FASHION from Milano in Italy currently has a number of positions for **shop assistants** in Germany to serve our customers at our fashion stores.
We need assistants for our Harz region (Bad Harzburg and Goslar) who have an excellent knowledge of English.
For further information, please contact Mr Werner, personnel manager, at …

Francesca Moreno
Kleeblattweg 27
38527 Meine

Latest Fashion
Königsallee 45
38667 Bad Harzburg

23 June 20…

Dear Mr Werner,

Application for a position as a shop assistant

I am writing to **1** ______________ for the position of shop assistant in your store in Bad Harzburg or Goslar, **2** ______________ in the *Abendzeitung* of 22 June 20….

As you can see from my enclosed CV, I recently **3** ______________ in retailing and sales as an Einzelhandelskauffrau. I did my traineeship at Fashion Meyer, a retailer in fashionable clothing in Meine, and **4** ______________ the Berufsbildende Schulen I in Gifhorn. During this three-year period I attended regular **5** ______________ in English for shop assistants and **6** ______________ my professional **7** ______________ skills. Last summer I worked for a fashion store in Manchester for four weeks.

The **8** ______________ you offer is just what I am looking for. I **9** ______________ working with people and would also like to have a job where I can use my English.

I would be very happy to be invited for a job interview and look forward to **10** ______________ from you soon.

Yours sincerely,

Francesca Moreno

P **2** **Writing a letter of application**
Write your own letter of application to Latest Fashion. Use your exercise book.

→ PHRASES: page 125

D | Writing a CV

R **1** **Curriculum vitae**
Read Francesca's CV. Then work with a partner and ask questions about her CV.

When was she born?

What computer programmes ...?

What qualifications/work experience did she get at ...?

Where did she go to ...?

How well does she speak ...?

What does she like doing in ...?

When did she start/ finish ...?

CURRICULUM VITAE

PERSONAL DETAILS

Name	Francesca Moreno
Address	Kleeblattweg 21 38527 Meine Tel.: 05304-87401 E-mail: f.moreno@mail...de
Date of birth:	1995

EDUCATION AND QUALIFICATIONS

Vocational school:	2011-2014	Berufsbildende Schulen I des Landkreises Gifhorn Qualification: Retail management assistant (Einzelhandelskauffrau)
Secondary school:	2005-2011	Schulzentrum Meine Qualification: Secondary school (erweiterter Sek-I Abschluss)
Primary school:	2001-2005	Grundschule Am Zellberg, Meine

WORK EXPERIENCE

Temporary work:	2014 2014	Job in the production department at VW, Wolfsburg Job at a fashion store in Manchester

SKILLS

Computer:	Microsoft Word, Microsoft Excel
Languages:	German (fluent), Italian (mother tongue), English (good)
Other:	Driving licence (since May 2014)

INTERESTS

Travelling, making clothes, singing

P **2** **Writing a CV**
Now write your own CV. Use your exercise book. Then exchange your CV with a partner's and ask each other about your qualifications.

WORD BANK

department – Abteilung
driving licence – Führerschein
education – Ausbildung
mother tongue – Muttersprache
primary school – Grundschule
production department – Produktion
secondary school – weiterführende Schule

E | A job interview

R **1** **Listening: A job interview**

A 2.10 Francesca is having a job interview at Latest Fashion. Listen to the conversation with Mr Werner.

Part 1

First, Mr Werner asks Francesca some questions about her CV. Tick (✓) the correct box.

1. Francesca loves
   - ☐ a) making her own clothes.
   - ☐ b) dancing in the disco.
   - ☐ c) travelling.
2. Francesca sings
   - ☐ a) on TV.
   - ☐ b) in a singing group.
   - ☐ c) at school.

Part 2

They are now talking about the work at Latest Fashion. Complete the following sentence.

Francesca thinks she would be a good shop assistant because she ______________

____.

Part 3

Listen to the end of the interview. Decide whether the statements are true or false.

	true	false
1. Francesca has one question for Mr Werner.	☐	☐
2. If Francesca got the job she would have to wear clothes from the store.	☐	☐
3. Mr Werner will contact Francesca tomorrow about the job.	☐	☐

2 **Telling the time** ○ → page 139

Write down the times.

Example: 17:25 *It's twenty-five minutes past five in the afternoon. / It's 5.25 p.m.*

1. 06:05 ______________
2. 09:15 ______________
3. 14:30 ______________
4. 21:45 ______________
5. 00:00 ______________
6. 02:57 ______________

INTERCULTURAL BOX **Uhrzeiten**

Um Uhrzeiten im Englischen anzugeben, benutzt man *o'clock* bei vollen Stunden. Wenn es sich nicht um Fahrpläne (z. B. Bus) oder Flugpläne handelt, verwendet man im Unterschied zum Deutschen immer die 12-Stunden-Uhr.

Beispiele:	15 Uhr	*It's three o' clock in the afternoon / 3 p.m.*
	7:15 Uhr	*It's (a) quarter past seven in the morning / 7.15 a.m.*
	16:30 Uhr	*It's half past four in the afternoon / 4.30 p.m.*
	13:45 Uhr	*It's (a) quarter to two in the afternoon / 1.45 p.m.*
	1:20 Uhr	*It's twenty (minutes) past one at night / 1.20. a.m.*

R **3**

Reading comprehension

Read Sophie's story and then answer the questions.

Hi friends!

As you know, I have just got my school leaving certificate from my Realschule in Flensburg, that's like a British secondary modern school, I think. I'm really excited because a couple of days ago I received an invitation for a job interview tomorrow morning at TOP, a local supermarket.

So to make sure that I'm there on time, I'll have to get up at a quarter to six tomorrow morning and finish my breakfast by half past six. I'll have to leave the house at exactly seven thirty, so that will give me enough time to dress up properly. The supermarket is in a suburb of Flensburg, and I've checked an app on my mobile phone to help me plan the route. It's a 20-minute walk to the bus stop and I'll have to take the bus at five to eight. That will drop me off at Ahornweg about 25 minutes later. From there it's only a 10-minute walk to the supermarket. As the job interview starts at a quarter to nine, I'll still have some time to relax before I go in for the interview.

Comment on this …

1. Where does Sophie have her interview?

   ____

2. What time will she have to get up tomorrow morning?

   ____

3. How long is the journey from her house to the supermarket?

   ____

4. When does the job interview start?

   ____

5. How long will she be able to relax before the job interview starts?

   ____

4

Using the passive

Make passive sentences. Use the simple present or the simple past.

Example: *Yesterday we were asked (ask) to make an offer for wristwatches.*

1. Once a week the products ______________ **(deliver)** by air mail.
2. Your goods ______________ **(damage)** in an accident last week.
3. The bathroom scale ______________ **(replace)** last Friday.
4. Usually the refunds ______________ **(send)** by our customer service office.
5. The best prices ______________ **(offer)** to loyal customers only.

→ **GRAMMAR:** page 156

Üben interaktiv
Das Passiv
r3xy5e

LANGUAGE BOX **Das Passiv**

Passivsätze werden mit *to be* und dem Partizip Perfekt (3. Form) gebildet. Die verschiedenen Zeiten werden mit den entsprechenden Formen von *to be* gebildet:

Beispiele: *The product **is made** in Britain. (simple present)*
*My wallet **was produced** in China. (simple past)*

WORD BANK

to dress up – sich feinmachen
to drop sb off – jdn. absetzen
invitation – Einladung
journey – Anfahrt, Reise
school leaving certificate – Abschlusszeugnis
secondary modern school – Realschule
suburb – Vorort

P **5**

Getting prepared for a job interview

Imagine you have been invited for a job interview. What should you think of in advance? Make a list. Then compare it with a partner's list.

F | Conducting job interviews

R **1** **Listening: A job interview in London**
◎ A 2.11 Florian Schäfer has been invited to a job interview at Home Tech Emporium's head office in London. He takes an early flight from Munich Airport to London Gatwick and arrives at their office at 10.30 a.m. Listen to the interview at Home Tech Emporium's personnel department and answer the following questions.

1. What type of company is Home Tech Emporium?

____

____

2. Where would Florian's new job be?

____

3. What would Florian be responsible for?

____

4. What does Mr Shannon offer with regard to accommodation?

____

5. If he got the job, when would Florian start?

____

6. When will Florian hear from Home Tech Emporium again?

____

7. What information will they send to Florian if they appoint him?

____

R **2** **Taking notes**
◎ A 2.11 During the interview Mr Shannon takes some notes about Florian. Listen again and complete the form for him.

Applicant's name:	_______________
Comes from:	_______________
Qualifications:	_______________
	_______________
	_______________
	_______________
Work experience:	_______________
	_______________
	_______________
	_______________
Languages:	_______________
	_______________

WORD BANK

head office – Hauptniederlassung
personnel department – Personalabteilung
with regard to – mit Bezug auf

WORD BANK ◎

accommodation – Unterkunft
to appoint sb – jdn. einstellen
confirmation – Bestätigung
familiar – vertraut
fluent – fließend
major – bedeutend
to move (to) – umziehen (nach)
personal affairs – persönliche Angelegenheiten
pleasure – Freude
repair – Reparatur
salary – Gehalt, Lohn

R/P **3** **Questions during an interview**

A 2.11

Listen to the interview once more and make a list of the questions asked by Mr Shannon and Florian Schäfer. Then think about other questions an interviewer and an applicant might ask and add them to your list.

Interviewer	Applicant

4 **Say it in English**

Put the following sentences into English.

1. Ich habe eine Ausbildung zum Einzelhandelskaufmann in einem Baumarkt in Bad Homburg absolviert.
2. Wir suchen Verkäufer mit fließenden Englischkenntnissen für unsere neue Filiale in Berlin.
3. Viele unserer Kunden kommen aus Deutschland, Großbritannien und den USA.
4. Arbeitsbeginn ist der 1. September.
5. Ich habe mich gefreut, Sie kennenzulernen.
6. Sie hören innerhalb von zwei Wochen von uns.

P **5** **At a job interview**

Describe the cartoon in about 50 words. Answer the questions on page 122.

- Who are the characters in the cartoon and where are they?
- What is happening?
- What might the interviewer say to the applicant?
- Will the applicant get the job? Why, or why not?

P **6** **Project work: Tips for a job interview**

Receiving an invitation to a job interview is the first important step towards finally getting the job. However, in order to be successful you have to behave correctly during the interview.

Step 1: Work in groups and make a list of dos and don'ts in a job interview. Think about the following aspects:

- preparing for the interview
- dress and appearance
- body language
- travelling to the interview

Dos in job interviews	Don'ts in job interviews

Step 2: Get together with other groups in your class, compare your results and complete your list.

Step 3: Decide on ten main tips and prepare a presentation, including some visual aids.

Step 4: Give your presentation in class and be prepared to answer questions.

WORD BANK

to travel – (an)reisen

G | Working in the EU

M **1** **Mediation**

Read the following information about working in the EU and summarise it in German. Use a dictionary if necessary.

As a European Union (EU) citizen, you have a basic right to travel to, live and work in any other EU country. The only document you need in order to move around the EU is a valid identity card or passport.
However, if you want to get a job in another EU country, you may need more documentation. You have a basic right to apply for all job vacancies advertised within the EU, including public sector jobs. But some EU countries require internationally recognized diplomas, titles, certificates or other special qualifications for certain types of jobs. For this reason, it may be difficult to have your own training and skills fully recognized. You may have to get certified translations of your qualifications and references into the language of the country you want to work in, and you may need to present a certificate that shows your level of knowledge of that country's language. You might also need a police certificate of good conduct from your home country to show that you do not have a current criminal record there.

WORD BANK

basic right – Grundrecht
certified translation – beglaubigte Übersetzung
citizen – Bürger/in
criminal record – Vorstrafenregister
European Union (EU) – Europäische Gemeinschaft (EG)
identity card – Personalausweis
passport – Pass
police certificate of good conduct – polizeiliches Führungszeugnis
public sector – öffentlicher Sektor
recognized – anerkannt
reference – *(hier:)* Arbeitszeugnis
vacancy – freie Stelle

R/P **2** **Internet research: Job offers in the EU**

Step 1: Search the internet for jobs offers for shop assistants in the EU. Choose five job adverts and take notes on the requirements and work conditions.

Step 2: Discuss whether or not you would apply for the jobs and give reasons for your decisions.

Step 3: Present your results to the class and discuss the advantages and disadvantages of different job offers.

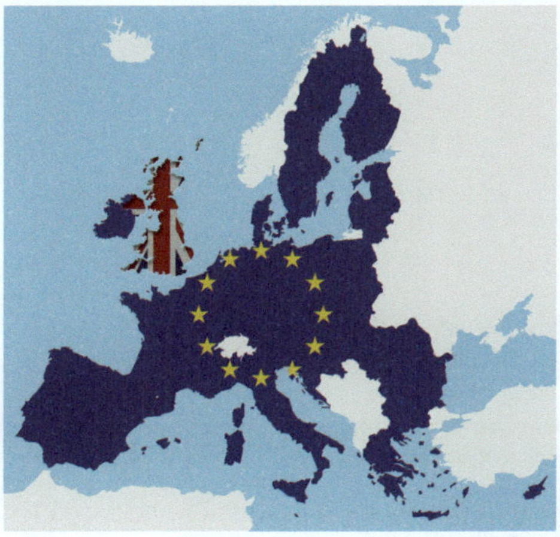

P **3** **Applying for a job**

Choose one of the jobs you found on the internet and write a letter of application for it. Look at the letter on page 116 for help.

→ **PHRASES:** page 125

H | Checking

1 **If I …**

Look at the photos and write a sentence about each picture.

Example: If I met my favourite singer I would be very happy.

1. ____________________

2. ____________________
3. ____________________
4. ____________________

1

2

3

4

2 **The passive**

Rewrite the sentences in the passive.

Example: *A customer studied your catalogue.*
→ *Your catalogue was studied by a customer.*

1. We appreciate payment in cash. ____________________
2. He sent two students to Britain. ____________________
3. Clive Smith reads the news on the BBC. ____________________
4. The owner offered Tom a job. ____________________

3 **Finding and translating words**

Find the words and phrases from Unit 10. Write them down and translate them into German.

primaryschoolcurriculumvitaetraineeshipqualificationsfullyqualifiedwantedparttime-furtherinformationknowledgeofEnglishexperiencefulltimecurrentlysecondaryschool-toapplyforajobretailmanagementassistant

____
____
____
____
____
____
____
____

ICH KANN JETZT …

1. über berufliche Vorstellungen reden. ○○○
2. über Stellenanzeigen und Bewerbungen sprechen. ○○○
3. mich auf eine Stelle mit einem Bewerbungsbrief und Lebenslauf bewerben. ○○○
4. mich in einem Vorstellungsgespräch richtig verhalten. ○○○

☺☺☺ = Kann ich schon!
☺☺ = Kann ich ein bisschen!
☺ = Kann ich bald!

I | Phrases: Job application

Job adverts	
We are currently looking for a fully qualified shop assistant / management assistant in retail business / retail management assistant.	Wir suchen momentan nach einer / einem vollausgebildeten Verkäuferin / Verkäufer / Einzelhandelskaufmann/-frau.
We can offer you a full-time / part-time job.	Wir können Ihnen einen Vollzeit- / Teilzeitarbeitsplatz anbieten.
It's a permanent / temporary job.	Es ist eine dauerhafte / befristete Stelle.
Applicants must have a good / an excellent knowledge of English.	Bewerber müssen über gute/hervorragende Englischkenntnisse verfügen.
The job is suitable for …	Der Job ist geeignet für …
You should have at least two years' experience.	Sie sollten über mindestens zwei Jahre Berufserfahrung verfügen.
Please send your application to …	Bitte schicken Sie Ihre Bewerbung an …
For further information, please contact …	Für weitere Informationen setzen Sie sich bitte mit … in Verbindung.
Our opening hours are from … to …	Unsere Öffnungszeiten sind von … bis …

Writing a letter of application	
I would like to apply for the position of …	Ich möchte mich auf die Stelle als … bewerben.
… as advertised in …	… wie ausgeschrieben/inseriert in …
I have qualified in retailing and sales.	Ich habe mich für Einzelhandel und Verkauf qualifiziert.
I have improved my professional communication skills.	Ich habe meine kommunikativen Fähigkeiten verbessert.
I enjoy working with people.	Es macht mir Spaß, mit Leuten zu arbeiten.

Writing a CV	
primary school / secondary school / secondary modern school / vocational school	Grundschule/weiterführende Schule / Realschule / Berufsschule
work experience / skills / interests	Arbeitserfahrung / Fähigkeiten / Interessen

At a job interview	
I'd like to do this job because …	Ich möchte gerne diesen Job machen, weil …
From your homepage on the internet I've learned that you …	Auf Ihrer Homepage im Internet habe ich erfahren, dass Sie …
My hobbies are …	Meine Hobbies sind …
When can I expect to receive an answer from you?	Wann kann ich von Ihnen eine Antwort erwarten?

Role play: Different lives

Work with a partner. Partner A uses the information on this page. Partner B uses the information on the next page.

Partner A

1. You are Frank from Germany and you are talking to a young woman from India. First read the information about Frank. Then answer her questions.

Frank

You are 18 and you are working as a trainee shop assistant for a big department store in Berlin. You are in the second year of your apprenticeship. You like your work because it is interesting and you enjoy having contact with customers.
From Monday to Friday you start work at 9 or 11 a.m. and finish at 6 or 8 p.m. Every second week you have to work on Saturdays from 9 a.m. to 6 p.m. Your boss and colleagues are very friendly. As a trainee you earn 690 euros a month during your second year. You spend most of your money on clothes, CDs, Blue-ray disks, your car and going out at the weekend. You have six weeks' holiday and in your holiday you usually go travelling with your girlfriend. You don't have any money problems because you still live with your parents. You have one older sister.

2. Now ask Sharin, a young woman from India, about her life and fill in the form below.

What's your …?
How old …?
How do you feel about/like …?
Where do you …?
What do you …?
How much do you …?
When …?
How long …?

Name: ______________________
Age: ______________________
City: ______________________
Job: ______________________
Place of work: ______________________
Boss: ______________________
Holidays: ______________________
Payment: ______________________
Working hours: ______________________
Spends money on: ______________________
Family: ______________________
Future plans: ______________________

Role play: Different lives

Work with a partner. Partner A uses the information on the previous page. Partner B uses the information on this page.

WORD BANK

to hit – schlagen
previous – vorherig

Partner B

1. You are Sharin from India and you are talking to a young man from Germany. Ask him questions about his life and fill in the form below.

What's your ...?
How much do you ...?
When ...?
How long ...?
Where do you ...?
How do you feel about/like ...?
What do you ...?
How old ...?

Name: ______
Age: ______
City: ______
Job: ______
Place of work: ______
Boss: ______
Holidays: ______
Payment: ______
Working hours: ______
Spends money on: ______
Family: ______
Future plans: ______

2. Read the information about Sharin. Then answer Frank's questions.

Sharin

You are 16 and come from New Delhi. You live with your four brothers and two sisters in one room. Your parents are very poor and they don't have enough money to send you to school. Your family needs the money that you earn from your work.
You work for a company that produces footballs. You work every day of the week from 6 a.m. until 6 p.m. Sometimes you have to work up to 14 hours a day. Then it is too late to go home and you sleep on the floor in the factory.
You earn 3,000 rupees a month which is about 37 euros. Your boss sometimes hits you when you don't work fast enough. You feel unhappy and you don't like your job. Sometimes you spend a bit of money on sweets. You only have twelve days' holiday a year.
You would like to open your own fashion shop in the future.

Communicative crossword

Find a partner. Then choose the left or the right side – your partner takes the other side. Don't look at your partner's side.

Partner A

You and your partner both have the same crossword, but some of the words are missing. Your partner's side shows the words that you need and your side shows the words that your partner needs. (All these words are from Units 1 to 7.)

Help your partner to finish the crossword. First think of good clues to the words on your own side and write them down. Then take turns to ask each other and tell each other your clues.

What's the clue for 2 down?

How do you call someone who …?

Yes, it is./No, …/ Yes, it does./No, …

Is the first letter a 'C'?/Does it start/ end with a/an …?

Is it …?

Do you spell it with a/an …?

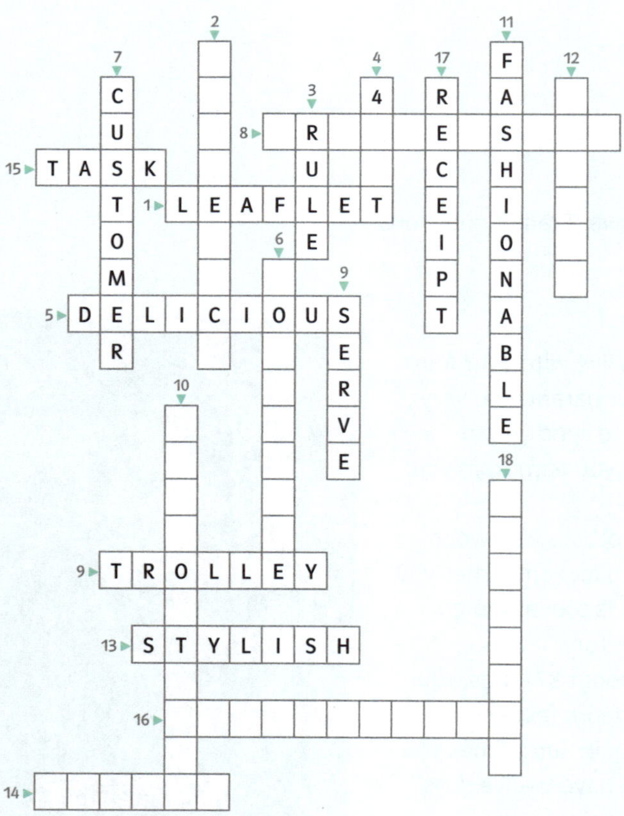

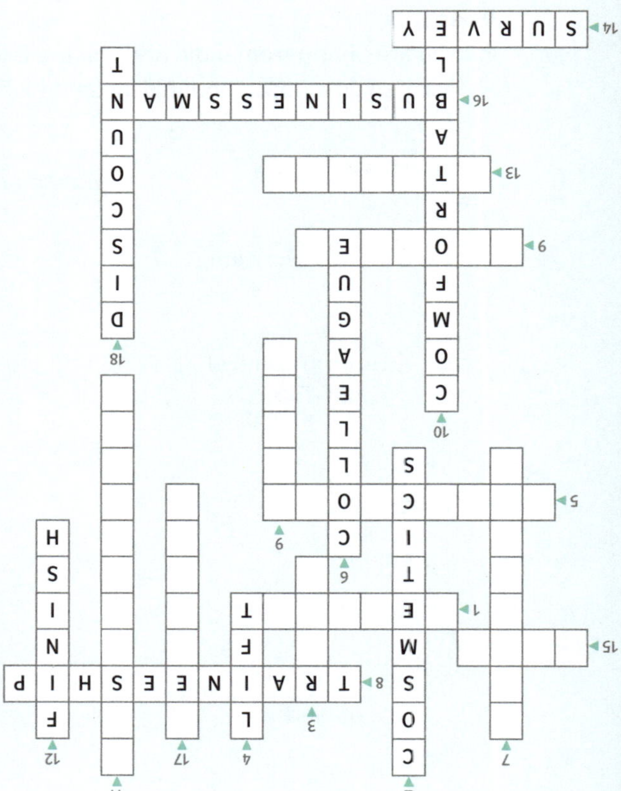

Yes, it is./No, …/ Yes, it does./No, …

Is it …?

Is the first letter a 'C'?/Does it start/ end with a/an …?

Do you spell it with a/an …?

How do you call someone who …?

What's the clue for 2 down?

Partner B

You and your partner both have the same crossword, but some of the words are missing. Your partner's side shows the words that you need and your side shows the words that your partner needs. (All these words are from Units 1 to 7.)

Help your partner to finish the crossword. First think of good clues to the words on your own side and write them down. Then take turns to ask each other and tell each other your clues.

WORD BANK

clue – Hinweis

Talking about statistics

Choose side A or B. Don't look at the side that you are not working with.

Partner A

You and your partner have got the same two graphs giving information about mobile phone sales and customer figures of shops in different cities in Britain. However, you each have only one of the two lines that should be on the graphs, so you have to help each other to draw the missing line. First tell your partner what your statistics are about. Then, use the figures at the bottom and the side of the graph and give the information to your partner.

The line starts in the year … • Between … and … sales rise/fall to … • The percentage rises from … to … • There is a gradual/sharp increase/decrease … • By … the percentage is …

Graph 1: Mobile phone sales to customers aged 18 to 26 in a shop in Liverpool

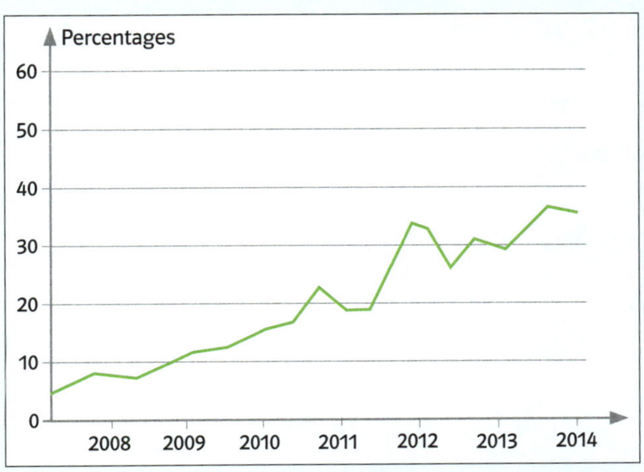

Graph 2: Customer figures of a fashion shop in London

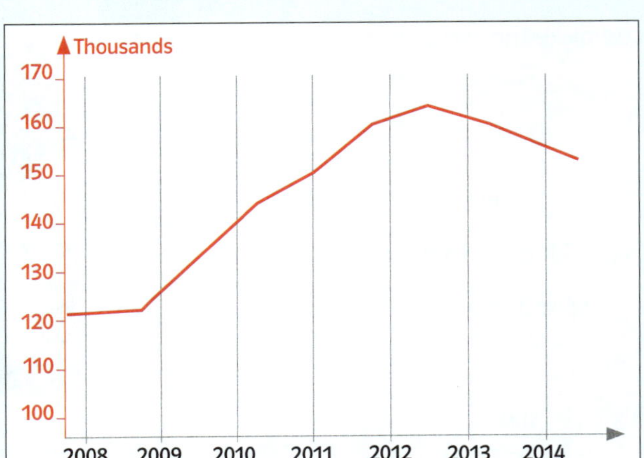

Partner B

You and your partner have got the same two graphs giving information about mobile phone sales and customer figures of shops in different cities in Britain. However, you each have only one of the two lines that should be on the graphs, so you have to help each other to draw the missing line. First tell your partner what your statistics are about. Then, use the figures at the bottom and the side of the graph and give the information to your partner.

The line starts in the year … • Between … and … sales rise/fall to … • The percentage rises from … to … • There is a gradual/sharp increase/decrease … • By … the percentage is …

Graph 1: Mobile phone sales to customers aged 18 to 26 in a shop in Bristol

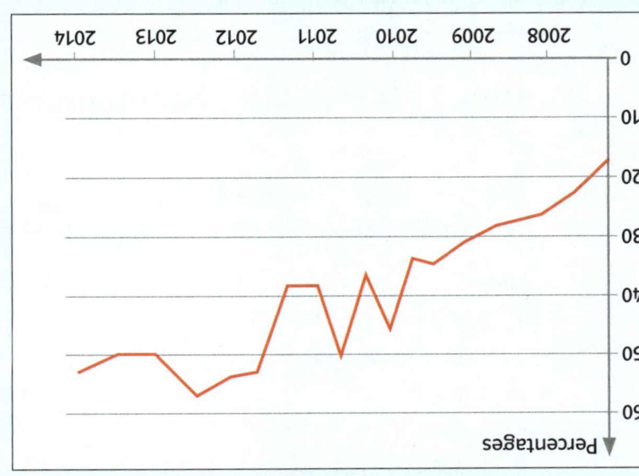

Graph 2: Customer figures of a fashion shop in Manchester

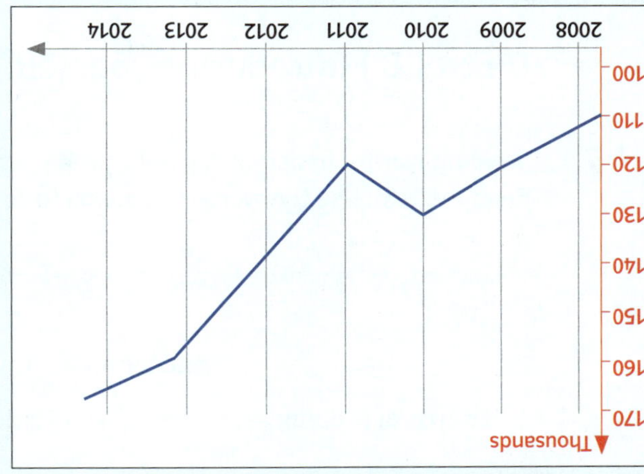

WORD BANK

figure – Zahl
gradual – allmählich
to rise – steigen

Helping Hand

Unit 1 | B | Introducing yourself

3 **Reading comprehension: A good friend from Manchester** → page 8
Read the text. Use the words in the box to complete the sentences.

Manchester • Franziska • grocery shop • work placement

1. ____________________ and Susan are trainees at a stationery shop in Rostock.
2. Franziska is doing a traineeship at a stationery shop while Susan is doing her ____________________ there.
3. Susan comes from ____________________ originally.
4. Dennis has just started his work placement at a ____________________ nearby.

Unit 1 | D | Talking about yourself and your job

2 **Your own blog** → page 11
Write a blog about yourself and your job. Use your exercise book.

Help
1. My name is …
2. I'm … years old.
3. I live in …
4. I'm training to become …
5. I start work at …
6. I finish work at …
7. I sell …
8. I like …
9. I don't like …

Unit 2 | A | Describing products

2 **Listening: Visiting a shoe shop** → page 18
Listen to the text. Use the words in the box and complete the sentences.

blouse • Manchester • pair • Susan • expensive

a) Franziska and Susan go to an ____________________ shoe shop.
b) Susan's friend in ____________________ doesn't like to go shopping with her.
c) Susan finds a ____________________ of shoes for Franziska.
d) Franziska finds a pair of shoes that matches her ____________________.
e) At the end, Franziska suggests they look for a pair of shoes for ____________________.

Unit 2 | D | Serving customers successfully

2 **Answer the questions. Use the words in italics.** → page 22

1. What product does Dennis want to buy?
   Dennis • tablet • buy • want • computer

   ____

   ____

2. What must be special about the product he is interested in?
   tablet • not be • heavy • fast • have • connectivity options • USB connection • memory card • room

   ____

   ____

3. Why doesn't he buy the product that the assistant shows him first?
   he • home • only • tablet • need • computer • WiFi

   ____

   ____

4. What is special about the product he finally buys?
   tablet • have • but • processor • more expensive • fast • to be • good quality • smaller

   ____

   ____

Unit 3 | C | Different types of shops

2 **Advantages of different shops** → page 33
Listen again. Use the words in the box to complete the sentences with the name of the right type of shop.

specialist shop • corner shop • specialist shop • discounter

1. Old people often buy products at a ____________________.
2. You can buy cheap food at a ____________________.
3. A ____________________ has products in different designs.
4. At a ____________________ there are shop assistants who can help you.

Unit 3 | D | Future plans

5 **Reading comprehension** → page 35

Read the text and complete the following summary. Choose the right words.

Shopping will be ____________________ (very different/very difficult) in the future. We'll do most of our shopping ____________________ (on the internet/ at local shops nearby). In the supermarket a ____________________ (shop assistant/ computer) will help us to do our shopping. It will tell us what we need and it will give us information about ____________________ (the shop/products). There won't be any ____________________ (shop assistants/trolleys).

Unit 4 | A | Talking about money

2 **Advantages of different shops** → page 42

Describe the cartoon.

Help

1. In the cartoon I can see …
2. The woman looks …
3. She is wearing …
4. She is shopping at …
5. She is pushing …
6. Her trolley has a front on it like a …

Unit 4 | D | At the cash desk

2 **Reading comprehension: At the corner shop** → page 44

Read the text on page 43 and answer the questions. Use the words in italics.

1. What problem does Steven have when the assistant greets him?
   problem • understand • can't/speak • German • have • Steven

   ____

   ____

2. Does Steven buy the cheap or the expensive bars of chocolate?
   buy • chocolate • cheap • bars • he

   ____

   ____

3. How much is a bottle of lemonade?
   lemonade • bottle • be • €0.95

   ____

   ____

4. Why can't Steven buy any pineapples?
   because • can't • them • buy • sold out • be • he • completely • they

   ____

   ____

5. Why does the assistant ask Steven if he has the exact change?
   have got • coins • this • few • morning • assistant • very

   ____

   ____

6. What does Steven get so that he can take his shopping items home safely?
   bag • carrier • get • he

   ____

   ____

Unit 5 | C | Finding different departments

2 **Listening: Finding the way** → page 57
Listen again. Use the words in the box to complete the sentences.

straight on • toy department • escalator • in the basement •
behind • go downstairs • lift • out of order

1. Please *(nach unten gehen)* ____________________ to the supermarket *(im Untergeschoss)* ____________________.
2. The *(Spielzeugabteilung)* ____________________ is on the third floor. You can take the *(Fahrstuhl)* ____________________ if you want.
3. You have to take the *(Rolltreppe)* ____________________ to go to the children's wear department. The lift is *(außer Betrieb)* ____________________.
4. The cosmetics department is *(hinter)* ____________________ this one. Just go *(geradeaus)* ____________________.

Unit 5 | D | Making comparisons

2 **Writing an SMS** → page 57
Susan's answer below to her friend Lilly is mixed up. Number the sentences in her SMS in the right order.

☐ Good that I know your size!
☐ I miss u a lot, too.
☐ And it doesn't really matter what u wear.
☐ Ino that the shoes there are less stylish and more expensive.
☐ They were cheaper and more beautiful than the ones u can buy in London.
☐ TXS
☐ I'm fine and I'm having a great time here in Germany.
☐ But don't worry: ur the prettiest girl anyway.
☐ CU, Susan
1 Hi Lilly,
☐ Write soon.
☐ Yesterday I bought a pair of really fashionable shoes with high heels for u.

Now write the SMS.

____

____

____

____

____

____

____

____

____

Unit 6 | B | Planning a product promotion

1 **Reading comprehension** → page 67

Read the flyer for eco-friendly cleaning products on page 67 and answer the questions. Use the in italics.

1. What is the problem with conventional cleaning products?
   have • *contain* • *chemicals* • *many of them* • *enviroment* • *be harmful* • *toxic side effects* • *which*

   ____

   ____

2. What are the two main characteristics of eco-friendly cleaners?
   be non-toxic • *products* • *bio-degradable* • *natural substances* • *that* • *contain*

   ____

   ____

3. What is the effect of eco-friendly cleaners on your household and the environment?
   on • *environment* • *impact* • *be minimal* • *on* • *bodies*

   ____

Unit 6 | C | Promoting online and offline sales

4 **Assessing the attractiveness of an online store** → page 70

Do some internet research together with your partner. Look at an online store of your choice and answer the following questions into your exercise book. Present your findings to the class.

a) How does the online store try to attract attention?
b) What are the advantages and disadvantages of the store?

Help

- The company's homepage makes a good/striking *(auffallend)* impression (on) … because …
- For customers it is easy to … / customers can easily find …
- The layout of the website is …
- On top of …/in the middle of …/at the bottom of the website you can see/find …
- The pictures on the website look emotional/inspiring/provocative *(provokant)*/ shocking.
- There is eye-catching *(ins Auge fallen)* information in large letters/capital letters *(Großbuchstaben)*/bold letters *(Fettdruck)*.
- The latest information is …
- The buttons *(Schaltflächen)* for the customers are …
- The website doesn't have a/an/any …
- … is/are missing *(fehlen)*
- There is no …

Unit 7 | C | Explaining rules and regulations

2 **Role play: Talking to a dissatisfied customer** → page 81

Put the dialogue into the right order. Number the parts of the dialogue from 1–9.

- ☐ Assistant: OK. No problem. Please come to the cash desk and I'll see that you get your money back.
- ☐ Customer: Hello. I have a complaint to make about this shirt I bought here last week.
- ☐ Assistant: Good afternoon. How can I help you?
- ☐ Customer: That's very kind of you. Thanks a lot.
- ☐ Assistant: What exactly happened?
- ☐ Customer: I'd really like to get a refund.
- ☐ Assistant: You're welcome.
- ☐ Customer: That's very kind of you. Thanks a lot.
- ☐ Assistant: I am sorry to hear that. But I must admit that the shirt looks really awful. I can certainly offer you a replacement or a refund.
- ☐ Customer: When I washed the shirt, it lost most of its colour. It looks terrible now and I'm very disappointed with the quality of it.

Unit 7 | E | Convincing upset customers

1 **Listening: Dealing with an upset customer** → page 83

Listen again and complete the sentences with the correct ending.

1. The customer is upset because …
   a) she has been waiting for more than half an hour.
   b) she has been waiting for more than 20 minutes.

2. In the future the customer thinks she is going to …
   a) to ask for a voucher if this happens again.
   b) to buy the products somewhere else.

3. The manager tries …
   a) to calm the customer down.
   b) to explain to the customer why she had to wait quite a long time.

Unit 8 | B | Dealing with product recalls

2 **Vocabulary work** → page 91

Read the press release on page 91 and choose the right word for these explanations.

1. You use it to weigh yourself.
   a) shoes b) body c) scale
2. It is like money and you get goods or services for it.
   a) voucher b) refund c) offer
3. The money that you get when you give back a product.
   a) voucher b) refund c) pocket money
4. Another word for 'hotline'.
   a) waiting room b) helpline c) operator

Unit 8 | D | Apologizing to customers

1 **Listening: Asking for a refund** → page 93

Listen to the dialogue on page 93 between a dissatisfied English-speaking customer and the customer service of a department store. Then answer the questions. Use the words in italics.

1. What did Mr Lindsay buy in the leather goods department?
   suitcase • buy • leather goods department

   ____

   ____

2. Why did he call the customer service?
   call • properly • not work • lock • customer service

   ____

   ____

3. What did the customer service offer Mr Lindsay first?
   lock • exchange • offer

   ____

   ____

4. But what did Mr Lindsay want to have?
   suitcase • refund • want • have • give back

   ____

   ____

5. How did the customer service react?
   Mr Lindsay • promise • refund • receive • give • suitcase

   ____

   ____

"I've got your letter in front of me now, sir."

Unit 9 | B | A business letter

6 **Writing an enquiry** → page 105
You are working in the toys department of a department store and you need a supplier of high-quality dolls. Complete the following enquiry by putting the jumbled letters of the words in brackets in the correct order.

Dear Sir or Madam,

__________________ *(QIYEUNR)*

We understand that you are a major __________________ *(ERPPSULI)* of high-quality dolls. We are currently looking for a new supplier of such dolls for our ______________ *(TYOS)* department in a large department __________________ *(ETORS)* in Dresden, Germany.

Please send us your current __________________ *(OGACTAUEL)*, a __________________ *(ERICP)* list and the trade __________________ *(SCODTSIUN)* that you can offer.

We would also appreciate further information about your __________________ (MERST) of delivery and __________________ *(APYNTME)*.

Thank you for your __________________ *(LEPH)* in advance. We look __________________ *(RAWRDFO)* to receiving an answer from you soon.

__________________ *(OUYSR)* faithfully,

____
name

____
suPghrnica satatnsis

Unit 9 | D | Placing an order

2 **Confirming an order** → page 106
British Jewellery confirms the order. Sum up the e-mail in German. Write in your exercise book.

Help

1. to be pleased to do sth *(sich über etwas freuen)*
2. free of charge *(kostenlos)*
3. to remind s.o. that … *(jemanden daran erinnern, dass …)*
4. settlement *(Begleichung)*
5. within *(innerhalb von …)*
6. to appreciate sth *(etwas zu schätzen wissen …)*
7. bank transfer *(Banküberweisung)*
8. to be certain *(überzeugt sein)*
9. to be fully satisfied with sth *(vollkommen zufrieden sein mit etwas)*

Unit 10 | A | Which job?

1 Different jobs → page 114

Look at the photos on page 114. Where do you think the people work? Describe the people and their jobs. Use the words below.

Photo A: *perfumery • help • find • right products*

____

Photo B: *fashion shop • sell • clothing • customers*

____

Photo C: *inform • functions • latest mobile phones*

____

Photo D: *cashier • scan products • cash desk*

____

____

____

____

____

Unit 10 | E | A job interview

2 Telling the time → page 118

a) Match the times. Write numbers 1–6 in the boxes.

1. 06:05	☐	It's midnight.
2. 09:15	☐	It's five minutes past six in the morning.
3. 14:30	☐	It's (a) quarter to ten in the evening.
4. 21:45	☐	It's three minutes to three in the morning.
5. 00:00	☐	It's half past two in the afternoon.
6. 02:57	☐	It's (a) quarter past nine in the morning.

b) Match these times. Write numbers 1–6 in the boxes.

1. 06:05	☐	It's 2.30 p.m.
2. 09:15	☐	It's 6.05 a.m.
3. 14:30	☐	It's 9.15 a.m.
4. 21:45	☐	It's 2.57 a.m.
5. 00:00	☐	It's 9.45 p.m.
6. 02:57	☐	It's 12 o'clock at night.

KMK-Prüfungssätze

KMK Stufe I (*100 VP*)

Schriftliche Prüfung
Zeit: 90 Minuten
Hilfsmittel: Allgemeines zweisprachiges Wörterbuch
Maximale Punktzahl: 100 Punkte

Im Folgenden werden Ihnen vier Aufgaben zur Bearbeitung vorgelegt. Die ersten beiden Aufgaben beziehen sich auf Ihre Fähigkeit, englische Texte (sowohl gesprochene als auch geschriebene) zu verstehen (= Rezeption). Die dritte Aufgabe verlangt das Schreiben eines englischen Textes (= Produktion). Bei der vierten Aufgabe wird von Ihnen erwartet, dass Sie englische Angaben ins Deutsche übertragen (= Mediation).
Die Prüfung beginnt mit der Hörverständnisaufgabe. Alle weiteren Aufgaben können in beliebiger Reihenfolge bearbeitet werden.

1 **Rezeption (Hörverstehen)** **20 VP**

◎ A 2.14 **Sie interessieren sich für eine Stelle im englischsprachigen Ausland, z. B. ein Praktikum oder eine längerfristige Anstellung nach Beendigung Ihrer Ausbildung. Die Virtual Employment Agency (VEA) vermittelt solche Praktika. Sie laden sich einen Podcast mit vier Stellenangeboten herunter. Hören Sie den Podcast zweimal an und füllen Sie die folgende Tabelle auf Englisch aus.**

Information number	1 (*5 VP*)	2 (*5 VP*)	3 (*5 VP*)	4 (*5 VP*)
1. position offered				
2. length of internship				
3. company and location of internship				
4. requirements				
5. extra information: e-mail address, telephone number if given				

2 Rezeption (Leseverstehen)

20 VP

Sie möchten während Ihrer Ausbildung gerne von Ihrem Arbeitgeber für ein Praktikum im Ausland freigestellt werden. Um Ihren Arbeitsgeber davon zu überzeugen, dass das eine sinnvolle Ergänzung zu Ihrer Arbeit im Betrieb darstellt, haben Sie sich dazu Informationsmaterial von der Internetseite der VEA heruntergeladen (siehe Seite 128). Sie werden nun von Ihrem Arbeitgeber gebeten, die folgenden Fragen zu diesem Text für ihn auf Deutsch zu beantworten.

1. Was ist die VEA für eine Organisation und was zeichnet sie aus? *(5 VP)*

2. Wie sieht das konkrete Angebot der VEA aus? *(3 VP)*

3. Mit welcher Bezahlung können die Teilnehmer der Praktika rechnen? *(3 VP)*

4. Was wird über die Dauer der Praktika gesagt? *(3 VP)*

5. Wer kann sich um einen Praktikumsplatz bewerben und welche Voraussetzungen müssen dafür erfüllt sein? *(3 VP)*

6. Wie kann man sich bewerben und was muss dazu eingereicht werden? *(3 VP)*

Manchester-based VEA offers lots of different job placements

Who we are	VEA is an organization financed by the European Union and European companies. We want to help to make European companies fit to operate more effectively worldwide. To this end, we want to give their trainees a chance to work in various countries in order to improve their language skills and also adapt to new cultures. The trainees taking part in the programme have a chance to see how goods are offered, advertised and sold in different ways and to learn to work under new working conditions.
What we offer	We help you to find work placements in different regions in Britain. All placements are in authentic work environments and we help potential trainees to establish contacts with companies and to plan their stay. If there are any problems, the trainees can contact us immediately by calling our telephone hotline.
What payment is given	We do not pay anything for the trainees except for a fixed amount to cover their travelling expenses. However, most companies we have under contract offer some small salaries for the work done so that the trainees will be able to cover at least their daily expenses such as food and accommodation.
How long do work placements last?	The duration depends on the companies and the offers they make. Normally, they run for between eight and ten weeks but flexible arrangements with the companies involved are also a possibility. The shortest possible placement is two weeks.
Who can apply	All trainees must have finished their first or second year of training if they want to apply. They should have at least a basic knowledge of English, although some companies are looking for applicants who speak English fluently. In addition, they should be communicative, open to new experiences and interested in English culture.
How to apply	It is best to send us an e-mail and a CV as an attachment in English telling us why you would like to take part in this work placement programme. In addition to that, it is important to attach a written letter of consent and a letter of recommendation from the company you work for. Please do not forget to mention the dates when you intend to do the placement and where you would like to work. Please send your application by email to info@vea...biz, subject line "Work placement in Britain."

3 Produktion

30 VP

Nach reiflicher Überlegung haben Sie sich dazu entschlossen, sich per E-Mail bei der VEA um ein Praktikum zu bewerben (Adresse: info@vea . . . biz). Schreiben Sie, dass Ihre Firma mit einem Auslandsaufenthalt von bis zu sechs Monaten einverstanden wäre. Geben Sie in Ihrer Mail Ihren Ausbildungsberuf an und in welchem Ausbildungsjahr Sie sich gerade befinden. Nennen Sie einen Zeitraum von sechs Monaten (mit genauem Datum), in dem Sie das Praktikum gerne absolvieren möchten.

From:

To:

Subject:

4 Mediation

30 VP

Auf der Internetseite der VEA befinden sich auch Erfahrungsberichte früherer Absolventen. Dabei halten Sie einen für besonders geeignet, um ihn Ihrem Arbeitgeber vorzulegen. Übertragen Sie ihn inhaltlich korrekt ins Deutsche. Beachten Sie dabei, dass Ihr Arbeitgeber auf eine wörtliche Übersetzung keinen Wert legt.

» My name is Tabea and I'm in my third year of training to become a management assistant in retail business next year. I've just come back from a three-month work placement in Leeds. I worked at a big department store right in the city centre.

When I arrived there, I started off in the cosmetics department. I had to fill the shelves, which was rather boring, but after some time I was allowed to serve customers, too. Customers often asked me where I came from as they probably noticed that I had a German accent. But the longer I stayed in the department the better my English got, and finally no one asked me where I originally came from. That was great. My colleagues were very friendly and helpful. In the last weeks of my stay I was also involved in designing flyers for products on offer. That was fun and I really enjoyed doing it.

All in all, this work placement was a great opportunity for me, and my boss sees it as a real plus for our company too, especially for our contacts with English-speaking customers. «

Mündliche Prüfung

Zeit:	15 Minuten (plus 20 Minuten Vorbereitungzeit)
Hilfsmittel:	Allgemeines zweisprachiges Wörterbuch
Maximale Punktzahl:	30 Punkte

Die mündliche Prüfung ist eine Partnerprüfung und sie besteht aus zwei Teilen. Im ersten Teil werden Sie gebeten, sich zu persönlichen oder beruflichen Themen zu äußern. Im zweiten Teil sollen Sie in Partnerarbeit ein Rollenspiel durchführen. Dazu erhalten Sie Rollenkarten auf denen eine Situation beschrieben ist, die Sie ausspielen sollen. Dabei wird von Ihnen erwartet, dass Sie mit der vorgegebenen Situation sprachlich angemessen umgehen.

Speaker A

Sie sind Praktikant/in in der britischen Filiale eines Mobilfunkanbieters in Liverpool, England. Es ist Ihr erster Arbeitstag und Sie unterhalten sich mit einem / einer Verkäufer/in in der Mittagspause über die tägliche Arbeit. Sie beginnen das Gespräch.

1. Stellen Sie sich kurz vor und sagen Sie, dass heute Ihr erster Arbeitstag ist und Sie einige Fragen hätten.
3. Erkundigen Sie sich nach den Öffnungszeiten des Geschäfts.
5. Sagen Sie, dass Sie heute Vormittag eine neue Warenlieferung ausgepackt und die Handys verschiedener Hersteller in die Regale eingeräumt haben. Erkundigen Sie sich nach weiteren Aufgaben, die in den nächsten Tagen auf Sie zukommen könnten.
7. Sagen Sie, dass Sie bereits viele Handys kennen, aber Sie noch unsicher sind, wenn Sie Kunden bedienen und ihnen alles auf Englisch erklären müssten.
9. Sagen Sie, dass Sie jetzt beruhigt sind und bedanken Sie sich für die Auskünfte.

Speaker B

Sie sind Verkäufer/in eines Mobilfunkanbieters in Liverpool, England. In Ihrer Mittagspause unterhalten Sie sich mit einem Praktikanten / einer Praktikantin aus Deutschland über Ihre tägliche Arbeit. Für den Praktikanten / die Praktikantin ist es der erste Arbeitstag. Der Praktikant / die Praktikantin eröffnet das Gespräch.

2. Stellen Sie sich ebenfalls kurz vor und sagen Sie, dass Sie gerne seine / ihre Fragen beantworten.
4. Teilen Sie ihm / ihr mit, dass das Geschäft montags bis freitags von 8 bis 21 Uhr geöffnet ist, sie an Samstagen von 9 bis 19 Uhr geöffnet haben und das Geschäft sonntags geschlossen bleibt.
6. Sagen Sie, dass er / sie die Besonderheiten und technischen Details einzelner Handys kennen lernen muss und wissen sollte, wie man sie bedient.
8. Weisen Sie den Praktikanten / die Praktikantin darauf hin, dass er / sie in den ersten zwei Wochen noch keine Kunden bedienen muss, sondern den anderen Verkäufern bei den täglichen Arbeiten helfen soll.
10. Bedanken Sie sich auch für das nette Gespräch und beenden Sie es mit dem Hinweis, dass Sie jederzeit gerne behilflich sind, wenn sie / er noch weitere Fragen haben sollte.

KMK Stufe II (*100 VP*)

Schriftliche Prüfung

Zeit:	90 Minuten
Hilfsmittel:	Allgemeines zweisprachiges Wörterbuch
Maximale Punktzahl:	100 Punkte

Im Folgenden werden Ihnen vier Aufgaben zur Bearbeitung vorgelegt. Die ersten beiden Aufgaben beziehen sich auf Ihre Fähigkeit, englische Texte (sowohl gesprochene als auch geschriebene) zu verstehen (= Rezeption). Bei der dritten Aufgabe wird von Ihnen erwartet, dass Sie englische Angaben ins Deutsche übertragen (= Mediation). Die vierte Aufgabe verlangt das Schreiben eines englischen Textes (= Produktion).
Die Prüfung beginnt mit der Hörverständnisaufgabe. Alle weiteren Aufgaben können in beliebiger Reihenfolge bearbeitet werden.

Situation
Sie sind Tina Heft, Assistentin der Einkaufsleitung der Modekette MODEWELT in Hamburg. Ihre Chefin, Frau Schmidt, ist durch eine Anzeige in einer Modezeitschrift auf den englischen Strickwarenhersteller Coolwool aufmerksam geworden. Da Sie über ausgezeichnete Englischkenntnisse verfügen, sind Sie aufgefordert, schriftlich und mündlich in Englisch zu kommunizieren.

1 **Rezeption (Hörverstehen)** 20 VP

A 2.15 **Tina Heft ruft bei Coolwool in England an. Hören Sie aufmerksam zu und notieren Sie Kurzantworten in deutscher Sprache, entsprechend den im untenstehenden Memo gemachten Angaben. Berücksichtigen Sie dabei die von Coolwool angebotene Produktpalette, die Qualitäten / Größen und die Garantie- und Liefermodalitäten. Sie hören den Dialog zweimal.**

MEMO

Für: ______________________

Von: ______________________

Gesprächspartner: ______________________

Firma: ______________________

Anruf vom (*heutiges Datum*): ______________________

Betreff: ______________________

____

____

____

____

____

____

____

2 Rezeption (Leseverstehen)

20 VP

Sie sind soeben von einem Woolmark Kongress in London zurückgekehrt. Frau Schmidt hat Sie gebeten, die Zahlen und Fakten über die Preisentwicklung auf dem Wollmarkt zu präsentieren. Dabei dient der folgende Text als Grundlage, um die Entwicklung von 2005 bis 2014 in einer Grafik darzustellen. Verwenden Sie bitte die untenstehende Tabelle für Ihre Eintragungen.

The international price for wool went up gradually from 650 cents per kg clean wool in 2005 to 760 cents/kg in the middle of 2007. One year later the price dropped to 450 cents/kg. In the following two years the price recovered and reached a maximum of 930 cents/kg at the end of 2009. Unfortunately, until the first quarter of the following year the price fell sharply to a low of 590 cents/kg. Then it picked up again in early 2012 to 810 cents/kg. At the beginning of 2013 it decreased by 40%. Since then it has picked up again and by the end of 2014 it is expected that the price will rise to 710 cents/kg.

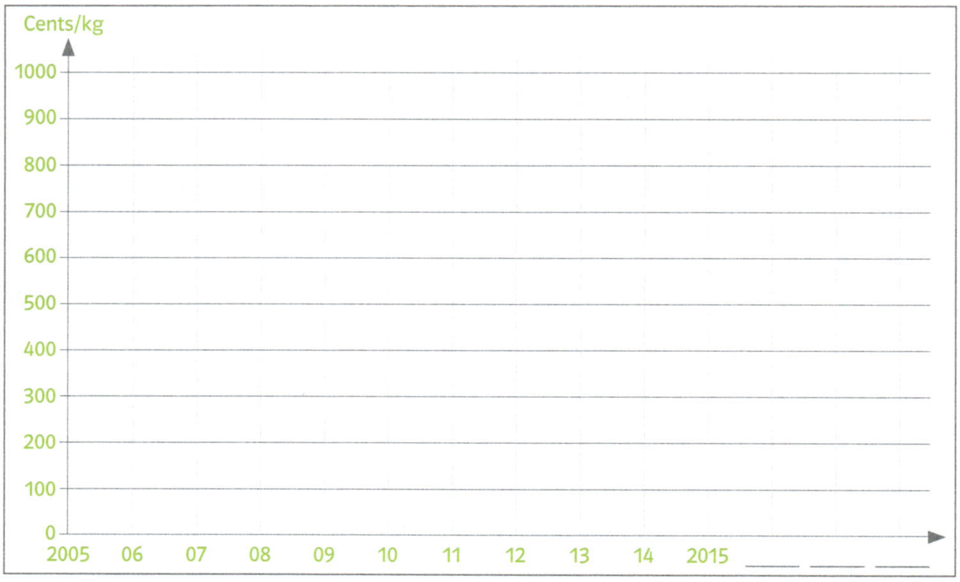

3 Mediation

30 VP

Ihre Chefin hat in einer internationalen Fachzeitschrift eine Anzeige der Gerarno Ltd, eines Großhändlers für Modebekleidung, gelesen. Frau Schmidt beauftragt Sie, die Anzeige ins Deutsche zu übertragen. Schreiben Sie Ihren deutschen Text in Ihr Heft.

... GERARNO Ltd *originated as a wholesale business*

Expansion continues in the UK and internationally with an emphasis on:

- the analysis of British and international markets to ensure the finest presentation of the products.
- preservation of brand integrity.
- development of the brand image and profile through visual merchandising.

As a result of successful placement in the UK's most greatly respected department stores the brand has a steadily increasing presence.

Our production centre in Hong Kong was established in 1978. The office has a very experienced team of people dedicated to finding new materials and techniques to improve the design aspect of the brand.

We specialise in advanced knitting and machine technology. Different quality garments are manufactured in Hong Kong and shipped to the UK and overseas. The emphasis is on quality, and all staff regularly attend courses to further their knowledge of the garment business.

Features of our ideal GERARNO customer:

- age group 28–55+ years
- classy
- money to invest

Nothing is more important than satisfied customers because:

- satisfied customers are repeat business.
- satisfied customers talk to and influence others.

4 Produktion

30 VP

Nach einer Woche liegen die gewünschten Unterlagen (Produktpalette, Qualitäten / Größen, Garantie- und Lieferbedingungen) der englischen Firma vor. Formulieren Sie nun ein Fax in englischer Sprache an den potentiellen Geschäftspartner Coolwool, 47 Brooklands Avenue, Great Wyrley, Walsall WS6 6LF, West Midlands, England, Tel.: 00 44 - (0) 15 42 - 77 42 90, Fax: 00 44 - (0) 15 42 - 77 42 91. Verwenden Sie dazu das untenstehende Formular und berücksichtigen Sie neben korrekter Anrede und Grußformel die folgenden Aspekte:

- Bedanken Sie sich höflich für die ausführlichen Informationen.
- Unterstreichen Sie, dass Ihre Kunden hochwertige Produkte erwarten.
- Betonen Sie, dass Sie hauptsächlich Strickjacken und Röcke für Damen in den Größen L bis XXL benötigen.
- Bitten Sie um einen Probeauftrag von je 500 Stück.
- Teilen Sie der Firma mit, dass Sie von regelmäßigen Lieferungen ausgehen, wenn die Probeartikel Ihren Erwartungen entsprechen.
- Bitten Sie um ein Preisangebot mit Angabe der Lieferungs- und Zahlungsbedingungen und sämtlicher Nachlässe über je 500 Stück.
- Gehen Sie darauf ein, dass Sie im Falle eines Vertragsabschlusses das Angebot des Transportes durch den englischen Hersteller annehmen.
- Schließen Sie Ihr Schreiben freundlich.

TELEFAX

Modewelt

Exklusive Bekleidung
Hafenstr. 27
23054 Hamburg
Tel.: (040) 24 24 24 - 0
Fax: (040) 24 24 24 - 12

Empfänger / Recipient: ______________________

Datum / Date: ______________________

Seiten / Pages: ______________________

Von / From: ______________________

Betreff / Subject: ______________________

Mündliche Prüfung

Zeit:	15 Minuten (plus 20 Minuten Vorbereitungzeit)
Hilfsmittel:	Allgemeines zweisprachiges Wörterbuch
Maximale Punktzahl:	30 Punkte

Die mündliche Prüfung ist eine Partnerprüfung und sie besteht aus zwei Teilen. Im ersten Teil werden Sie gebeten, sich zu persönlichen oder beruflichen Themen zu äußern. Im zweiten Teil sollen Sie in Partnerarbeit ein Rollenspiel durchführen. Dazu erhalten Sie Rollenkarten auf denen eine Situation beschrieben ist, die Sie ausspielen sollen. Dabei wird von Ihnen erwartet, dass Sie mit der vorgegebenen Situation sprachlich angemessen umgehen.

Speaker A

Sie sind Angestellte/r der Filiale der Autovermietungsgesellschaft Travis United in Falmouth, Cornwall. Es ist 10 Uhr. Das Telefon klingelt und Sie bereiten sich auf eine Anfrage bezüglich der Anmietung eines Fahrzeuges vor.

1. Nennen Sie Ihren Firmennamen und Ihren eigenen Namen und fragen Sie höflich, was Ihr Telefonpartner wünscht.
3. Fragen Sie den Kunden, ob er einen besonderen Fahrzeugwunsch hat.
5. Fragen Sie, für wie lange das Fahrzeug gemietet werden soll.
7. Erklären Sie, dass das Fahrzeug 55£ pro Tag kostet, inklusive Mehrwertsteuer und Vollkaskoversicherung. Es gibt keine Meilenbegrenzung.
9. Sagen Sie, dass Sie das Fahrzeug zum Hotel bringen können und die Mietgebühr den Transport zu einem vereinbarten Treffpunkt beinhaltet. Bitten Sie Ihren Gesprächspartner um den Namen, die momentane Adresse und die Telefonnummer.
11. Fragen Sie, ob das Alter des Kunden zwischen 21 und 70 liegt und die Führerscheindauer mindestens zwei Jahre beträgt.
13. Bitten Sie um die Nummer und das Ablaufdatum der Kreditkarte.
15. Sichern Sie zu, dass das Auto in der nächsten halben Stunde zum Hotel gebracht wird und der Fahrer die Dokumente zum Unterschreiben mitbringt.
17. Bedanken Sie sich für den Anruf und wünschen Sie dem Anrufer einen angenehmen und sicheren Aufenthalt in Großbritannien.

Speaker B

Sie sind geschäftlich für eine Woche in Großbritannien unterwegs. In Falmouth, Cornwall, gehen Sie zu Ihrem vorgebuchten Hotel und erhalten dort die Telefonnummer der Autovermietungsgesellschaft Travis United, die Sie nun anrufen. Es ist 10 Uhr.

2. Eröffnen Sie das Telefongespräch und erklären Sie, dass Sie eine viertürige Limousine mieten möchten.
4. Sagen Sie, dass Sie ein deutsches Fahrzeug bevorzugen.
6. Sagen Sie, dass Sie das Auto für vier Tage benötigen.
8. Geben Sie Ihr Einverständnis zu den unterbreiteten Kosten. Bitten Sie darum, Ihnen das Fahrzeug nun zum Hotel zu bringen.
10. Geben Sie Ihren Namen und Ihre momentane Adresse an: Sea View Hotel, Nelson Street Nr. 15, Tel.: 01326-250544.
12. Bejahen Sie die Frage und sagen Sie, dass Sie 28 Jahre alt sind und Ihren Führerschein seit zehn Jahren haben.
14. Ihre Kreditkartennummer lautet: 5232 2436 2007 und die Karte ist bis Juni 2025 gültig.
16. Bedanken Sie sich und beenden Sie angemessen das Telefongespräch.

Grammar overview

Das *simple present*

A Allgemein

Das *simple present* wird verwendet:
- für Aussagen, die längere Zeit gültig sind.
- um auszudrücken, was jemand regelmäßig tut.

B Mit *sometimes, often* usw.

Da man mit dem *simple present* ausdrückt, was man regelmäßig tut, wird es oft mit Wörtern wie *usually, normally, sometimes, often, always, never* verwendet. Diese Wörter (Adverbien) stehen immer:
- **vor** einem Vollverb.
- **nach** *to be*.

C Bildung: Aussagen

Das *simple present* wird aus der Grundform des Verbs (Infinitiv ohne *to*) gebildet.

Vorsicht!
Nach *he / she / it* endet das Verb immer auf *-s* oder *-es*:
1. An die meisten Verben wird einfach *-s* angehängt.
2. Die Endung *-es* wird bei Verben benutzt, die auf *-s, -ss, -x, -ch* oder *-sh* enden (z. B. *to finish*), da es schwer wäre, nur ein *-s* auszusprechen.
3. Auch die Verben *go* und *do* enden mit *-es*.
4. Ein Sonderfall sind Verben, die auf *-y* enden: *to tidy* → *he tidi**es***.

1. to work	**2. to finish**
I work	I finish
he / she / it work**s**	he / she / it finish**es**
we work	we finish
you work	you finish
they work	they finish

3. to go	**4. to tidy**
I go	I tidy
he / she / it go**es**	he / she / it tid**ies**
we go	we tidy
you go	you tidy
they go	they tidy

D Bildung: Fragen und Verneinungen

- Fragen im *simple present* werden mit *do* (bei *he / she / it*: *does*) gebildet.
- Verneinungen bildet man mit *don't* (nach *he / she / it*: *doesn't*).

Vorsicht!
Nach *does / doesn't* kommt immer die Grundform des Verbs:
*Does he work? (**!** Does he ~~works~~?)*
*She doesn't work. (**!** She doesn't ~~works~~.)*

Fragen	**Verneinungen**
Do I work?	I don't work
Does he / she / it wor**k**?	he / she / it doesn't wor**k**
Do we work?	we don't work
Do you work?	you don't work
Do they work?	they don't work

Das *present continuous*

A Allgemein

Das *present continuous* benutzt man für Aktivitäten, die gerade im Augenblick des Sprechens stattfinden. Oder auch um ein Bild zu beschreiben. Es wird häufig mit Zeitangaben wie *at the moment* und *right now* verwendet.

*I'**m reading** this text at the moment.*

What can you see in this photo?
*– A hairdresser. Right now, she'**s cutting** a customer's hair.*

B Mit *this week, this month* usw.

Das *present continuous* kann auch für längere, befristete Handlungen verwendet werden, die gerade stattfinden, z. B. *this week, this month*.

*We'**re visiting** a friend in England this week.*
*Julia **is learning** English on a course in London.*

C Bildung: Aussagen

Das *present continuous* wird mit *to be* und Verb + *-ing* gebildet.

I'm he's / she's / it's we're you're they're	working

D Bildung: Fragen und Verneinungen

Fragen und Verneinungen werden mit den Frage- und Verneinungsformen von *to be* gebildet.

Fragen	**Verneinungen**
Am I working? Are you working? Are they working?	I'm not working she isn't working

E Verb + *-ing*: Schreibregeln

- An die meisten Verben wird einfach *-ing* angehängt: *work – work**ing**, do – do**ing**.*
- Verben, die auf *-e* enden, verlieren das *-e*: *us**e** – us**ing**, danc**e** – danc**ing**.*
- Kurze Verben, die auf einen Vokal und einen Konsonanten (außer *-y*, *-w* und *-x*) enden, verdoppeln den Konsonanten: *cu**t** – cu**tt**ing* (ABER: *pla**y** – pla**y**ing*).
- Längere Verben, die auf einen Vokal und einen Konsonanten enden, verdoppeln den Konsonanten nicht: *visi**t** – visi**t**ing, delive**r** – delive**r**ing.* (Ausnahmen: *trave**ll**ing, begi**nn**ing*)
- Bei Verben, die auf *-ie* enden, wird *-ie* zu *-y*: *-**ie** – d**y**ing*

F *Simple present* oder *present continuous?*

This is Patrick. He lives in England. He works in a supermarket five days a week.

It's 8.30 in the morning. Patrick is going to the supermarket by bus.

Das *simple past*

A Allgemein

Das *simple past* wird verwendet, um Ereignisse in der Vergangenheit zu schildern, die jetzt abgeschlossen sind. Es wird häufig mit Zeitangaben wie *then, in 1970, last week* und *30 years ago* benutzt.

B Bildung: Aussagen

- Regelmäßige Verben bilden das *simple past* mit *-ed*. Diese Form bleibt in allen Personen gleich.
- Unregelmäßige Verben haben Sonderformen im *simple past* (eine Liste findest du auf dem Klappumschlag). Diese Formen (außer bei *to be*) bleiben ebenfalls in allen Personen gleich.

regelmäßig	**unregelmäßig**	
to work	**to go**	**to be**
I worked	I went	I **was**
he worked	he went	he was
she worked	she went	she was
it worked	it went	it was
we worked	we went	we **were**
you worked	you went	you were
they worked	they went	they were

C Bildung: Fragen und Verneinungen

- Fragen im *simple past* werden in allen Personen mit *did* gebildet.
- Verneinungen bildet man durchgehend mit *didn't*.
- *to be* bildet Fragen und Verneinungen im *simple past* mit eigenen Formen.

Vorsicht!
Nach *did / didn't* steht immer die Grundform des Verbs:
Did he work? (! Did he ~~worked~~?)
She didn't work. (! She didn't ~~worked~~.)

Fragen	**Verneinungen**
Did I work?	I didn't work
Did he / she / it work?	he / she / it didn't work
Did we work?	we didn't work
Did you work?	you didn't work
Did they work?	they didn't work
to be	
Was I?	I wasn't
Was he / she / it?	he / she / it wasn't
Were we / you / they?	we / you / they / weren't

D Verb + *-ing*: Schreibregeln

- An die meisten Verben wird einfach *-ed* angehängt: *work – work**ed***.
- An Verben, die auf *-e* enden, hängt man nur *-d* an: ***use** – use**d**, **dance** – dance**d***.
- Kurze Verben, die auf einen Vokal (*a, e, i o, u*) und einen Konsonanten (außer *-y, -w* und *-x*) enden, verdoppeln den Konsonanten: *sho**p** – sho**pp**ed, jo**g** – jo**gg**ed.*
- Längere Verben, die auf einen Vokal und einen Konsonanten enden, verdoppeln den Konsonanten nicht: ***visit** – visit**ed**, deliver – deliver**ed**.* (Ausnahme: *trave**ll**ed*)
- Bei Verben, die auf *-y* enden, wird *-y zu -i: stud**y** – stud**ied***.

Das *present perfect*

A Allgemein

Mit dem *present perfect* und *since / for* kann man Fragen beantworten, die sich darauf beziehen, wie lange etwas andauert (*How long ...?*)

- *Since* wird mit einem Zeitpunkt (z. B. *2001, 3 January, last year*) benutzt.
- *For* verwendet man für einen Zeitraum (z. B. *two years, six months*).

B Bildung: Aussagen

Das *present perfect* wird mit *to have* und der 3. Form (Partizip Perfekt) gebildet.

- Regelmäßige Verben (z. B. *to work*) bilden ihre 3. Form mit *-ed*.
- Unregelmäßige Verben (z. B. *to go*) haben Sonderformen, die in der Liste auf dem Klappumschlag zu finden sind.

I have (I've) he / she / it (he's / she's / it's) we / you / they (we've / you've / they've)	worked gone

C Bildung: Fragen und Verneinungen

Fragen und Verneinungen werden mit Frage- und Verneinungsformen von *to have* + 3. Form des Verbs gebildet.

Fragen	Verneinungen
Have you worked? Has he worked?	I haven't worked he / she / it hasn't worked we / you / they haven't worked

Das *past perfect*

A Allgemein

Das *past perfect* wird für ein Ereignis in der Vergangenheit verwendet, das noch vor einem zweiten Ereignis in der Vergangenheit stattfand. Für das länger zurückliegende Ereignis verwendet man das *past perfect*, für das nicht ganz so lange zurückliegende das *simple past*. Wir verwenden das *past perfect* häufig mit *after*.

*She **chose** her job after she **had visited** an interesting company.*

B Bildung

Das *past perfect* wird mit *had* + 3. Form (Partizip Perfekt) des Verbs gebildet. Fragen werden auch mit *had*, Verneinungen mit *hadn't* gebildet.

After Jamie had run in the marathon, he went home and went to sleep!

Aussagen	Verneinungen
I had worked he / she / it had worked we / you / they had worked	I hadn't worked he / she / it hadn't worked we / you / they hadn't worked

Fragen
Had I worked? Had he / she / it worked? Had we / you / they worked?

Das *will-future*

A Allgemein

Will wird für feststehende Ereignisse in der Zukunft sowie für Vorhersagen und Vermutungen verwendet.	*I'll **have** a family in 10 years.* *She **won't leave** her job when she has a family.*

B Bildung

- **Aussagen** werden mit *will* + Grundform des Verbs gebildet. Die Kurzform (*'ll*) wird fast immer beim Sprechen und häufig auch beim Schreiben verwendet.
- **Fragen** bildet man, indem man *will* und das Subjekt umstellt. Hier sind die Kurzformen nicht möglich.
- **Verneinungen** werden mit *won't* + Grundform des Verbs gebildet.

I will (I'll) come	Will I come?
he will (he'll) come	Will he come?
she will (she'll) come	Will she come?
it will (it'll) come	Will it come?
we will (we'll) come	Will we come?
you will (you'll) come	Will you come?
they will (they'll) come	Will they come?

I won't come
he / she / it won't come
we / you / they won't come

Das *going to-future*

A Allgemein

Going to verwendet man, um über Pläne und Vorhaben zu sprechen: *I'm going to buy a new jacket* entspricht auf Deutsch: „Ich habe vor, eine neue Jacke zu kaufen."	***I'm going to** have a new job next month.* ***Are** you **going to** leave home?*

B Bildung

- **Aussagen** bildet man mit *to be* + *going to* + Hauptverb.
- **Fragen** bildet man mit den Frageformen von *to be* + *going to* + Hauptverb.
- Für **Verneinungen** benutzt man die Verneinung von *to be* + *going to* + Hauptverb.

I'm he's / she's / it's we're / you're / they're	going to	work
Am I Is he / she / it Are we / you / they	going to	work?
I'm not he / she / it isn't we / you / they aren't	going to	work

C *Will* oder *going to*?

Modale Hilfsverben: *must, have to, mustn't* und *don't / doesn't have to*

A Allgemein

Mit den modalen Hilfsverben *must, have to, mustn't* und *don't / doesn't have to* wird ausgedrückt, was man tun muss, nicht tun darf und nicht zu tun braucht (nicht tun muss).

must / have to

In England you must / have to drive on the left.

Must und *have to* haben etwa die gleiche Bedeutung. Sie drücken aus, was man tun **muss**.

mustn't

You mustn't drive on the right!

Mustn't drückt aus, was man **nicht darf**.

Vorsicht!

Mustn't bedeutet **nicht** „nicht müssen".

don't / doesn't have to

He doesn't have to drive!
He has a driver.

Don't / Doesn't have to drückt aus, was man **nicht zu tun braucht**.

Vorsicht!

don't have to = nicht müssen

B Bildung: *must* und *have to*

- *Must* bleibt in allen Personen gleich. Auf *must* folgt die Grundform des Verbs.
- *Have to* bildet man mit *to have* + Grundform des Verbs.

must	have to
I must go he / she / it must go we / you / they must go	I have to go he / she / it has to go we / you / they have to go

C Bildung: *mustn't*

Mustn't bleibt ebenfalls bei allen Personen gleich. Auf *mustn't* folgt die Grundform des Verbs.

I mustn't he / she / it mustn't we / you / they mustn't	go

D Verneinung: *don't / doesn't have to*

Die Verneinungsform von *have to* bildet man mit *don't / doesn't have to* + Grundform des Verbs.

I don't have to he / she / it doesn't have to we / you / they don't have to	go

If-Sätze (Bedingungssätze)

A Allgemein

- Ein Bedingungssatz besteht aus einem *if*-Teil und einem Hauptsatz. Der *if*-Teil beschreibt eine Bedingung und der Hauptsatz drückt aus, was passieren wird oder passieren könnte (oder hätte passieren können), wenn diese Bedingung erfüllt wird.
- Bedingungssätze können entweder mit dem *if*-Teil oder mit dem Hauptsatz beginnen. Beginnt ein Satz mit dem *if*-Teil, dann steht immer ein Komma vor dem Hauptsatz.

B *If*-Sätze Typ 1

***If** you **ask** the robot, it **will clean** the house.*

- Typ 1 drückt aus, was unter bestimmten Bedingungen in der Zukunft geschehen wird oder nicht geschehen wird.

If + simple present	will (not) + verb
If you go to the party,	you'll see Mitch.

C *If*-Sätze Typ 2

***If** I **worked** for that company, I **would need** a good qualification.*

- Wir benutzen Typ 2, um über eventuelle Situationen zu sprechen oder wenn man bezweifelt, dass eine Bedingung erfüllbar ist.
- ***Vorsicht!***
  Anders als im Deutschen darf *would* nur im Hauptsatz, nicht im *if*-Teil stehen.

If + simple past	would(n't) + verb
If you went to the party,	you would see Mitch.

D *If*-Sätze Typ 1 oder Typ 2?

Typ 1: Für Sachen, die passieren werden, wenn …

Typ 2: Für imaginäre, schwer vorstellbare Situationen

Das Passiv

A Allgemein

- Aktivsätze betonen, **wer** etwas tut. Passivsätze betonen, was getan wird – die Handlung steht im Vordergrund.
- In einem **Aktivsatz** steht das Subjekt vor dem Verb. Gibt es ein Objekt, so steht dieses nach dem Verb.
- **Passivsätze** kann man als ‚umgedrehte' Aktivsätze ansehen: Das Objekt des Aktivsatzes wird zum Subjekt des Passivsatzes.

Aktivsatz		
Subjekt	**Verb**	**Objekt**
The man	bought	the flowers.
Passivsatz		
The man	bought	the flowers.
The flowers	were bought	by the man.

B Bildung

- Das Passiv wird mit *to be* + 3. Form des Verbs (Partizip Perfekt) gebildet.

simple present		simple past	
I'm he's she's it's we're you're they're	made	I was he was she was it was we were you were they were	made

C Mit oder ohne *by*?

Meist wird das Subjekt des Aktivsatzes in einem Passivsatz nicht genannt. Wollen wir aber das Subjekt besonders betonen, können wir es mit *by* am Satzende anfügen. In Satz **1.** ist der Name des Regisseurs besonders wichtig. In Satz **2.** ist es uninteressant, von wem die Blumen angebaut werden.

1. *The film was made* ***by Steven Spielberg****.*
2. *These flowers are grown in* ***Kenya*** *(by …).*

They delivered oranges to the supermarket yesterday.

Too many oranges were delivered to the supermarket yesterday!

Adjektive und Adverbien

A Allgemein

- Adjektive beschreiben Personen und Sachen. Sie stehen meist vor einem Substantiv oder nach *to be*.
- Adverbien sagen etwas über Verben aus. Sie sagen uns, wie etwas passiert.

*It is a **big** robot.*
*The robot is **big**.*
*The robot loads the lorries **quickly**.*

B Bildung

- Ein Adverb wird gebildet, indem *-ly* an das Adjektiv angehängt wird.
- Die Endung *-y* wird zu *-ily*.
- Die Endung *-le* wird zu *-ly*.
- *-ic* wird zu *-ically*.
- Das Adverb von *good* ist *well*.

Adjektiv	Adverb
quick	quick**ly**
easy	eas**ily**
simple	simp**ly**
automatic	automat**ically**
good	**well**

Boris can do things very quickly.

Relativsätze

A Allgemein

Relativsätze sind Sätze, die eines der Relativpronomen *who, which* oder *where* enthalten. Sie beschreiben das Wort, auf das sie sich beziehen, näher.

***The woman who** is helping him is Frau Bliscz.*
***The document which** she has in her hand is Herr Krueger's letter.*

B *who, which* oder *where*?

- *who* für Personen
- *which* für Sachen
- *where* für Orte

Vorsicht!
Anders als im Deutschen steht kein Komma vor *who, which* und *where*.

*A passenger is a person **who** travels by plane.*
*A plane is a machine **which** carries people.*
*The place **where** peopl check in is the check-in desk.*

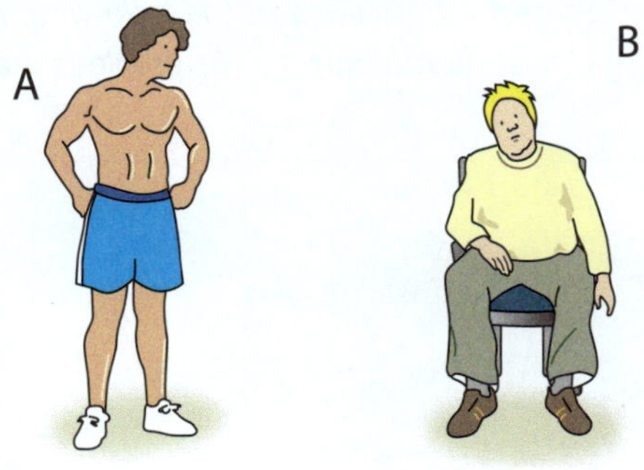

The guy who goes to a fitness club every day is A or B?

Indirekte Rede

A Allgemein

Die indirekte Rede wird verwendet, um zu berichten, was jemand sagt oder in der Vergangenheit sagte.

***She says (that) she likes** her new job at the department store.*
***The shop manager told him (that) he couldn't finish** work before 8 p.m. that day.*

B Bildung: einleitendes Verb im *simple present*

- Steht das einleitende Verb im *simple present* (z. B. *say, tell, ask*), dann ändert sich die Zeitform in der indirekten Rede nicht.
- Pronomen wie *I* und *we* werden in der indirekten Rede zu *he / she* und *they*, Possessivpronomen wie *my* zu *his / her* usw.

Direkte Rede → Indirekte Rede

Tom: "I **like** my job."
→ Tom **says** (that) he **likes** his job.
Susan and Paul: "We **serve** customers every day."
→ They **tell us** (that) they **serve** customers every day.

C Bildung: einleitendes Verb im *simple past*

- Steht das einleitende Verb im *simple past* (z. B. *said, told, asked*), dann ändern sich die Zeitformen wie folgt:
  - *simple present* wird zu *simple past.*
  - *simple past* wird zu *past perfect.*
  - *present perfect* wird zu *past perfect.*
- Pronomen wie *I* und *we* werden ebenfalls zu *he / she* und *they*, Possessivpronomen wie *my* zu *his / her* usw.

Direkte Rede → Indirekte Rede

Joe: "I **love** my job a lot."
→ Joe **said** (that) he **loved** his job a lot.
Julia: "Ali **didn't like** school very much."
→ Julia **told me** (that) Ali **hadn't liked** school very much.

- Bei Hilfsverben treten folgende Änderungen ein:
  - *can* wird zu *could.*
  - *must* wird zu *had to.*
  - *may* wird zu *might.*
  - *shall* wird zu *should.*
  - *will* wird zu *would.*

Direkte Rede → Indirekte Rede

Bill: "Mary **can't** come today."
→ Bill **told me** that Mary **couldn't** come on that day.
Leo: "John **may** be able to help you."
→ Leo **said** that John **might** be able to help us.
Sue: "**Will** you be ready on time?"
→ Sue **asked** me if I **would** be ready on time.

- Bei den Adverbialbestimmungen kommt es zu folgenden Änderungen:
  - *now* wird zu *then.*
  - *today* wird zu *that day.*
  - *ago* wird zu *before.*
  - *here* wird zu *there.*
  - *next month* wird zu *the following month.*
  - *last month* wird zu *the previous month.*

Direkte Rede → Indirekte Rede

Lucy: "I'll call you **tomorrow**."
→ She said that she would call me **the next day**.
Cathy: "**This** is the first time I've been **here**!"
→ Cathy said that **that** was the first time she had been **there**.
Mark: "I saw Jim three days **ago**."
→ Mark said that he had seen Jim three days **before**.

Basic vocabulary

Diese Liste umfasst die Vokabeln, die für die Arbeit mit dem Lehr-/Arbeitsbuch **Retail Milestones** vorausgesetzt werden. Da nicht in allen Fällen Mehrfachbedeutungen in der Übersetzung angegeben werden können, ersetzt diese Liste nicht ein umfassendes zweisprachiges Wörterbuch.
Beim Verwenden der Liste als Übersetzungshilfe muss immer der Kontext beachtet werden.
Zahlwörter (*one, two, first, second, ...*), Pronomen (*I, you, my, your, myself, yourself, ...*), die Wochentage (*Monday, Tuesday, ...*) sowie die Monatsnamen (*January, February, ...*) sind nicht enthalten.

* = unregelmäßige Verbform

A

a, an ein/e
a little ein wenig
a lot viel/e
about über, um
across (quer) über (hinüber)
address Adresse
after nach, nachdem
afternoon Nachmittag
again wieder
air Luft
airport Flughafen
all alle/s
all right in Ordnung
always immer
a.m. vormittags
and und
animal Tier
to answer antworten
any irgendein/e/er
apple Apfel
around um (herum)
to ask fragen
at an, in, zu
away weg

B

baby Baby
back zurück
bad schlecht
bag Tasche
ball Ball
banana Banane
bank Bank
baseball Baseball
bath Bad
bathroom Badezimmer
***to be** sein
beautiful schön
because weil
bed Bett
bedroom Schlafzimmer
before vor, bevor
***to begin** anfangen, beginnen
beginning Anfang, Beginn
big groß
bike Fahrrad
bird Vogel
birthday Geburtstag
black schwarz
blue blau
boat Boot
body Körper
book Buch
bottle Flasche
box Karton, Schachtel
boy Junge
bread Brot
***to break** (zer)brechen, kaputt machen
breakfast Frühstück
***to bring** bringen
brother Bruder
brown braun
building Gebäude
bus Bus
business Geschäft, Business
but aber
***to buy** kaufen
by durch, mit

C

cake Kuchen
to call rufen, nennen, heißen
camping Camping
can können
cannot (can't) nicht können
car Auto
careful vorsichtig
to carry tragen
cat Katze
***to catch** fangen
centre Zentrum, Mitte
centimetre Zentimeter
chair Stuhl
cheap billig
to check prüfen
cheese Käse
chicken Hähnchen
child Kind
chocolate Schokolade
Christmas Weihnachten
cigarette Zigarette
city Stadt
class Klasse
classroom Klassenzimmer
clean sauber
clever schlau, clever
clock Uhr
closed geschlossen
club Club
coach Reisebus; Trainer/in
coffee Kaffee
cold kalt
colour Farbe
***to come** kommen
computer Computer
to cook kochen
correct richtig
***to cost** kosten
could könnte/n, konnte/n
country Land
of course (not) natürlich (nicht)
cup Tasse
***to cut** schneiden

D

dad Papa
to dance tanzen
date Datum
daughter Tochter
day Tag
dead tot
dear lieb
deep tief

desk Schreibtisch
to dictate diktieren
dictation Diktat
dinner Abendessen
discussion Diskussion
***to do** tun, machen
doctor Arzt, Ärztin
dog Hund
door Tür
down (nach) unten
***to dream** träumen
dress Kleid
***to drink** trinken
***to drive** fahren
driver Fahrer/in
dry trocken

E

early früh
east (nach) Osten; östlich
easy leicht
***to eat** essen
empty leer; leeren
to end beenden
England England
English englisch
evening Abend
every jede/r/s
exact genau
exam Prüfung
example Beispiel
exercise Übung
to explain erklären
eye Auge

F

face Gesicht
***to fall** fallen
false falsch
family Familie
fat dick; fett
father Vater
***to feel** fühlen
to fill füllen
***to find** finden
film Film
fine gut, schön
finger Finger
to finish aufhören, beenden
first erste/r/s; zuerst
to fish fischen
flower Blume
food Essen, Lebensmittel
foot Fuß
football Fußball
for für
***to forget** vergessen
form formen; Form
free frei; kostenlos
friend Freund/in
from von
fruit Frucht
full (of) voll (von, mit)

G

game Spiel
garage Garage
garden Garten
***to get** erhalten, bekommen, werden
to get up aufstehen
girl Mädchen
***to give** geben
glass Glas
***to go** gehen, fahren
gold Gold
good gut
Goodbye. Auf Wiedersehen!
grandfather Großvater
grandmother Großmutter
grass Gras
great groß; großartig
green grün
group Gruppe

H

hair Haar
half halb
happy glücklich
***to have (got)** haben
head Kopf
***to hear** hören
heavy schwer
hello hallo
to help helfen
here hier
high hoch
hobby Hobby
holiday(s) Ferien, Urlaub
home nach / zu Hause; Zuhause
homework Hausaufgabe(n)
to hope hoffen
hospital Krankenhaus
hot heiß
hotel Hotel
hour Stunde
house Haus
how wie
how much wie viel
how old wie alt
hungry hungrig

I

ice cream Eis
idea Idee
if wenn, falls, ob
ill krank
in in
interest Interesse
interesting interessant
into in (hinein)

J

jacket Jacke
jeans Jeans
job Job

K

***to keep** (be)halten
kilo(gramme) Kilo(gramm)
kilometre Kilometer
king König
to kiss küssen
kitchen Küche
***to know** wissen

L

lady Dame
late spät
to learn lernen
left links; übrig
lesson Stunde
letter Brief
***to lie (down)** (sich hin)legen; liegen
life Leben
light hell; leicht; Licht
to like mögen
line Linie
list Liste
to listen (to) zuhören
litre Liter
little klein; wenig
to live leben, wohnen
living room Wohnzimmer
long lang
to look schauen, (aus)sehen; Blick
to love lieben; Liebe
lucky Glück haben
lunch Mittagessen

M

machine Maschine
***to make** machen
man Mann, Mensch
many viele

marmalade Marmelade
metal Metall
metre Meter
middle Mitte
milk Milch
minute Minute
mistake Fehler
moment Moment
money Geld
month Monat
more mehr
morning Morgen
most meiste/r/s
mother Mutter
much viel
mum Mama
music Musik
must müssen

N

name Name
to need brauchen
never nie(mals)
new neu
news Nachricht(en)
newspaper Zeitung
next nächste/r/s
nice schön, nett, gut
night Nacht
no nein; kein
not nicht
nothing nichts
now jetzt
number Zahl, Nummer

O

o'clock Uhr *(Zeitangabe bei vollen Stunden)*
of von, bei, aus
off weg
office Büro
often oft
old alt
one ein/e
only nur
to open öffnen
or oder
to order bestellen; befehlen
other andere/r/s
out aus
over über

P

page Seite
pair Paar
paper Papier
parents Eltern
park Park
partner Partner/in
party Party
passenger Passagier/in
***to pay** (be)zahlen
pen Füller; Stift
people Leute
person Person
to phone anrufen
photo Foto
picture Bild
place Ort
to plan planen
plastic (aus) Plastik
to play spielen
play Theaterstück
player Spieler/in
p.m. nachmittags
police Polizei
policeman Polizist
poor arm
pop Pop
post office Post
postcard Postkarte
postman Postbote
to press drücken
pretty hübsch
price Preis
programme Programm
to pronounce aussprechen
to pull ziehen
pupil Schüler/in
to push schieben
***to put** stellen, legen, setzen
to put on anziehen; auftragen

Q

queen Königin
question Frage
quick schnell

R

radio Radio
to rain regnen
rainy regnerisch
***to read** lesen
to record aufnehmen
red rot
to remember sich erinnern
to repair reparieren
to report berichten
rest Rest
restaurant Restaurant
rich reich
***to ride** reiten
right rechts; richtig
***to ring** klingeln
river Fluss
road Straße
room Zimmer; Platz
round rund; um (herum)
***to run** laufen, rennen

S

sad traurig
safe sicher
same gleiche/r/s
sand Sand
sandwich Sandwich
***to say** sagen
school Schule
sea Meer
second zweite/r/s; Sekunde
***to see** sehen
***to sell** verkaufen
***to send** schicken, senden
sentence Satz
ship Schiff
shirt Hemd
shoe Schuh
shop Laden, Geschäft
short kurz
***to show** zeigen
side Seite
***sing** singen
single einzel/n
sister Schwester
***to sit** sitzen
***to sleep** schlafen
slow langsam
small klein
to smoke rauchen
so so
sock Socke
soft weich
some etwas, einige
son Sohn
song Lied, Song
(I'm) sorry! Entschuldigung!
soup Suppe
***to speak** sprechen
sport Sport
***to stand** stehen
to start anfangen
station Bahnhof
to stop aufhören, anhalten
story Geschichte
street Straße
strong stark
stupid dumm

summer Sommer
sun Sonne
supermarket Supermarkt
***to swim** schwimmen

T

table Tisch
***to take** nehmen, mitnehmen
to talk reden, sprechen
taxi Taxi
tea Tee
***to teach** unterrichten
teacher Lehrer/in
team Team
to telephone telefonieren
television Fernseher
***to tell** erzählen
text Text
to thank (sich) bedanken
that (one) der / die / das da
the der / die / das
theatre Theater
then dann
there da, dort
these diese
thing Ding
***to think** denken, meinen
this diese/r/s
those jene
ticket Fahr-/Eintrittskarte
time Zeit
today heute
together zusammen
toilet Toilette
tomato Tomate
tomorrow morgen
too auch; zu
top Spitze
tourist Tourist/in
town Stadt
to train trainieren
train Zug
to translate übersetzen
tree Baum
trip Reise
trouble Ärger
true richtig; wahr
TV Fernseher

U

uncle Onkel
under unter
***to understand** verstehen
until bis
us uns

V

very sehr
to visit besuchen

W

***to wake (up)** aufwachen
to walk laufen, gehen
to want wollen
warm warm
to wash waschen
to watch beobachten, anschauen
water Wasser
way Weg
week Woche
weekend Wochenende
well gut; gesund; also
what was
what about was ist mit
when wann
where wo(hin)
which welche/r/s
white weiß
who wer
whole ganz
why warum
will ('ll) werden
to win gewinnen
winter Winter
with mit
woman Frau
word Wort
to work arbeiten
***to write** schreiben
to write down aufschreiben
wrong falsch

Y

year Jahr
yes ja
yesterday gestern
young jung

Z

zoo Zoo

Chronological word list

Videotraining: Englische Aussprache

Perfekte englische Aussprache leicht gemacht:
Mit dem Lernprogramm zur englischen Lautschrift können Sie alle Laute einüben. Wählen Sie einfach in der Navigation rechts den entsprechenden Reiter (*Vowels* oder *Consonants*) aus und klicken Sie dann auf das gewünschte phonetische Symbol. Sprechen Sie die Wörter laut nach.
Unter www.klett.de geben Sie bitte den Code unter der Abbildung rechts ein.

n633sn

Abkürzungen und Zeichen

etw. = etwas	sb = somebody	*AE* = American English
jdn. = jemanden	sth. = something	*BE* = British English
jdm. = jemandem	*pl.* = plural	⊙ = Vokabeln zu den Hörtexten und Videos

Unit 1 Meeting colleagues

to meet ['mi:t] (sich) treffen
colleague ['kɒli:g] Kollege / Kollegin

A | Jobs and places of work

place of work [pleɪs ɒv wɜ:k] Arbeitsplatz
statement ['steɪtmənt] Aussage
to match ['mætʃ] zuordnen
mobile phone shop [ˌməʊbaɪl 'fəʊn ˌʃɒp] Mobilfunkgeschäft

B | Introducing yourself

to sum up [ˌsʌm‿'ʌp] zusammenfassen
phrase [freɪz] Redewendung
exchange student [ɪks'tʃeɪndʒ ˌstju:dənt] Austauschschüler/in
vocational school [vəʊ'keɪʃənl ˌsku:l] Berufsschule
twice a week [ˌtwaɪs‿ə 'wi:k] zweimal pro Woche
remaining [rɪˌmeɪnɪŋ] verbleibend
stationery shop ['steɪʃənrɪ ˌʃɒp] Schreibwarenladen
opposite ['ɒpəzɪt] gegenüber
traineeship [ˌtreɪ'ni:ʃɪp] Ausbildung
work placement *(BE)*, internship *(AE)* [ˌwɜk 'pleɪs‿mənt, 'ɪntɜ:nʃɪp] Praktikum
apprenticeship [ə'prentɪsʃɪp] Ausbildung
intern ['ɪntɜ:n] Praktikant/in
sales area ['seɪlz‿eərɪə] Verkaufsfläche
item [ˌaɪtəm] Artikel
to hang up [ˌhæŋ‿'ʌp] aufhängen
mechanical pencil [məˌkænɪkl 'pensl] Druckbleistift
to sharpen ['ʃɑ:pn] anspitzen
shelf, *(pl.)* shelves [ʃelf, ʃelvz] Regal
to contain [kən'teɪn] beinhalten
to survive [sə'vaɪv] überleben
survival kit [sə'vaɪvl ˌkɪt] Überlebensausrüstung
remark [rɪ'mɑ:k] Bemerkung
grocery store ['grəʊsərɪ ˌstɔ:] Lebensmittelgeschäft
nearby [ˌnɪə'baɪ] in der Nähe
to have a few days off [ˌhæv‿ə ˌfju: deɪz‿'ɒf] ein paar Tage frei haben
to introduce sb to sb [ˌɪntrə'dju:s ˌsʌmbədɪ tu: ˌsʌm‿bədɪ] jdn. jdm. vorstellen
originally [ə'rɪdʒnəlɪ] ursprünglich
Pleased to meet you. [ˌpli:zd tə 'mi:t ju:] Schön Sie / dich / euch kennen zu lernen.
to complete [kəm'pli:t] vervollständigen

C | Job duties

job duty ['dʒɒb ˌdju:tɪ] Arbeitsaufgabe
table ['teɪbl] Tabelle
company ['kʌmpənɪ] Firma
task [tɑ:sk] Aufgabe
to serve [sɜ:v] bedienen
customer ['kʌstəmə] Kunde / Kundin

to weigh [weɪ] (ab)wiegen
fresh food [ˌfreʃ 'fu:d] Frischkost
to tag [tæg] auszeichnen
to unpack [ʌn'pæk] auspacken
goods [gʊdz] Waren

shop assistant ['ʃɒp‿əˌsɪstənt] Verkäufer/in
retail chain [ˌri:teɪl 'tʃeɪn] Einzelhandelskette
branch manager [brɑ:ntʃ ˌmænɪdʒər] Filialleiter/in
cashier [kæ'ʃɪə] Kassierer/in

D | Talking about yourself and your job

to be training to become [bi: 'treɪnɪŋ tʊ bɪ'kʌm] in der Ausbildung sein zum/zur
department [dɪ'pɑ:tmənt] Abteilung
department store [dɪ'pɑ:tmənt stɔ:] Kaufhaus, Warenhaus
once [wʌnts] einmal
to have contact with [hæv 'kɒntækt wɪð] Kontakt haben mit
mood [mu:d] Stimmung
to be afraid [bi:‿ə'freɪd] Angst haben
management assistant in retail business [ˌmænɪdʒmənt‿ə'sɪstənt‿ɪn ˌri:teɪl 'bɪznɪs] Kaufmann/-frau im Einzelhandel
retail management assistant [ˌri:teɪl ˌmænɪdʒmən‿ə'sɪstənt] Kaufmann/-frau im Einzelhandel
to take notes [ˌteɪk 'nəʊts] Notizen machen
meaning ['mi:nɪŋ] Bedeutung

E | Personal skills of sales staff

skills [skɪlz] Fähigkeiten, Fertigkeiten
staff [stɑ:f] Personal, Belegschaft
home entertainment shop [ˌhəʊm‿entə'teɪnmənt ˌʃɒp] Geschäft für Unterhaltungselektronik
to belong to [bɪ'lɒŋ tu:] gehören zu
daily routine [ˌdeɪlɪ ru:'ti:n] Tagesablauf
to worry ['wʌrɪ] sich Sorgen machen
to deliver [dɪ'lɪvə] (aus)liefern, zustellen
on offer [ɒn‿'ɒfə] im Angebot
to display [dɪ'spleɪ] auslegen, zur Schau stellen
shop entrance [ˌʃɒp‿'entrəns] Ladeneingang
further away [ˌfɜ:ðər‿ə'weɪ] weiter weg
besides [bɪ'saɪdz] außerdem
to wander around [ˌwɒndər‿ə'raʊnd] herumirren
advice [əd'vaɪs] Ratschlag
case [keɪs] Fall
to deal with ['di:l wɪð] umgehen mit, es zu tun haben mit
complaint [kəm'pleɪnt] Beschwerde
refund ['ri:fʌnd] Erstattung, Rückzahlung
shoplifter ['ʃɒplɪftə] Ladendieb/in
elderly ['eldəlɪ] älter
cash desk ['kæʃ ˌdesk] Kasse
queue [kju:] Warteschlange

to advise [əd'vaɪz] beraten
service ['sɜ:vɪs] Service, Dienstleistung
to handle sth ['hændl ˌsʌmθɪŋ] mit etw. umgehen, behandeln
special needs [ˌspeʃl 'ni:dz] spezielle Bedürfnisse, Sonderanforderungen
required [rɪ'kwaɪəd] benötigt
employer [ɪm'plɔɪə] Arbeitgeber
to search ['sɜ:tʃ] durchsuchen
appropriate [ə'prəʊprɪət] geeignet, passend
requirement [rɪ'kwaɪəmənt] Bedingung, Voraussetzung
outgoing [ˌaʊt'gəʊɪŋ] kontaktfreudig
personality [ˌpɜ:sn'ælətɪ] Persönlichkeit

F | Checking

odd one out [ɒd wʌn‿'aʊt] nicht dazugehören

Unit 2 Products and services

A | Describing products

comfortable ['kʌmftəbl] bequem
delicious [dɪ'lɪʃəs] köstlich
colourful ['kʌləfəl] farbenfroh
elegant ['elɪgənt] elegant
healthy ['helθɪ] gesund
solid ['sɒlɪd] stabil
stylish ['staɪlɪʃ] elegant, stilvoll
useful ['ju:sfl] nützlich
well-designed [ˌweldɪ'zaɪnd] gut gestaltet
trousers ['traʊzəz] Hose
wheelbarrow ['wi:lˌbærəʊ] Schubkarre
expensive [ɪk'spensɪv] teuer
inexpensive [ˌɪnɪk'spensɪv] preisgünstig

B | Explaining the benefits of products

benefit ['benəfɪt] Nutzen
to decide [dɪ'saɪd] entscheiden
latest ['leɪtɪst] neueste/r/s
to enter ['entə] betreten
size [saɪz] Größe
to fit sb [fɪt ˌsʌmbədɪ] jdm. passen
to suit sb [su:t ˌsʌmbədɪ] jdm. stehen
to match sth ['mætʃ ˌsʌmθɪŋ] zu etw. passen, zueinanderpassen
to go well with [ˌgəʊ 'wel wɪð] gut passen zu
to describe [dɪ'skraɪb] beschreiben
to change [tʃeɪndʒ] tauschen, wechseln
to store [stɔ:] (ab)speichern
to guess [ges] (er)raten

C | Different ways of selling products

to collect [kə'lekt] abholen
stationary ['steɪʃənri] stationär, ortsgebunden

retail store ['ri:teɪl ˌstɔ:] Ladengeschäft
channel ['tʃænl] Kanal
distribution [ˌdɪstrɪ'bju:ʃn] Vertrieb, Verkauf
garden center ['gɑ:dn ˌsentə] Gartencenter
to rent [rent] mieten
to be in urgent need [bɪ‿ɪn‿ɜ:dʒənt 'ni:d] dringend benötigen
lawnmower ['lɔ:nˌməʊə] Rasenmäher
self-propelled [ˌselfprə'peld] mit Eigenantrieb
to mow [məʊ] mähen
to run on sth ['rʌn‿ɒn ˌsʌmθɪŋ] betrieben werden mit etw.
cord [kɔ:d] Kabel
corded ['kɔ:dɪd] mit Kabel
features ['fi:tʃəz] Eigenschaften
cutting width ['kʌtɪŋ ˌwɪtθ] Schnittbreite
adjust [ə'dʒʌst] anpassen
cutting height ['kʌtɪŋ ˌhaɪt] Schnitthöhe
price tag ['praɪs ˌtæg] Preisschild
bargain ['bɑ:gɪn] Schnäppchen
discount ['dɪskaʊnt] Preisnachlass
initial order [ɪˌnɪʃl‿'ɔ:də] Erstauftrag
search engine ['sɜ:tʃ‿endʒɪn] Suchmaschine
to key in [ˌki:‿'ɪn] eingeben
to be passed on [ɪ ˌpɑ:st‿'ɒn] weitergeleitet werden

D | Serving customers successfully

successfully [sək'sesfəlɪ] erfolgreich
to miss [mɪs] fehlen, vermissen
change [tʃeɪndʒ] Wechselgeld
receipt [rɪ'si:t] Quittung, Kassenzettel
sausage ['sɒsɪdʒ] Würstchen
certainly ['sɜ:tnlɪ] sicherlich
of course [əv 'kɔ:s] selbstverständlich
drill [drɪl] Bohrmaschine
acceptable [ək'septəbl] akzeptabel
connectivity [ˌkɒnek'tɪvətɪ] Netzwerkfähigkeit
connection [kə'nekʃn] Anschluss
to have room for [ˌhæv 'ru:m fə] Platz haben für
memory card ['memrɪ ˌkɑ:d] Speicherkarte
WiFi internet access [ˌwaɪfaɪ‿'ɪntənet‿ækses] drahtloser Internetzugang
to make a contract [ˌmeɪk‿ə 'kɒntrækt] einen Vertrag abschließen
special offer [ˌspeʃl‿'ɒfə] Sonderangebot
mobile service provider [ˌməʊbaɪl 'sɜ:vɪs prəˌvaɪdə] Mobilfunkanbieter
on the move [ˌɒn ðə 'mu:v] unterwegs
without jerking [wɪˌðaʊt 'dʒɜ:kɪŋ] ohne Ruckeln
I'm afraid [aɪm‿ə'freɪd] leider
actually ['æktʃʊəlɪ] eigentlich, tatsächlich
slot [slɒt] Steckplatz
You're welcome. [ˌjɔ: 'welkʌm] Bitte schön, gern geschehen.

V1 Fairtrade clothing line

to launch [lɔ:ntʃ] einführen, starten
clothing line ['kləʊðɪŋ ˌlaɪn] Modelinie
conventionally made [kənˌvenʃnəlɪ'meɪd] herkömmlich gefertigt
grower ['grəʊə] Erzeuger/in, Bauer / Bäuerin
factory-made [ˌfæktərɪ'meɪd] industriell gefertigt
available [ə'veɪləbl] verfügbar
guarantee [ˌgærən'ti:] Garantie
ethically made [ˌeθɪklɪ'meɪd] nach ethischen Maßstäben hergestellt
labour standard ['leɪbə ˌstændəd] Arbeitsnorm
to trade [treɪd] handeln
to grow in popularity [ˌgrəʊ‿ɪn ˌpɒpjə'lærətɪ] an Beliebtheit gewinnen

E | Products at a DIY store

DIY store, do-it-yourself store [ˌdi:aɪ'waɪ ˌstɔ:, ˌdu:ɪtjɔ:'self ˌstɔ:] Heimwerkermarkt, Baumarkt
to paint [peɪnt] streichen
paint roller ['peɪnt ˌrəʊlə] Farbroller
to demonstrate ['demənstreɪt] zeigen
usage ['ju:sɪdʒ] Gebrauch
to take turns [ˌteɪk 'tɜ:nz] sich abwechseln
convenient [kən'vi:nɪənt] zweckmäßig, praktisch
tool [tu:l] Werkzeug
to drill [drɪl] bohren
hole [həʊl] Loch

to brighten up [ˌbraɪtn‿'ʌp] aufhellen
to replace [rɪ'pleɪs] ersetzen
bathroom cabinet [ˌbɑ:θru:m 'kæbɪnət] Badezimmerschrank
to hang sth up [hæŋ ˌsʌmθɪŋ‿'ʌp] etwas aufhängen
to get sth done [get ˌsʌmθɪŋ 'dʌn] etwas schaffen
to suppose [sə'pəʊz] annehmen, vermuten
to worry ['wʌrɪ] sich Sorgen machen
wall plug ['wɔ:l ˌplʌg] Wanddübel
plasterboard screw ['plɑ:stəbɔ:d ˌskru:] Rigipsschraube
to be supplied with [bɪ sə'plaɪd wɪð] mitgeliefert werden mit

open day ['əʊpn ˌdeɪ] Tag der offenen Tür
to centre ['sentə] zentrieren
spirit level ['spɪrɪt ˌlevl] Wasserwaage
levelled ['levəld] *(hier:)* waagerecht
tape measure ['teɪp ˌmeʒə] Maßband, Metermaß
to measure ['meʒə] messen
width [wɪdθ] Breite, Weite
centre point ['sentə ˌpɔɪnt] Mittelpunkt
to screw [skru:] (an)schrauben
screwdriver ['skru:ˌdraɪvə] Schraubenzieher

bracket hole ['brækɪt ˌhəʊl] Loch für die Halterung
procedure [prə'siːdʒə] Ablauf, Verfahren
explanation [ˌeksplə'neɪʃn] Erklärung

F | Shopping for clothes

tie [taɪ] Krawatte
tight [taɪt] eng
what a pity [ˌwɒt‿ə 'pɪtɪ] wie schade
fitting room ['fɪtɪŋ ˌruːm] Umkleidekabine

G | Checking

to draw [drɔː] zeichnen
to enjoy [ɪn'dʒɔɪ] genießen

Unit 3 Customers

A | Types of customers and their shopping habits

habit ['hæbɪt] Gewohnheit

behaviour [bɪ'heɪvjə] Verhalten
carefully ['keəfəlɪ] sorgfältig
to distinguish [dɪ'stɪŋgwɪʃ] unterscheiden
environmentally friendly [ɪnˌvaɪərənˌmentəlɪ 'frendlɪ] umweltfreundlich
in a hurry [ɪn‿ə 'hʌrɪ] in Eile
packaging ['pækɪdʒɪŋ] Verpackung
to take one's time [ˌteɪk wʌnz 'taɪm] sich Zeit nehmen
hectic ['hektɪk] hektisch
sceptical ['skeptɪkl] skeptisch, kritisch

to identify [aɪ'dentɪfaɪ] identifizieren, erkennen

B | Keeping customers satisfied

to keep sb satisfied [kiːp ˌsʌmbədɪ 'sætɪsfaɪd] jdn. zufrieden stellen
to adapt to [ə'dæpt tə] (sich) anpassen an
trolley ['trɒlɪ] Einkaufswagen
couple ['kʌpl] Paar, Pärchen
plant [plɑːnt] Pflanze
to make eye contact with sb [ˌmeɪk 'aɪˌkɒntækt wɪð ˌsʌmbədɪ] Blickkontakt mit jdm. aufnehmen
natural ['nætʃərl] *(hier:)* naturbelassen
to compare [kəm'peə] vergleichen
disabled [dɪ'seɪbld] behindert
wheelchair ['wiːltʃeə] Rollstuhl
to choose [tʃuːz] wählen
Greece [griːs] Griechenland
sports and leisure shop [ˌspɔːt‿ən 'leʒə ʃɒp] Sport- und Freizeitgeschäft
tracksuit ['træksuːt] Trainingsanzug

over there [ˌəʊvə 'ðeə] dort drüben
kind [kaɪnd] freundlich
rack [ræk] Regal
a range of [reɪndʒ əv] eine Reihe von, zahlreiche
to wear [weə] tragen
outdoors [ˌaʊt'dɔːz] draußen, im Freien
wide variety of [ˌwaɪd və'raɪətɪ‿əv] große Auswahl / Vielfalt an
picture frame ['pɪktʃə ˌfreɪm] Bilderrahmen
photographic shop [ˌfəʊtəʊgræfɪk 'ʃɒp] Fotogeschäft
to get on sb's nerves [ˌget ɒn ˌsʌmbədɪz 'nɜːvz] jdm. auf die Nerven gehen
to disturb [dɪ'stɜːb] stören
kids' zone ['kɪdz‿ˌzəʊn] Kinderbereich
to take care of [ˌteɪk‿'keər‿əv] aufpassen auf
to pick sb up [pɪk ˌsʌmbədɪ 'ʌp] jdn. abholen
to finish ['fɪnɪʃ] beenden
to read out [riːd 'aʊt] vorlesen

C | Different types of shops

far away [ˌfɑːr‿ə'weɪ] weit weg
owner ['əʊnə] Besitzer/in
to collect [kə'lekt] (ein)sammeln
discounter [dɪs'kaʊntə] Billigsupermarkt
to earn [ɜːn] verdienen
shop fittings [ʃɒp 'fɪtɪŋz] Ladenausstattung
to count [kaʊnt] zählen
specialist shop ['speʃəlɪst ˌʃɒp] Fachgeschäft
design [dɪ'zaɪn] Gestaltung

advantage [əd'vɑːntɪdʒ] Vorteil
to add [æd] hinzufügen
corner shop ['kɔːnə ˌʃɒp] (kleines) Lebensmittelgeschäft
result [rɪ'zʌlt] Ergebnis

D | Future plans

to take part [ˌteɪk 'pɑːt] teilnehmen
survey ['sɜːveɪ] Umfrage, Befragung
to own [əʊn] besitzen
married ['mærɪd] verheiratet
showroom ['ʃəʊruːm] Ausstellungsraum
screen [ˌskriːn] Bildschirm
fridge [frɪdʒ] Kühlschrank
disadvantage [ˌdɪsəd'vɑːntɪdʒ] Nachteil
development [dɪ'veləpmənt] Entwicklung
to translate [trænz'leɪt] übersetzen
word for word [ˌwɜːd‿fə 'wɜːd] wortwörtlich

V2 Oranges: Healthy and full of vitamins

valuable ['væljʊəbl] wertvoll
to harvest ['hɑːvɪst] ernten

to develop [dɪ'veləp] *(hier:)* ausbilden
organic [ɔ:'gænɪk] organisch, biologisch
pesticide ['pestɪsaɪd] Pflanzenschutzmittel
daily requirement [ˌdeɪlɪ rɪ'kwaɪəmənt] Tagesbedarf
skin [skɪn] *(hier:)* Schale

to treat [tri:t] behandeln
taste [teɪst] Geschmack

E | The importance of different types of customer

importance [ɪm'pɔ:təns] Wichtigkeit, Bedeutung
branch [brɑ:ntʃ] Filiale
to give sb attention [ˌgɪv ˌsʌmbədɪ‿ə'tenʃn] jdm. Aufmerksamkeit schenken
need [ni:d] Bedarf, Bedürfnis
desire [dɪ'zaɪə] Wunsch
to make up [ˌmeɪk‿'ʌp] *(hier:)* ausmachen
impulse shopper ['ɪmpʌls ʃɒpə] Impulskäufer/in
definitely ['defɪnətlɪ] eindeutig, auf jeden Fall
to convince sb [kən'vɪns ˌsʌmbədɪ] jdn. überzeugen
to increase [ɪn'kri:s] erhöhen, steigen
expectation [ˌekspek'teɪʃn] Erwartung
introduction [ˌɪntrə'dʌkʃn] Einleitung, Einführung
main body [ˌmeɪn 'bɒdɪ] Hauptteil
conclusion [kən'klu:ʒn] Abschluss, Schlussfolgerung
visual aid [ˌvɪʒʊəl‿'eɪd] visuelles Hilfsmittel
graph [grɑ:f] Diagramm, Grafik
audience ['ɔ:dɪəns] Publikum, Zuhörer
to avoid [ə'vɔɪd] vermeiden
confident ['kɒnfɪdənt] selbstbewusst
characteristic [ˌkærɪktə'rɪstɪk] Eigenschaft

F | Consumer rights

consumer rights [kənˌsju:mə 'raɪts] Verbraucherrechte
to peel [pi:l] schälen
promise ['prɒmɪs] Versprechen
receipt [rɪ'si:t] *(hier:)* Erhalt
to credit ['kredɪt] gutschreiben
method of payment [ˌmeθəd‿əv 'peɪmənt] Zahlungsform
seal [si:l] Siegel
to exclude [ɪk'sklu:d] ausschließen
to apply [ə'plaɪ] zutreffen
processing ['prəʊsesɪŋ] Bearbeitung
proof [pru:f] Nachweis
tracking reference number ['trækɪŋ ˌrefrəns ˌnʌmbə] Nachverfolgungsnummer

G | Checking

gap [gæp] Lücke

Unit 4 Money

A | Talking about money

to deal with ['di:l wɪð] umgehen mit, es zu tun haben mit
to borrow ['bɒrəʊ] sich ausleihen
to withdraw [wɪð'drɔ:] abheben
cash dispenser ['kæʃ dɪˌspensə] Geldautomat

B | Goods and quantities

quantity ['kwɒntətɪ] Menge
a bar of [ə 'bɑ:r‿əv] eine Tafel
difference ['dɪfrəns] Unterschied
to cost [kɒst] kosten
twice as much as [ˌtwaɪs‿əz 'mʌtʃ‿əz] zweimal so viel wie
honey ['hʌnɪ] Honig
pineapple ['paɪnæpl] Ananas
to have sth left [hæv ˌsʌmθɪŋ 'left] etw. übrig haben
completely sold out [kəmˌpli:tlɪ səʊld 'aʊt] vollständig ausverkauft
a packet of [ə 'pækɪt‿əv] ein Paket
a roll of [ə 'rəʊl‿əv] eine Rolle
a loaf of [ə 'ləʊf‿əv] ein Laib
to have exact change [hæv ɪgˌzækt‿'tʃeɪndʒ] es passend haben
carrier bag ['kærɪə ˌbæg] Tragetasche
safely ['seɪflɪ] sicher

C | Talking about prices

toys department ['tɔɪz dɪˌpɑ:tmənt] Spielwarenabteilung
to pop into [pɒp‿ˌɪntʊ] schnell vorbeischauen
remote-controlled [rɪˌməʊt kən'trəʊld] ferngesteuert
to be ... percent off [bɪ pəˌsent‿'ɒf] ... Prozent weniger kosten
to save [seɪv] sparen
overpriced [ˌəuvə'praɪst] überteuert
truck [trʌk] Laster
leaflet ['li:flət] Prospekt
brand-name product [ˌbrændˌneɪm 'prɒdʌkt] Markenprodukt
no-name product [ˌnəʊˌneɪm 'prɒdʌkt] No-Name-Produkt, kein Markenprodukt
to keep one's eyes open [ˌki:p wʌnz‿'aɪz‿əʊpn] die Augen offen halten
to take advantage of sth [ˌteɪk‿əd'vɑ:ntɪdʒ‿əv ˌsʌmθɪŋ] etw. ausnutzen
reduction [rɪ'dʌkʃn] Ermäßigung
discount ['dɪskaʊnt] Nachlass, Rabatt
to bargain ['bɑ:gɪn] handeln
incredibly [ɪn'kredɪblɪ] unglaublich, unvorstellbar
to cross out [ˌkrɒs‿'aʊt] durchstreichen
particularly [pə'tɪkjələlɪ] besonders

D | At the cash desk

to cancel ['kænsl] *(hier:)* stornieren
repayment [rɪ'peɪmənt] Rückzahlung

V3 Black Friday

◎
pastime ['pɑ:staɪm] Zeitvertreib
to outbid [ˌaʊt'bɪd] überbieten
to rake [reɪk] einstreichen, erzielen
takings ['teɪkɪŋz] Einnahmen
to indicate sth ['ɪndɪkeɪt ˌsʌmθɪŋ] hindeuten auf etw.
outlook ['aʊtlʊk] Perspektive, Aussicht
crowds [kraʊdz] Menschenmassen
economic crisis [ˌi:kənɒmɪk 'kraɪsɪs] Wirtschaftskrise
rush [rʌʃ] *(hier:)* Andrang
to descend upon sth [dɪ'send‿əˌpɒn ˌsʌmθɪŋ] *(hier:)* etw. stürmen
to fulfill [fʊl'fɪl] erfüllen
to get a glimpse of sth [ˌget‿ə 'glɪmps‿əv ˌsʌmθɪŋ] einen Blick auf etw. erhaschen
to take place [ˌteɪk 'pleɪs] stattfinden
Thanksgiving [ˌθæŋks'gɪvɪŋ] Erntedankfest in den USA
to kick off [ˌkɪk‿'ɒf] beginnen
season ['si:zn] Saison, Jahreszeit

E | Dealing with customers professionally

irritated ['ɪrɪteɪtɪd] verärgert
similar ['sɪmɪlə] ähnlich
unpleasant [ʌn'plezənt] unangenehm
row [rəʊ] Reihe
operator [ˌɒpəreɪtə] Kassierer/in
alongside [əˌlɒŋ'saɪd] nebeneinander
supervisor ['su:pəvaɪzə] Vorgesetzte/r
fault [fɔ:lt] Fehler
policy ['pɒləsɪ] Strategie, Grundsatz, Politik
to take sb by surprise [ˌteɪk ˌsʌmbədɪ baɪ sə'praɪz] jdn. überraschen
look on sb's face [ˌlʊk‿ɒn ˌsʌmbədɪz 'feɪs] Gesichtsausdruck von jdm.
to lift [lɪft] hochhalten
to reply [rɪ'plaɪ] antworten, reagieren
to be aware of sth [bɪ‿ə'weər‿əv ˌsʌmθɪŋ] sich etw. bewusst sein
to come across [ˌkʌm‿ə'krɒs] wirken, rüberkommen
to scan [skæn] einscannen
to complete a transaction [kəmˌpli:t‿ə træn'zækʃn] einen Kaufvorgang abschließen
to raise [reɪz] erheben
merrily ['merɪlɪ] fröhlich, vergnügt
honoured ['ɒnəd] verehrt, geschätzt
attention [ə'tenʃn] Aufmerksamkeit
to deserve [dɪ'zɜ:v] verdienen

F | Product pricing

product pricing [ˌprɒdʌkt 'praɪsɪŋ] Preisfestsetzung
pricing strategy ['praɪsɪŋ ˌstrætədʒɪ] Preisstrategie
practical use [ˌpræktɪkl 'ju:s] praktische Anwendung
competitive [kəm'petətɪv] konkurrierend
competition [ˌkɒmpə'tɪʃn] Wettbewerb, Konkurrenz

G | Checking

announcement [ə'naʊnsmənt] Durchsage

Unit 5 At the department store

A | Different floors

floor ['flɔ:] Stock(werk)
children's wear ['tʃɪldrənz ˌweə] Kinderbekleidung
cosmetics [kɒz'metɪks] Kosmetik
ground floor [ˌgraʊnd 'flɔ:] Erdgeschoss
top floor [ˌtɒp 'flɔ:] Obergeschoss
basement ['beɪsmənt] Untergeschoss

◎
to look forward to [ˌlʊk 'fɔ:wəd tə] sich freuen auf
news [nju:z] Nachricht(en)

B | Finding products

according to [ə'kɔ:dɪŋ tə] entsprechend, gemäß
instruction [ɪn'strʌkʃn] Anweisung
to follow sb ['fɒləʊ ˌsʌmbədɪ] jdm. folgen
lunch break ['lʌntʃ breɪk] Mittagspause
to suggest [sə'dʒest] vorschlagen
lift [lɪft] Aufzug
Here we are. [ˌhɪə wɪ‿'ɑ:] Hier wären wir.
lipstick ['lɪpstɪk] Lippenstift
bright [braɪt] hell
colour ['kʌlə] Farbe
aisle [aɪl] Gang
on the left [ɒn ðə 'left] auf der linken Seite
round [raʊnd] um … herum
to hide [haɪd] verbergen, verstecken
a must-have [ə ˌmʌst'hæv] ein Muss
next to ['nekst tʊ] neben
across from [ə'krɒs frəm] gegenüber von

C | Finding different departments

information desk [ˌɪnfə'meɪʃn ˌdesk] Informationsschalter
doll [dɒl] Puppe
barbecue ['bɑ:bɪkju:] Grillparty
downstairs [ˌdaʊn'steəz] nach unten
escalator ['eskəleɪtə] Rolltreppe
out of order [ˌaʊt‿əv 'ɔ:də] außer Betrieb

to repair [rɪ'peə] reparieren
to stay [steɪ] bleiben
straight on [ˌstreɪt‿'ɒn] geradeaus

D | Making comparisons

abbreviation [əˌbri:vɪ'eɪʃn] Abkürzung
favour ['feɪvə] Gefallen
heel [ˌhi:l] (Schuh-)Absatz
promise ['prɒmɪs] Versprechen
to remember [rɪ'membə] sich erinnern (an)
bracket ['brækɪt] Klammer
spelling ['spelɪŋ] Rechtschreibung

E | Department stores and product information

exhausting [ɪg'zɔ:stɪŋ] anstrengend, ermüdend
luckily ['lʌkɪlɪ] glücklicherweise
amazing [ə'meɪzɪŋ] toll, unglaublich
square foot, *(pl.)* square feet [ˌskweə 'fʊt, ˌskweə 'fi:t] Quadratfuß (Fuß = 0,3048 Meter)
selling space ['selɪŋ ˌspeɪs] Verkaufsraum, Verkaufsfläche
huge [hju:dʒ] riesig
selection [sə'lekʃn] Auswahl
to offer ['ɒfə] anbieten
impressive [ɪm'presɪv] beeindruckend
Egyptian [ɪ'dʒɪpʃn] ägyptisch
motive ['məʊtɪv] Motiv
curious ['kjʊərɪəs] neugierig
to forget [fə'get] vergessen
soft toy [ˌsɒft 'tɔɪ] Plüschtier
to keep in mind [ˌki:p‿ɪn 'maɪnd] im Hinterkopf behalten
worn out [ˌwɔ:n'aʊt] verschlissen
to turn sb away [ˌtɜ:n ˌsʌmbədɪ‿ə'weɪ] jdn. abweisen
Are you kidding? [ˌɑ: jʊ 'kɪdɪŋ] Machst du Witze?
to decorate ['dekəreɪt] dekorieren
dress code ['dres ˌkəʊd] Kleidervorschriften

detail ['di:teɪl] Detail, Einzelheit
jewellery *(BE)*, jewelry *(AE)* ['dʒu:əlrɪ] Schmuck
value ['vælju:] Wert
to be ready to do sth [bɪ ˌredɪ tə 'du: ˌsʌmθɪŋ] bereit sein etw. zu tun
purchase ['pɜ:tʃəs] (Ein-)Kauf, Ware
to involve [ɪn'vɒlv] beinhalten, umfassen
unique [ju:'ni:k] einzigartig
to expect [ɪk'spekt] erwarten
to appear [ə'pɪə] auftreten
knowledgeable ['nɒlɪdʒəbl] sachkundig
to achieve [ə'tʃi:v] erreichen, erzielen
ability [ə'bɪlətɪ] Fähigkeit
to provide [prə'vaɪd] liefern, bereitstellen
customer service [ˌkʌstəmə 'sɜ:vɪs] Kundenbetreuung

E | Checking

to move [mu:v] (sich) bewegen

Unit 6 Sales promotion

sales promotion ['seɪlz‿prə'məʊʃn] Verkaufsförderung

A | Promoting products online and offline

to promote [prə'məʊt] fördern
caption ['kæpʃn] Bildunterschrift
trial [traɪəl] Probe
tasting ['teɪstɪŋ] Kostprobe, Verköstigung
to advertise ['ædvətaɪz] Werbung machen für
measure ['meʒə] Maßnahme

B | Planning a product promotion

eco-friendly [ˌi:kəʊ'frendlɪ] umweltfreundlich
to introduce [ˌɪntrə'dju:s] einführen
challenge ['tʃælɪndʒ] Herausforderung
toxic ['tɒksɪk] giftig
harmful ['hɑ:mfəl] schädlich
environment [ɪn'vaɪərənmənt] Umwelt
solution [sə'lu:ʃn] Lösung
to reduce [rɪ'dju:s] reduzieren
bio-degradable [ˌbaɪəʊdɪ'greɪdəbl] biologisch abbaubar
impact ['ɪmpækt] Auswirkung, Einfluss
chance [tʃɑ:ns] Möglichkeit, Gelegenheit

C | Promoting online and offline sales

category ['kætəgrɪ] Kategorie
search function ['sɜ:tʃ ˌfʌŋkʃn] Suchfunktion
basket of all goods [ˌbɑ:skɪt‿əv‿ɔ:l 'gʊdz] gesamter Warenkorb
to delete [dɪ'li:t] löschen
entry ['entrɪ] Eingabe
confirmation [ˌkɒnfə'meɪʃn] Bestätigung
to place an order [ˌpleɪs‿ən‿'ɔ:də] eine Bestellung aufgeben
chat button ['tʃæt ˌbʌtn] Chat-Schaltfläche
to assist [ə'sɪst] helfen
in case [ɪn 'keɪs] im Falle, dass
social networking site [ˌsəʊʃl 'netwɜ:kɪŋ ˌsaɪt] Seite in den sozialen Netzwerken
besides [bɪ'saɪdz] darüber hinaus
promotion video [prə'məʊʃn ˌvɪdɪəʊ] Werbevideo
treadmill ['tredmɪl] Laufband

D | The history of shopping habits

tremendous [trə'mendəs] gewaltig enorm
competitive [kəm'petətɪv] wettbewerbsfähig

limited ['lɪmɪtɪd] begrenzt, eingeschränkt
motorway service [ˌməʊtəweɪ 'sɜ:vɪs] Autobahnraststätte
federal state [ˌfedrəl 'steɪt] Bundesland
to fix [fɪks] festlegen

E | Promoting and advertising products

subject ['sʌbdʒekt] Betreff, Thema

tiny ['taɪnɪ] winzig
extraordinary [ɪk'strɔ:dɪnərɪ] außergewöhnlich
Go ahead, please. [ˌgəʊ‿ə'hed ˌpli:z] Fahren Sie bitte fort.
lightweight ['laɪtweɪt] Leichtgewicht
furthermore [ˌfɜ:ðə'mɔ:] außerdem
front-facing [ˌfrʌnt'feɪsɪŋ] nach vorne zeigend
back-facing [ˌbæk'feɪsɪŋ] nach hinten zeigend
capable ['keɪpəbl] fähig
storage space ['stɔ:rɪdʒ ˌspeɪs] Speicherplatz
on-board [ˌɒn'bɔ:d] *(hier:)* auf der Platine
to expand [ɪk'spænd] erweitern
additional [ə'dɪʃənl] zusätzlich
operating system ['ɒpəreɪtɪŋ ˌsɪstəm] Betriebssystem
unique selling point (USP) [ju:ˌni:k 'selɪŋ ˌpɔɪnt, ˌju:es'pi:] Alleinstellungsmerkmal

choice [tʃɔɪs] Wahl
timeless ['taɪmləs] zeitlos
gift [gɪft] Geschenk
to frame [freɪm] (ein)rahmen
rear-side [ˌrɪə 'saɪd] Rückseite
favourite ['feɪvərɪt] Lieblings-
sturdy ['stɜ:dɪ] fest, stabil
flap [flæp] Klappe
to imagine [ɪ'mædʒɪn] sich vorstellen
to address sb [ə'dres ˌsʌmbədɪ] jdn. ansprechen
heading ['hedɪŋ] Überschrift
to highlight ['haɪlaɪt] hervorheben
to prove [pru:v] beweisen
superlative [su'pɜ:lətɪv] Superlativ, Übertreibung
effect [ɪ'fekt] Wirkung
workplace ['wɜ:kpleɪs] Arbeitsplatz

Unit 7 Special sales situations

A | Handling goods

to touch [tʌtʃ] anfassen
to be allowed to [bɪ‿ə'laʊd‿tʊ] dürfen
sample ['sɑ:mpl] Muster
to smell [smel] riechen
fragile ['frædʒaɪl] zerbrechlich

B | Giving instructions

to price sth ['praɪs ˌsʌmθɪŋ] etw. auszeichnen
content ['kɒntent] Inhalt
to climb (onto) [klaɪm] hinaufklettern
furniture ['fɜ:nɪtʃə] Möbel
to press [pres] drücken
button ['bʌtn] Knopf
to go wrong [ˌgəʊ 'rɒŋ] schief gehen
to go off [gəʊ‿'ɒf] schlecht werden
carpet ['kɑ:pɪt] Teppich
travel guide ['trævl ˌgaɪd] Reiseführer
rule [ru:l] Regel
care instructions ['keə ɪnˌstrʌkʃnz] Pflegehinweise
to bleach [bli:tʃ] bleichen
to iron [aɪən] bügeln
heat [hi:t] Hitze
to protect [prə'tekt] schützen
humidity [hju:'mɪdɪtɪ] Feuchtigkeit
flammable ['flæməbl] entflammbar

C | Explaining rules and regulations

regulation [ˌregjə'leɪʃn] Vorschrift
to keep (to) [ki:p‿tʊ] sich halten (an)
politely [pə'laɪtlɪ] höflich
unfortunately [ʌn'fɔ:tʃənətlɪ] leider
dirty ['dɜ:tɪ] dreckig
credit card ['kredɪt ˌkɑ:d] Kreditkarte
smoking area ['sməʊkɪŋ ˌeərɪə] Raucherzone
condition [kən'dɪʃn] Zustand

D | Dealing with customer complaints

to appreciate [ə'pri:ʃieɪt] (wert)schätzen
exception [ɪk'sepʃn] Ausnahme
to exchange [ɪks'tʃeɪndʒ] (um)tauschen
replacement [rɪ'pleɪsmənt] Ersatz
return [rɪ'tɜ:n] Rückgabe
ruined [ruɪ'nd] ruiniert
suggestion [sə'dʒestʃn] Vorschlag
voucher ['vaʊtʃə] Gutschein
glove [glʌv] Handschuh
upset [ʌp'set] aufgebracht, verärgert
to see a point [ˌsi:‿ə 'pɔɪnt] einen Standpunkt verstehen
dissatisfied [dɪs'sætɪsfaɪd] unzufrieden
to solve [sɒlv] lösen
operating instructions ['ɒpreɪtɪŋ‿ɪnˌstrʌkʃnz] Bedienungsanleitung
quick start guide [ˌkwɪk 'stɑ:t ˌgaɪd] Schnellstartanleitung
to feel annoyed [ˌfi:l‿ə'nɔɪd] sich verärgert fühlen
to do sb a favour [du: ˌsʌmbədɪ‿ə 'feɪvə] jemandem einen Gefallen tun

E | Convincing upset customers

to calm down [kɑ:m 'daʊn] sich beruhigen
inconvenience [ˌɪnkən'vi:nɪəns] Unannehmlichkeit

V4 Food expiry dates

expiry date [ɪk'spaɪərɪ ˌdeɪt] Verfallsdatum, Ablaufdatum

minced meat [ˌmɪnst 'mi:t] Hackfleisch
legible ['ledʒɪbl] lesbar
to retain [rɪ'teɪn] bewahren
flavour ['fleɪvə] Geschmack
dairy product ['deərɪ ˌprɒdʌkt] Milchprodukt
to spoil [spɔɪl] verderben
to judge [dʒʌdʒ] beurteilen, bewerten
heat-treated [ˌhi:t'tri:tɪd] wärmebehandelt, pasteurisiert
caution ['kɔ:ʃn] Vorsicht
to pose a health risk [ˌpəʊz‿ə 'helθ ˌrɪsk] ein Gesundheitsrisiko darstellen
to estimate ['estɪmeɪt] schätzen

F | Dealing with dissatisfied customers

sportswear ['spɔ:tsweə] Sportbekleidung

spot [spɒt] Fleck
scratch [skrætʃ] Kratzer
Hold the line, please. [ˌhəʊld ðə 'laɪn ˌpli:z] Bleiben Sie bitte am Apparat.
annoying [ə'nɔɪɪŋ] ärgerlich
in stock [ɪn 'stɒk] vorrätig
in the meantime [ɪn ðə 'mi:ntaɪm] zwischenzeitlich
at sb's expense [ət ˌsʌmbədɪz‿ɪk'spens] auf jdns. Kosten
by mail [baɪ 'meɪl] per Post

low-value [ˌləʊ'vælju:] von geringem Wert
original packaging [əˌrɪdʒɪnl 'pækɪdʒɪŋ] Originalverpackung
playability [ˌpleɪə'bɪlətɪ] Abspielbarkeit
diving goggles ['daɪvɪŋ ˌgɒglz] Taucherbrille
to praise [preɪz] loben
customer service agent [ˌkʌstəmə 'sɜ:vɪs‿eɪdʒənt] Kundenbetreuer/in
prepaid address label [ˌpri:peɪd‿ə'dres ˌleɪbl] frankierte Adressenaufkleber
to recommend [ˌrekə'mend] empfehlen
to reflect on sth [rɪ'flekt‿ɒn ˌsʌmθɪŋ] über etw. nachdenken
to put the blame on sb [ˌpʊt ðə 'bleɪm‿ɒn ˌsʌmbədɪ] jdm. die Schuld geben
to yell at sb ['jel‿ət ˌsʌmbədɪ] jdn. anschreien
to escalate ['eskəleɪt] eskalieren
to interrupt [ˌɪntə'rʌpt] unterbrechen
to let off steam [ˌlet‿ɒf 'sti:m] Dampf ablassen
uncrossed [ʌn'krɒst] nicht gekreuzt
genuine ['dʒenjʊɪn] echt, ehrlich

G | Handling shoplifters

shoplifting ['ʃɒpˌlɪftɪŋ] Ladiendiebstahl
theft [θeft] Diebstahl
violently ['vaɪələntlɪ] gewalttätig
to confront sb [kən'frʌnt ˌsʌmbədɪ] jdm. entgegentreten
indiscriminate [ˌɪndɪ'skrɪmɪnət] wahllos
to sue sb for damages [ˌsu: ˌsʌmbədɪ fə 'dæmɪdʒɪz] jdn. auf Schadenersatz verklagen
to accuse sb of sth [ə'kju:z ˌsʌmbədɪ‿əv ˌsʌmθɪŋ] jdn. wegen etw. beschuldigen
nevertheless [ˌnevəðə'les] trotzdem, dennoch
average ['ævərɪdʒ] durchschnittlich
cart [kɑ:t] Einkaufswagen
proposal [prə'pəʊzl] Vorschlag

H | Checking

to burn [bɜ:n] (ver)brennen
to lock [lɒk] abschließen

Unit 8 After-sales services

A | Product recall

product recall [ˌprɒdʌkt 'ri:kɔ:l] Produktrückrufaktion
to damage ['dæmɪdʒ] beschädigen
in the long run [ɪn ðə 'lɒŋ ˌrʌn] auf lange Sicht
construction fault [kən'strʌkʃn ˌfɒlt] Konstruktionsfehler
reputation [ˌrepjə'teɪʃn] Ruf, Ansehen
to lose trust in [ˌlu:z 'trʌst ɪn] Vertauen verlieren in
to unsettle [ʌn'setl] beunruhigen

B | Dealing with product recalls

helpline ['helplaɪn] telefonischer Beratungsdienst
press release ['pres rɪˌli:s] Pressemitteilung
bathroom scale [ˌbɑ:θru:m 'skeɪl] Gewichtswaage
weight [weɪt] Gewicht
to replace [rɪ'pleɪs] ersetzen
to apologize [ə'pɒlədʒaɪz] sich entschuldigen
compensation [ˌkɒmpen'seɪʃn] Schadensersatz
to meet sb's needs [ˌmi:t ˌsʌmbədɪz 'ni:dz] die Bedürfnisse von jdm. befriedigen

C | Customer feedback

to share [ʃeə] teilen
on time [ɒn 'taɪm] pünktlich

to push [pʊʃ] schieben
past [pɑ:st] vorbei

D | Apologizing to customers

countable ['kaʊntəbl] zählbar
uncountable [ʌn'kaʊntəbl] unzählbar
careers advisor [kərɪəz‿əd͵vaɪzə] Berufsberater/in
changing cubicle ['tʃeɪndʒɪŋ ͵kju:bɪkl] Umkleidekabine

to rely on [rɪ'laɪ‿ɒn] verlassen auf
suitcase ['su:tkeɪs] Koffer

signature ['sɪgnətʃə] Unterschrift
salutation [͵sæljə'teɪʃn] Anrede
subject line ['sʌbdʒekt ͵laɪn] Betreffzeile
reference line ['refrəns ͵laɪn] Bezugszeichenzeile
recently ['ri:səntlɪ] kürzlich
documentary [͵dɒkjʊ'mentrɪ] Dokumentarfilm
factory ['fæktrɪ] Fabrik
to admit [əd'mɪt] zugeben
to assure sb of sth [ə'ʃɔ: ͵sʌmbədɪ‿əv ͵sʌmθɪŋ] jdm. etw. zusichern
in keeping with [ɪn 'ki:pɪŋ wɪð] in Einklang mit
health and safety standards [͵helθ‿ən 'seɪftɪ ͵stæn‿dədz] Arbeitsschutzstandards
national average [͵næʃənəl‿'ævərɪdʒ] Landesdurchschnitt
to hesitate ['hezɪteɪt] zögern
bar chart ['bɑ: ͵tʃɑ:t] Balkendiagramm
percentage [pə'sentɪdʒ] Prozentsatz

E | Understanding safety instructions

safety instructions ['seɪftɪ‿ɪn͵strʌkʃns] Sicherheitshinweise
user manual ['ju:zə ͵mænjʊəl] Bedienungsanleitung
to tip over [͵tɪp‿'əʊvə] umkippen
to direct towards [dɪ'rekt tə͵wɔ:dz] (aus)richten auf
to arrange [ə'reɪndʒ] anordnen
to stack [stæk] übereinanderstellen
to connect [kə'nekt] verbinden
to disconnect [͵dɪskə'nekt] trennen
to insert [ɪn'sɜ:t] hineinstecken, einfügen
designated ['dezɪgneɪtɪd] vorgesehen
port [pɔ:t] *(hier:)* Anschluss, Schnittstelle
to use force [͵ju:z 'fɔ:s] Kraft anwenden
power surge ['paʊə ͵sɜ:dʒ] Überspannung
short-circuit [͵ʃɔ:t'sɜ:kɪt] Kurzschluss
overheating [͵əuvə'hi:tɪŋ] Überhitzung
instability [͵ɪnstə'bɪlətɪ] Instabilität

F | Giving guarantees

opening hours ['əʊpənɪŋ‿͵aʊəz] Öffnungszeiten
portable ['pɔ:təbl] tragbar
to turn on [͵tɜ:n‿'ɒn] anschalten, einschalten
loudspeaker [͵laʊd'spi:kə] Lautsprecher

sleep timer ['sli:p ͵taɪmə] Schlaffunktion, (automatische) Abschaltfunktion
to dispatch [dɪ'spætʃ] versenden, verschicken
trendy ['trendɪ] modisch, schick

backpacking ['bæk͵pækɪŋ] Wandern
tent [tent] Zelt
to exceed [ɪk'si:d] hinausgehen über
legal regulation [͵li:gl ͵regjə'leɪʃn] gesetzliche Vorschrift
favourable ['feɪvrəbl] günstig

G | Customer satisfaction

satisfaction [͵sætɪs'fækʃn] Zufriedenheit
graded ['greɪdɪd] abgestuft
interviewee [͵ɪntəvjʊ'i:] Befragte/r
beverage ['bevrɪdʒ] Getränk
to disagree [͵dɪsə'gri:] nicht zustimmen
to improve [ɪm'pru:v] verbessern
to conduct [kən'dʌkt] durchführen
questionnaire [͵kwestʃə'neə] Fragebogen

Unit 9 Getting goods delivered

A | Making an enquiry

enquiry [ɪn'kwaɪrɪ] Anfrage
potential [pə'tenʃl] potenziell
supplier [sə'plaɪə] Zulieferer

wristwatch ['rɪstwɒtʃ] Armbanduhr

B | A business letter

with reference to [wɪð 'refrəns tə] mit Bezug auf
to request [rɪ'kwest] bitten
to extend [ɪk'stend] erweitern
range of products [͵reɪndʒ‿əv 'prɒdʌkts] Produktpalette
trade discount [͵treɪd 'dɪskaʊnt] Handelsrabatt
terms of delivery and payment [͵tɜ:mz‿əv ͵peɪmənt‿ən dɪ'lɪvərɪ] Lieferungs- und Zahlungsbedingungen
in advance [ɪn‿əd'vɑ:ns] im Voraus
to paraphrase ['pærəfreɪz] umschreiben, paraphrasieren
complimentary close [͵kɒmplɪmentrɪ 'kləʊz] Grußformel

C | Receiving an offer

enc (enclosure) [ɪn'kləʊʒə] Anlage
delivery [dɪ'lɪvərɪ] Lieferung
total price [͵təʊtl 'praɪs] Gesamtpreis
willing ['wɪlɪŋ] bereit

order ['ɔ:də] Bestellung
cash discount [ˌkæʃ 'dɪskaʊnt] Barzahlungsrabatt, Skonto
settlement ['setlmənt] Bezahlung
to desire [dɪ'zaɪə] wünschen
air mail ['eəmeɪl] Luftpost
receipt of order [rɪˌsi:t‿əv 'ɔ:də] Auftragseingang

D | Placing an order

to place an order [ˌpleɪs‿ən‿'ɔ:də] eine Bestellung aufgeben
to confirm [kən'fɜ:m] bestätigen
to remind [rɪ'maɪnd] erinnern
bank transfer ['bæŋk ˌtrænsfɜ:] Banküberweisung

E | Delivery and payment

means of payment [ˌmi:nz‿əv 'peɪmənt] Zahlungsmittel, Bezahlungsverfahren
in instalments [ɪn‿ɪn'stɔ:lmənts] in Raten
on receipt [ɒn‿rɪ'si:t] bei Erhalt
invoice ['ɪnvɔɪs] Rechnung

F | Ordering goods

based in ['beɪst‿ɪn] mit Sitz in

◎
straight [streɪt] gerade
skirt [skɜ:t] Rock
to cover [kʌvə] bedecken
slim [slɪm] schlank
conversion chart [kən'vɜ:ʃn ˌtʃɑ:t] Umrechnungstabelle
pattern ['pætən] Muster
plain [pleɪn] einfach, nur
foot (= 0.3048 m), *(pl.)* feet [fʊt, 'fi:t] Fuß (= 0,3048 m)
inch (= 2.54 cm) [ɪntʃ] Zoll (= 2,54 cm)
cut [kʌt] Schnitt
to read sth back [ˌri:d sʌmθɪŋ 'bæk] etw. nochmal vorlesen
verification code [ˌverɪfɪ'keɪʃn ˌkəʊd] Sicherheitsziffer(n), Bestätigungscode
valid until ['vælɪd‿ənˌtɪl] gültig bis

to keep sth [ki:p ˌsʌmθɪŋ] etw. behalten
delivery date [dɪ'lɪvərɪ ˌdeɪt] Lieferdatum

G | Making a complaint

to insist on sth [ɪn'sɪst‿ɒn ˌsʌmθɪŋ] auf etw. bestehen
to carry out [ˌkærɪ‿'aʊt] ausführen
to close [kləʊz] *(hier:)* beenden, abschließen
duty ['dju:tɪ] Verpflichtung, Aufgabe
relegated ['reləgeɪtɪd] heruntergestuft (in eine niedrigere Liga)

H | Evaluating different methods of delivery

to evaluate [ɪ'væljʊeɪt] bewerten
pros and cons [ˌprəʊz‿ən 'kɒnz] Für und Wider, Pro und Kontra
speed [spi:d] Geschwindigkeit
slide presentation ['slaɪd preznˌteɪʃn] Folienpräsentation

Unit 10 Job hunting

to hunt [hʌnt] *(hier:)* suchen

A | Which job?

◎
rejection [rɪ'dʒekʃn] Absage, Ablehnung
letter of application [ˌletər‿əv‿æplɪ'keɪʃn] Bewerbungsschreiben
career [kə'rɪə] Karriere
to fire ['faɪə] entlassen
to give up [gɪv‿'ʌp] aufgeben
job centre ['dʒɒb ˌsentə] Arbeitsamt

B | Looking at job adverts

job advert ['dʒɒb ˌædvɜ:t] Stellenanzeige
mark [mɑ:k] Note
to employ [ɪm'plɔɪ] einstellen, beschäftigen
to apply [ə'plaɪ] sich bewerben
temporary job [ˌtemprərɪ 'dʒɒb] befristete Stelle

C | Writing a letter of application

to advertise ['ædvətaɪz] *(hier:)* inserieren
to attend [ə'tend] teilnehmen, besuchen
personnel manager [ˌpɜ:sən'el ˌmænɪdʒə] Personalchef/in
CV (= curriculum vitae) [ˌsi:'vi:] Lebenslauf
to invite [ɪn'vaɪt] einladen
job interview ['dʒɒb ˌɪntəvju:] Bewerbungsgespräch

D | Writing a CV

education [ˌedjʊ'keɪʃn] Ausbildung
secondary school ['sekəndrɪ ˌsku:l] weiterführende Schule
primary school ['praɪmərɪ ˌsku:l] Grundschule
production department [prə'dʌkʃn dɪˌpɑ:tmənt] Produktion
mother tongue [ˌmʌðə 'tʌŋ] Muttersprache
driving licence ['draɪvɪŋ ˌlaɪsəns] Führerschein

E | A job interview

school leaving certificate ['sku:l‚li:vɪŋ sə‚tɪfɪkət] Abschlusszeugnis
secondary modern school [‚sekəndrɪ 'mɒdən ‚sku:l] Realschule
invitation [‚ɪnvɪ'teɪʃn] Einladung
to dress up [‚dres‿'ʌp] sich feinmachen
suburb ['sʌbɜ:b] Vorort
to drop sb off [‚drɒp ‚sʌmbədɪ‿'ɒf] jdn. absetzen
journey ['dʒɜ:nɪ] Anfahrt, Reise

F | Conducting job interviews

head office [‚hed‿'ɒfɪs] Hauptniederlassung
personnel department [‚pɜ:sən'el dɪ‚pɑ:tmənt] Personalabteilung

major [['meɪdʒə] bedeutend
fluent ['flu:ənt] fließend
familiar [fə'mɪlɪə] vertraut
repair [rɪ'peə] Reparatur
to move (to) ['mu:v (tə)] umziehen (nach)
accomodation [ə‚kɒmə'deɪʃn] Unterkunft
to appoint sb [ə'pɔɪnt ‚sʌmbədɪ] jdn. einstellen
confirmation [‚kɒnfə'meɪʃn] Bestätigung
salary ['sælərɪ] Gehalt, Lohn
personal affairs [‚pɜ:sənl‿ə'feəz] persönliche Angelegenheiten
pleasure ['pleʒə] Freude

with regard to [wɪð rɪ'gɑ:d tə] mit Bezug auf
to travel ['trævl] (an)reisen

G | Working in the EU

European Union (EU) [‚jʊərəpɪən 'ju:nɪən, ‚i:'ju:] Europäische Gemeinschaft (EG)
citizen ['sɪtɪzn] Bürger/in
basic right [‚beɪsɪk 'raɪt] Grundrecht
identity card [aɪ'dentɪtɪ ‚kɑ:d] Personalausweis
passport ['pɑ:spɔ:t] Pass
vacancy ['veɪkənsɪ] freie Stelle
public sector [‚pʌblɪk 'sektə] öffentlicher Sektor
recognized ['rekəgnaɪzd] anerkannt
certified translation [‚sɜ:tɪfaɪ'd træns'leɪʃn] beglaubigte Übersetzung
reference ['refrəns] Arbeitszeugnis
police certificate of good conduct [pə‚li:s sə'tɪfɪkət‿əv ‚gʊd 'kɒndʌkt] polizeiliches Führungszeugnis
criminal record [‚krɪmɪnl 'rekɔ:d] Vorstrafenregister

Conversion table inch – cm / foot – metre

1 *inch* (in) = 2.54 cm   1 *foot* = 30.48 cm

Die Angaben sind gerundet. Die bei den Umrechnungen in *inches* und *feet* angegebene Dezimale dient nur der Verdeutlichung.

in	cm	cm	in	ft	m	m	ft
1	2.54	3	1.18	1	0.3048	1	3.28
2	5.08	4	1.57	2	0.6096	2	6.56
3	7.62	5	1.97	3	0.9144	3	9.84
4	10.16	10	3.94	4	1.2192	4	13.12
5	12.70	15	5.91	5	1.5240	5	16.40
6	15.24	20	7.87	6	1.8288	6	19.68
7	17.78	25	9.84	7	2.1336	7	22.96
8	20.32	30	11.81	8	2.4384	8	26.24
9	22.86	35	13.78	9	2.7432	9	29.52
10	25.40	40	15.75	10	3.0480	10	32.80
11	27.94	45	17.72	11	3.3528	11	36.08
12	30.48	50	19.69	12	3.6576	12	39.36

Hinweis:

- Eine Länge von ca. 35 cm würde man statt mit 13 ¾" eher mit 1'1¾" (1 *foot* 1¾ *inches*) angeben.
- *Feet* wird in der Luftfahrt für Höhenangaben verwendet: Flughöhe 10,000 ft.
- Die Körpergröße eines Menschen von 1,79 m würde man mit 5'10" angeben.

Alphabetical word list

Die Seitenzahl bezieht sich auf das erste Vorkommen der Vokabel im Buch.

Abkürzungen

AE = American English
BE = British English
pl. = plural
* = irregular verb

A

B

C

to **centre** zentrieren 25
centre point Mittelpunkt 25
certainly sicherlich 22
certified translation beglaubigte Übersetzung 123
challenge Herausforderung 67
chance Möglichkeit, Gelegenheit 67
to **change** tauschen, wechseln 19
change Wechselgeld 22
changing cubicle Umkleidekabine 93
characteristic Eigenschaft 38
channel Kanal 20
chat button Chat-Schaltfläche 68
children's wear Kinderbekleidung 54
choice Wahl 74
*to **choose** wählen 32
citizen Bürger/in 123
to **climb (onto)** hinaufklettern 79
to **close** *(hier:)* beenden, abschließen 109
clothing line Modelinie 23
colleague Kollege/Kollegin 6
to **collect** abholen 20; (ein)sammeln 33
colour Farbe 55
*to **come across** wirken, rüberkommen 49
comfortable bequem 18
company Firma 9
to **compare** vergleichen 31
compensation Schadensersatz 91
competition Wettbewerb, Konkurrenz 50
competitive konkurrierend 50; wettbewerbsfähig 72
complaint Beschwerde 13
to **complete** vervollständigen 8
to **complete a transaction** einen Kaufvorgang abschließen 49
completely sold out vollständig ausverkauft 43
complimentary close Grußformel 104
conclusion Abschluss, Schlussfolgerung 37
condition Zustand 80
to **conduct** durchführen 99
confident selbstbewusst 37
to **confirm** bestätigen 106
confirmation Bestätigung 68
to **confront sb** jdm. entgegentreten 87
to **connect** verbinden 96
connection Anschluss 22
connectivity Netzwerkfähigkeit 22
construction fault Konstruktionsfehler 90
consumer rights Verbraucherrechte 39
to **contain** beinhalten 7
content Inhalt 79
convenient zweckmäßig, praktisch 24
conventionally made herkömmlich gefertigt 23
conversion chart Umrechnungstabelle 108
to **convince sb** jdn. überzeugen 37
cord Kabel 21
corded mit Kabel 21
corner shop (kleines) Lebensmittelgeschäft 33
cosmetics Kosmetik 54
*to **cost** kosten 43
to **count** zählen 33
countable zählbar 93
couple Paar, Pärchen 31
to **cover** bedecken 108
to **credit** gutschreiben 39
credit card Kreditkarte 80
criminal record Vorstrafenregister 123
to **cross out** durchstreichen 46
crowds Menschenmassen 47
curious neugierig 60
customer Kunde / Kundin 9
customer service Kundenbetreuung 63
cut Schnitt 108
cutting width Schnittbreite 21
cutting height Schnitthöhe 21
CV (= curriculum vitae) Lebenslauf 116

D

daily requirement Tagesbedarf 35
daily routine Tagesablauf 12
dairy product Milchprodukt 83
to **damage** beschädigen 90
*to **deal with** umgehen mit, es zu tun haben mit 13
to **decide** entscheiden 19
to **decorate** dekorieren 60
definitely eindeutig, auf jeden Fall 37
to **delete** löschen 68
delicious köstlich 18
to **deliver** (aus)liefern, zustellen 12
delivery Lieferung 105
delivery date Lieferdatum 109
to **demonstrate** zeigen 24
department Abteilung 10
department store Kaufhaus, Warenhaus 10
to **descend upon sth** *(hier:)* etw. stürmen 47
to **describe** beschreiben 19
to **deserve** verdienen 49
design Gestaltung 33
designated vorgesehen 96
desire Wunsch 36
to **desire** wünschen 105
detail Detail, Einzelheit 61
to **develop** *(hier:)* ausbilden 35
development Entwicklung 35
difference Unterschied 43
to **direct towards** (aus)richten auf 96
dirty dreckig 80
disabled behindert 31
disadvantage Nachteil 35
to **disagree** nicht zustimmen 99
to **disconnect** trennen 96
discount Nachlass, Rabatt 21
discounter Billigsupermarkt 33
to **dispatch** versenden, verschicken 97
to **display** auslegen, zur Schau stellen 12
dissatisfied unzufrieden 81
to **distinguish** unterscheiden 30
distribution Vertrieb, Verkauf 20
to **disturb** stören 32
diving goggles Taucherbrille 85
DIY store, do-it-yourself store Heimwerkermarkt, Baumarkt 24
to **do sb a favour** jemandem einen Gefallen tun 82
documentary Dokumentarfilm 94
doll Puppe 56
downstairs nach unten 56
*to **draw** zeichnen 28
dress code Kleidervorschriften 60
to **dress up** sich feinmachen 119
drill Bohrmaschine 22
to **drill** bohren 24
driving licence Führerschein 117
to **drop sb off** jdn. absetzen 119
duty Verpflichtung, Aufgabe 110

E

to earn verdienen 33
eco-friendly umweltfreundlich 67
economic crisis Wirtschaftskrise 47
education Ausbildung 117
effect Wirkung 75
Egyptian ägyptisch 60
elderly älter 13
to **employ** einstellen, beschäftigen 115
employer Arbeitgeber 15
enc (enclosure) Anlage 105
to **enjoy** genießen 28
enquiry Anfrage 102
to **enter** betreten 19
entry Eingabe 68
environment Umwelt 67
environmentally friendly umweltfreundlich 30
to **escalate** eskalieren 86
escalator Rolltreppe 56
to **estimate** schätzen 83
ethically made nach ethischen Maßstäben hergestellt 23
European Union (EU) Europäische Gemeinschaft (EG) 123
to **evaluate** bewerten 111
to **exceed** hinausgehen über 97
exception Ausnahme 81
to **exchange** (um)tauschen 81
exchange student Austauschschüler/in 7
to **exclude** ausschließen 39
exhausting anstrengend, ermüdend 60
to **expand** erweitern 73
to **expect** erwarten 63
expectation Erwartung 37
expensive teuer 18
expiry date Verfallsdatum, Ablaufdatum 83
explanation Erklärung 25
to **extend** erweitern 103
extraordinary außergewöhnlich 73

F

factory Fabrik 94
factory-made industriell gefertigt 23
familiar vertraut 120
far away weit weg 33
fault Fehler 49
favour Gefallen 57
favourable günstig 97
favourite Lieblings- 74
features Eigenschaften 21
federal state Bundesland 72
to **feel annoyed** sich verärgert fühlen 82
to **finish** beenden 32
to **fire** entlassen 114
*to **fit sb** jdm. passen 19
fitting room Umkleidekabine 27
to **fix** festlegen 72
flammable entflammbar 79
flap Klappe 74
flavour Geschmack 83
floor Stock(werk) 54
fluent fließend 120
to **follow sb** jdm. folgen 55
foot (= 0.3048 m), *(pl.)* feet Fuß (= 0,3048 m) 108
*to **forget** vergessen 60
fragile zerbrechlich 78
to **frame** (ein)rahmen 74
fresh food Frischkost 9
fridge Kühlschrank 35
front-facing nach vorne zeigend 73
to **fulfill** erfüllen 47
furniture Möbel 79
further away weiter weg 12
furthermore außerdem 73

G

garden center Gartencenter 21
gap Lücke 40
genuine echt, ehrlich 86
*to **get a glimpse of sth** einen Blick auf etw. erhaschen 47
*to **get on sb's nerves** jdm. auf die Nerven gehen 32
*to **get sth done** etwas schaffen 25
gift Geschenk 74
*to **give sb attention** jdm. Aufmerksamkeit schenken 36
*to **give up** aufgeben 114
glove Handschuh 81
Go ahead, please. Fahren Sie bitte fort. 73
goods Waren 9
*to **go off** schlecht werden 79
*to **go well with** gut passen zu 19
*to **go wrong** schief gehen 79
graded abgestuft 98
graph Diagramm, Grafik 37
Greece Griechenland 32
grocery store Lebensmittelgeschäft 7
ground floor Erdgeschoss 54
grower Erzeuger/in, Bauer/Bäuerin 23
*to **grow in popularity** an Beliebtheit gewinnen 23
guarantee Garantie 23
to **guess** (er)raten 19

H

habit Gewohnheit 30
to **handle sth** mit etw. umgehen, behandeln 14
*to **hang up** aufhängen 7
harmful schädlich 67
to **harvest** ernten 35
*to **have a few days off** ein paar Tage frei haben 7
*to **have contact with** Kontakt haben mit 10
*to **have exact change** es passend haben 43
*to **have sth left** etw. übrig haben 43
heading Überschrift 74
head office Hauptniederlassung 120
health and safety standards Arbeitsschutzstandards 94
healthy gesund 18
heat Hitze 79
heat-treated wärmebehandelt, pasteurisiert 83
hectic hektisch 30
heel (Schuh-)Absatz 57
helpline telefonischer Beratungsdienst 91
Here we are. Hier wären wir. 55
to **hesitate** zögern 94
*to **hide** verbergen, verstecken 55
to **highlight** hervorheben 74
Hold the line, please. Bleiben Sie bitte am Apparat. 84
hole Loch 24
home entertainment shop Geschäft für Unterhaltungselektronik 12
honey Honig 43
honoured verehrt, geschätzt 49
huge riesig 60
humidity Feuchtigkeit 79
to **hunt** *(hier:)* suchen 114

I

I'm afraid leider 22
to **identify** identifizieren, erkennen 30

natural *(hier:)* naturbelassen 31
nearby in der Nähe 7
need Bedarf, Bedürfnis 36
nevertheless trotzdem, dennoch 87
news Nachricht(en) 54
next to neben 55
no-name product No-Name-Produkt, kein Markenprodukt 45

O

odd one out nicht dazugehören 16
of course selbstverständlich 22
to **offer** anbieten 60
on-board *(hier:)* auf der Platine 73
once einmal 10
on offer im Angebot 12
on receipt bei Erhalt 106
on the left auf der linken Seite 55
on the move unterwegs 22
on time pünktlich 92
open day Tag der offenen Tür 25
opening hours Öffnungszeiten 97
operating instructions Bedienungsanleitung 82
operating system Betriebssystem 73
operator Kassierer/in 49
opposite gegenüber 7
order Bestellung 105
organic organisch, biologisch 35
originally ursprünglich 7
original packaging Originalverpackung 85
*to **outbid** überbieten 47
outdoors draußen, im Freien 32
outgoing kontaktfreudig 15
outlook Perspektive, Aussicht 47
out of order außer Betrieb 56
overheating Überhitzung 96
overpriced überteuert 45
over there dort drüben 32
to **own** besitzen 34
owner Besitzer/in 33

P

packaging Verpackung 30
a packet of ein Paket 43
to **paint** streichen 24
paint roller Farbroller 24
to **paraphrase** umschreiben, paraphrasieren 104
particularly besonders 46
to **be passed on** weitergeleitet werden 21
passport Pass 123
past vorbei 92
pastime Zeitvertreib 47
pattern Muster 108
to **peel** schälen 39
percentage Prozentsatz 95
personal affairs persönliche Angelegenheiten 122
personality Persönlichkeit 15
personnel department Personalabteilung 120
personnel manager Personalchef/in 116
pesticide Pflanzenschutzmittel 35
photographic shop Fotogeschäft 32
phrase Redewendung 7
to **pick sb up** jdn. abholen 32
picture frame Bilderrahmen 32
pineapple Ananas 43
to **place an order** eine Bestellung aufgeben 68
place of work Arbeitsplatz 6
plain einfach, nur 108
plant Pflanze 31
plasterboard screw Rigipsschraube 25
playability Abspielbarkeit 85
Pleased to meet you. Schön Sie/dich/euch kennen zu lernen. 7
pleasure Freude 120
police certificate of good conduct polizeiliches Führungszeugnis 123
policy Strategie, Grundsatz, Politik 49
politely höflich 80
to **pop into** schnell vorbeischauen 45
port *(hier:)* Anschluss, Schnittstelle 96
portable tragbar 97
to **pose a health risk** ein Gesundheitsrisiko darstellen 83
potential potenziell 102
power surge Überspannung 96
practical use praktische Anwendung 50
to **praise** loben 85
to **press** drücken 79
press release Pressemitteilung 91
to **price sth** etw. auszeichnen 79
price tag Preisschild 21
pricing strategy Preisstrategie 50
primary school Grundschule 117
procedure Ablauf, Verfahren 25
processing Bearbeitung 39
production department Produktion 117
product pricing Preisfestsetzung 50
product recall Produktrückrufaktion 90
promise Versprechen 39
to **promote** fördern 66
promotion video Werbevideo 70
proof Nachweis 39
proposal Vorschlag 87
pros and cons Für und Wider, Pro und Kontra 111
to **protect** schützen 79
to **prove** beweisen 74
to **provide** liefern, bereitstellen 63
public sector öffentlicher Sektor 123
purchase (Ein-)Kauf, Ware 63
to **push** schieben 92
*to **put the blame on sb** jdm. die Schuld geben 86

Q

quantity Menge 43
questionnaire Fragebogen 99
queue Warteschlange 13
quick start guide Schnellstartanleitung 82

R

rack Regal 32
to **raise** erheben 49
to **rake** einstreichen, erziehlen 47
a range of eine Reihe von, zahlreiche 32
range of products Produktpalette 103
*to **read out** vorlesen 32
*to **read sth back** etw. nochmal vorlesen 108
rear-side Rückseite 74
receipt Quittung, Kassenzettel 22, Erhalt 39
receipt of order Auftragseingang 105
recently kürzlich 94
recognized anerkannt 123
to **recommend** empfehlen 85
to **reduce** reduzieren 67

reduction Ermäßigung 45
reference Arbeitszeugnis 123
reference line Bezugszeichenzeile 94
to **reflect on sth** über etw. nachdenken 86
refund Erstattung, Rückzahlung 13
regulation Vorschrift 80
rejection Absage, Ablehnung 114
relegated heruntergestuft (in eine niedrigere Liga) 110
to **rely on** verlassen auf 93
to **rent** mieten 21
remaining verbleibend 7
remark Bemerkung 7
to **remember** sich erinnern (an) 59
to **remind** erinnern 106
remote-controlled ferngesteuert 45
to **repair** reparieren 56
repair Reparatur 120
repayment Rückzahlung 46
to **replace** ersetzen 25
replacement Ersatz 81
to **reply** antworten, reagieren 49
reputation Ruf, Ansehen 90
to **request** bitten 103
required benötigt werden 15
requirement Bedingung, Voraussetzung 15
result Ergebnis 33
retail chain Einzelhandelskette 9
retail management assistant Kaufmann/-frau im Einzelhandel 10
retail store Ladengeschäft 20
to **retain** bewahren 83
return Rückgabe 81
a roll of eine Rolle 43
to **have room for** Platz haben für 22
round um ... herum 55
row Reihe 49
ruined ruiniert 81
rule Regel 79
to **run on sth** betrieben werden mit etw. 21
rush *(hier:)* Andrang 47

S

safely sicher 44
safety instructions Sicherheitshinweise 96
salary Gehalt, Lohn 120
sales area Verkaufsfläche 7
sales promotion Werbung, Werbeaktion 66
salutation Anrede 94
sample Muster 78
satisfaction Zufriedenheit 98
sausage Würstchen 22
to **save** sparen 45
to **scan** einscannen 49
sceptical skeptisch, kritisch 30
school leaving certificate Abschlusszeugnis 119
scratch Kratzer 84
screen Bildschirm 35
to **screw** (an)schrauben 25
screwdriver Schraubenzieher 25
seal Siegel 39
to **search** durchsuchen 15
search engine Suchmaschine 21
search function Suchfunktion 68
season Saison, Jahreszeit 47
secondary modern school Realschule 119
secondary school weiterführende Schule 117
*to **see a point** einen Standpunkt verstehen 81
selection Auswahl 60
self-propelled mit Eigenantrieb 21
selling space Verkaufsraum, Verkaufsfläche 60
to **serve** bedienen 9
service Service, Dienstleistung 14
settlement Bezahlung 105
to **share** teilen 92
to **sharpen** anspitzen 7
shelf, *(pl.)* shelves Regal 7
shop assistant Verkäufer/in 9
shop entrance Ladeneingang 12
shop fittings Ladenausstattung 33
shoplifter Ladendieb/in 13
shoplifting Ladiendiebstahl 87
short-circuit Kurzschluss 96
showroom Ausstellungsraum 35
signature Unterschrift 94
similar ähnlich 48
size Größe 19
skills Fähigkeiten, Fertigkeiten 12
skin *(hier:)* Schale 35
skirt Rock 108
sleep timer Schlaffunktion, (automatische) Abschaltfunktion 97
slide presentation Folienpräsentation 111
slim schlank 108
slot Steckplatz 22
*to **smell** riechen 78
smoking area Raucherzone 80
social networking site Seite in den sozialen Netzwerken 70
soft toy Plüschtier 60
solid stabil 18
solution Lösung 67
to **solve** lösen 81
specialist shop Fachgeschäft 33
special needs spezielle Bedürfnisse, Sonderanforderungen 14
special offer Sonderangebot 22
speed Geschwindigkeit 111
spelling Rechtschreibung 59
spirit level Wasserwaage 25
to **spoil** verderben 83
sports and leisure shop Sport- und Freizeitgeschäft 32
sportswear Sportbekleidung 84
spot Fleck 84
square foot, *(pl.)* square feet Quadratfuß (Fuß = 0,3048 Meter) 60
to **stack** übereinanderstellen 96
staff Personal, Belegschaft 12
statement Aussage 6
stationary stationär, ortsgebunden 20
stationery shop Schreibwarenladen 7
to **stay** bleiben 56
storage space Speicherplatz 73
to **store** (ab)speichern 19
straight gerade 108
straight on geradeaus 56
sturdy fest, stabil 74
stylish elegant, stilvoll 18
subject Betreff, Thema 73
subject line Betreffzeile 94
suburb Vorort 119
successfully erfolgreich 22
to **sue sb for damages** jdn. auf Schadenersatz verklagen 87
to **suggest** vorschlagen 55
suggestion Vorschlag 81
suitcase Koffer 93
to **suit sb** jdm. stehen 19
to **sum up** zusammenfassen 7
superlative Superlativ, Übertreibung 74
supervisor Vorgesetzte/r 49
supplier Zulieferer 102
to **suppose** annehmen, vermuten 25
survey Umfrage, Befragung 34

survival kit Überlebensausrüstung 7
to **survive** überleben 7

T

table Tabelle 9
to **tag** auszeichnen 9
*to **take advantage of sth** etw. ausnutzen 45
*to **take care of** aufpassen auf 32
*to **take notes** Notizen machen 11
*to **take one's time** sich Zeit nehmen 30
*to **take part** teilnehmen 34
*to **take place** stattfinden 47
*to **take sb by surprise** jdn. überraschen 49
*to **take turns** sich abwechseln 24
takings Einnahmen 47
tape measure Maßband, Metermaß 25
task Aufgabe 9
taste Geschmack 35
tasting Kostprobe, Verköstigung 66
temporary job befristete Stelle 115
tent Zelt 97
terms of delivery and payment Lieferungs- und Zahlungsbedingungen 103
Thanksgiving Erntedankfest in den USA 47
theft Diebstahl 87
tie Krawatte 26
tight eng 26
timeless zeitlos 74
tiny winzig 73
to **tip over** umkippen 96
tool Werkzeug 24
top floor Obergeschoss 54
total price Gesamtpreis 105
to **touch** anfassen 78
toxic giftig 67
toys department Spielwarenabteilung 45
tracking reference number Nachverfolgungsnummer 39
tracksuit Trainingsanzug 32
to **trade** handeln 23
trade discount Handelsrabatt 103
traineeship Ausbildung 7
to **translate** übersetzen 35
to **travel** (an)reisen 122
travel guide Reiseführer 79
treadmill Laufband 70
to **treat** behandeln 35
tremendous gewaltig enorm 72
trendy modisch, schick 97
trial Probe 66
trolley Einkaufswagen 31
trousers Hose 18
truck Laster 45
to **turn on** anschalten, einschalten 97
to **turn sb away** jdn. abweisen 60
twice as much as zweimal so viel wie 43
twice a week zweimal pro Woche 7

U

uncountable unzählbar 93
uncrossed nicht gekreuzt 86
unfortunately leider 80
unique einzigartig 63
unique selling point (USP) Alleinstellungsmerkmal 73
to **unpack** auspacken 9
unpleasant unangenehm 49
to **unsettle** beunruhigen 90
upset aufgebracht, verärgert 81
to **be in urgent need** dringend benötigen 21
usage Gebrauch 24
to **use force** Kraft anwenden 96
useful nützlich 18
user manual Bedienungsanleitung 96

V

vacancy freie Stelle 123
valid until gültig bis 108
valuable wertvoll 35
value Wert 63
verification code Sicherheitsziffer(n), Bestätigungscode 108
violently gewalttätig 87
visual aid visuelles Hilfsmittel 37
vocational school Berufsschule 7
voucher Gutschein 81

W

wall plug Wanddübel 25
to **wander around** herumirren 13
*to **wear** tragen 32
to **weigh** (ab)wiegen 9
weight Gewicht 91
well-designed gut gestaltet 18
what a pity wie schade 26
wheelbarrow Schubkarre 18
wheelchair Rollstuhl 31
wide variety of große Auswahl/Vielfalt an 32
width Breite, Weite 25
WiFi internet access drahtloser Internetzugang 22
willing bereit 105
*to **withdraw** abheben 42
without jerking ohne Ruckeln 22
with reference to mit Bezug auf 103
with regard to mit Bezug auf 120
word for word wortwörtlich 35
workplace Arbeitsplatz 75
work placment *(BE)*, internship *(AE)* Praktikum 7
worn out verschlissen 60
to **worry** sich Sorgen machen 12
wristwatch Armbanduhr 102

Y

to **yell at sb** jdn. anschreien 86
Yours sincerely Mit freundlichen Grüßen 82
You're welcome. Bitte schön, gern geschehen. 22

Irregular verbs

be, was/were, been	sein	**lead, led, led**	führen
become, became, become	werden	**leave, left, left**	(ver)lassen
begin, began, begun	anfangen	**lend, lent, lent**	(ver)leihen
bind, bound, bound	binden	**let, let, let**	lassen
bite, bit, bitten	beißen	**lie, lay, lain**	liegen
break, broke, broken	(zer)brechen	**lose, lost, lost**	verlieren
bring, brought, brought	(mit)bringen	**make, made, made**	machen
build, built, built	bauen	**mean, meant, meant**	meinen, bedeuten
burn, burnt, burnt	(ver)brennen	**meet, met, met**	treffen
buy, bought, bought	kaufen	**pay, paid, paid**	bezahlen
can, could, –	können	**put, put, put**	legen, stellen, setzen
catch, caught, caught	fangen		
choose, chose, chosen	wählen	**read, read, read**	lesen
come, came, come	kommen	**ride, rode, ridden**	reiten, fahren
cost, cost, cost	kosten	**ring, rang, rung**	klingeln
cut, cut, cut	schneiden	**rise, rose, risen**	steigen
deal, dealt, dealt (with)	(be)handeln	**run, ran, run**	laufen
do, did, done	tun, machen	**say, said, said**	sagen
draw, drew, drawn	zeichnen	**see, saw, seen**	sehen
drink, drank, drunk	trinken	**sell, sold, sold**	verkaufen
drive, drove, driven	fahren	**send, sent, sent**	senden
eat, ate, eaten	essen	**show, showed, shown**	zeigen
fall, fell, fallen	fallen	**shut, shut, shut**	schließen
feel, felt, felt	(sich) fühlen	**sing, sang, sung**	singen
find, found, found	finden	**sit, sat, sat**	sitzen
fly, flew, flown	fliegen	**sleep, slept, slept**	schlafen
forbid, forbade, forbidden	verbieten	**speak, spoke, spoken**	sprechen
forget, forgot, forgotten	vergessen	**spend, spent, spent**	ausgeben
get, got, got	bekommen	**stand, stood, stood**	stehen
give, gave, given	geben	**swim, swam, swum**	schwimmen
go, went, gone	gehen, fahren	**take, took, taken**	nehmen
grow, grew, grown	wachsen	**teach, taught, taught**	unterrichten
hang, hung, hung	hängen	**tell, told, told**	sagen; erzählen
have, had, had	haben	**think, thought, thought**	denken
hear, heard, heard	hören	**understand, understood, understood**	verstehen
hide, hid, hidden	(sich) verstecken		
hit, hit, hit	schlagen	**wear, wore, worn**	tragen
hold, held, held	(fest)halten	**win, won, won**	gewinnen
keep, kept, kept	aufbewahren; (sich) halten (an)	**withdraw, withdrew, withdrawn**	abheben
know, knew, known	wissen; kennen	**write, wrote, written**	schreiben

Phrases: Communication

Giving your opinion	
I think (that) ...	Ich denke/meine, dass ...
In my opinion .../In my view ...	Meiner Meinung/Ansicht nach ...
My view/opinion is that ...	Meine Ansicht/Meinung ist, ...
I find ... (really) good/interesting/boring.	Ich finde ... (echt) gut/interessant/langweilig.

Agreeing and disagreeing	
I agree (with ...).	Ich stimme (...) zu.
I disagree/don't agree (with ...).	Ich stimme (...) nicht zu.
Yes, I think the same./I think so, too.	Ja, ich denke das Gleiche./Das meine ich auch.
Rubbish!	Quatsch/Unsinn!

Adding points	
Furthermore ...	Des Weiteren/Außerdem ...
Moreover ...	Außerdem/Ferner ...
It's also important to mention that ...	Es ist auch wichtig zu erwähnen, ...

Pointing out alternatives	
Although .../Though ...	Obwohl ...
On the one hand ... But on the other hand ...	Einerseits ... Aber andererseits ...
However, ...	Jedoch ...

Dates	
Write …	Say …
1 October	the first of October
2 January	the second of January
3 August	the third of August
20 April	the twentieth of April

Years	
1995	nineteen ninety-five
2000	two thousand
2001	two thousand and one
2005	two thousand and five
2010	two thousand and ten

The 12-hour clock

- twelve o'clock midday/midnight
- five past ten
- ten past ten
- (a) quarter past ten
- twenty past ten
- twenty-five past ten
- half past ten
- twenty-five to eleven
- (a) quarter to eleven
- five to eleven

The 24-hour clock			
12:00	twelve o'clock midday	13:00	one o'clock in the afternoon / thirteen hundred
00:00	twelve o'clock midnight		
10:05	ten oh five	13:07	thirteen oh seven
10:10	ten ten	15:30	fifteen thirty
10:15	ten fifteen	18:56	eighteen fifty-six

Bildquellennachweis

Cover 1 iStockphoto (courtneyk), Calgary, Alberta; **Cover 2** iStockphoto (kali9), Calgary, Alberta. **4.1** Thinkstock (Purestock), München; **4.2** Thinkstock (iStock/Danilin), München; **4.3** iStockphoto (adventtr), Calgary, Alberta; **5.1** shutterstock (frica Studio), New York, NY; **5.2** iStockphoto (Feverpitched), Calgary, Alberta; **6.1** Corbis (Erik Isakson/Blend Images), Berlin; **6.2** Thinkstock (iStock/Adam Gregor), München; **6.3** Thinkstock (Digital Vision/Jack Hollingsworth), München; **6.4** Thinkstock (Fuse), München; **7** iStockphoto (JackF), Calgary, Alberta; **9.1** JupiterImages photos.com, Tucson, AZ; **9.2** iStockphoto (36clicks), Calgary, Alberta; **9.3** iStockphoto (kali9), Calgary, Alberta; **9.4** iStockphoto (IPGGutenbergUKLtd), Calgary, Alberta; **10** shutterstock (Goodluz), New York, NY; **11.1** Thinkstock (Purestock), München; **11.2** Thinkstock (Ingram Publishing), München; **11.3** Fotolia.com (Sergey Ryzhov), New York; **11.4** iStockphoto (pederk), Calgary, Alberta; **12** Alamy stock photo (Juice Images), Abingdon, Oxon; **13** iStockphoto (97), Calgary, Alberta; **15** Fotolia.com (contrastwerkstatt), New York; **18.1** iStockphoto (Maarigard), Calgary, Alberta; **18.2** Fotolia.com (agcreativelab), New York; **18.3** iStockphoto (Kondor83), Calgary, Alberta; **18.4** Fotolia.com (scharfsinn86), New York; **19** shutterstock (milanzeremski), New York, NY; **20.1** Thinkstock (Jack Hollingsworth / Digital Vision), München; **20.2** Getty Images (Asia Images), München; **20.3** Thinkstock (Digital Vision), München; **20.4** Thinkstock (Purestock), München; **20.5** shutterstock (Macrovector), New York, NY; **22.1** iStockphoto (zokara), Calgary, Alberta; **22.2** Masterfile, Düsseldorf; **22.3** shutterstock (racorn), New York, NY; **22.4** iStockphoto (Krystian Nawrocki), Calgary, Alberta; **23** Video(s) supplied by BBC Worldwide Learning, London; **24** BigStockPhoto.com (Kadmy), Davis, CA; **25** Fotolia.com (Agence DER), New York; **26.1** iStockphoto (shironosov), Calgary, Alberta; **26.2** iStockphoto (kadmy), Calgary, Alberta; **26.3** Thinkstock (BananaStock), München; **27** iStockphoto (mediaphotos), Calgary, Alberta; **30.1** Thinkstock (iStock/Danilin), München; **30.2** Thinkstock (Digital Vision/Photodisc), München; **30.3** Thinkstock (Digital Vision/Noel Hendrickson), München; **30.4** BigStockPhoto.com (Andres), Davis, CA; **31** BigStockPhoto.com (CandyBox Images), Davis, CA; **32** Thinkstock (JackF), München; **33.1** iStockphoto (Monkeybusinessimages), Calgary, Alberta; **33.2** BigStockPhoto.com (06photo), Davis, CA; **33.3** BigStockPhoto.com (Kadmy), Davis, CA; **34** iStockphoto (gpointstudio), Calgary, Alberta; **35** contunico - ZDF Enterprises, Mainz; **36** iStockphoto (vnlit), Calgary, Alberta; **38** iStockphoto (Svetlana Braun), Calgary, Alberta; **39.1** www.CartoonStock.com, Bath; **39.2** iStockphoto (JaysonPhotography), Calgary, Alberta; **40** iStockphoto (Dangubic), Calgary, Alberta; **42.1** iStockphoto (skynesher), Calgary, Alberta; **42.2** Fotolia.com (Edler von Rabenstein), New York; **42.3** Fotolia.com (Robert Kneschke), New York; **42.4** iStockphoto (KatarzynaBialasiewicz), Calgary, Alberta; **42.5** www.CartoonStock.com (Stan Eales), Bath;.**43** Fotolia.com (industrieblick), New York; **44.1** shutterstock (Ocean Image Photography), New York, NY; **44.2** Fotolia.com (Andrey Zyk), New York; **44.3** Fotolia.com (Nitr), New York; **44.4** Avenue Images GmbH (Stockbyte), Hamburg; **45** shutterstock (terekhov igor), New York, NY; **46.1** dreamstime.com (Andrey Burkov), Brentwood, TN; **46.2** dreamstime.com (Michaelnivelet), Brentwood, TN; **47** contunico - ZDF Enterprises, Mainz; **48** Fotolia.com (Tyler Olson), New York; **49** shutterstock (lithian), New York, NY; **50.1** iStockphoto (adventtr), Calgary, Alberta; **50.2** iStockphoto (Jitalia17), Calgary, Alberta; **50.3** iStockphoto (Daniel Raustadt), Calgary, Alberta; **50.4** shutterstock (Tom Gowanlock), New York, NY; **51.1** iStockphoto (Mystock88photo), Calgary, Alberta; **51.2** iStockphoto (peter zelei), Calgary, Alberta; **51.3** dreamstime.com (Olivier Le Moal), Brentwood, TN; **51.4** iStockphoto (zaniman), Calgary, Alberta; **52.1** Fotolia.com (Sergey Ryzhov), New York; **52.2** iStockphoto (ShotShare), Calgary, Alberta; **52.3** iStockphoto (vuk8691), Calgary, Alberta; **52.4** iStockphoto (ljubaphoto), Calgary, Alberta; **54.1** Fotolia.com (flashpics), New York; **54.2** iStockphoto (ImageGap), Calgary, Alberta; **54.3** BigStockPhoto.com (CandyBox Images), Davis, CA; **54.4** dreamstime.com (Pavel Losevsky), Brentwood, TN; **55** Thinkstock (Jacob Wackerhausen), München; **56** Alamy stock photo (Cultura Creative), Abingdon, Oxon; **57** shutterstock (pkchai), New York, NY; **58.1** shutterstock (Strawberry Mood), New York, NY; **58.2** iStockphoto (zilli), Calgary, Alberta; **58.3** Fotolia.com (Voyagerix), New York; **59.1-2** Dream Maker Software (RF), Colorado; **60.1** dreamstime.com (Clearvista), Brentwood, TN; **60.2** dreamstime.com (Sjankauskas), Brentwood, TN; **60.3** iStockphoto (Clicknique), Calgary, Alberta; **60.4** iStockphoto (franckreporter), Calgary, Alberta; **61** iStockphoto (TonyBaggett), Calgary, Alberta; **63** dreamstime.com (Agencyby), Brentwood, TN; **66.1** Fotolia.com (Eisenhans), New York; **66.2** BigStockPhoto.com (pressmaster), Davis, CA; **66.3** iStockphoto (CarmenMurillo), Calgary, Alberta; **66.4** dreamstime.com (Thinglass), Brentwood, TN; **67** iStockphoto (fcafotodigital), Calgary, Alberta; **68** iStockphoto (kizilkayaphotos), Calgary, Alberta; **69** Fotolia.com (hedgehog94), New York; **70** Thinkstock (iStock / Adam Gregor), München; **71** iStockphoto (Yuri), Calgary, Alberta; **72.1** dreamstime.com (Sgc), Brentwood, TN; **72.2** shutterstock (photocritical), New York, NY; **73** iStockphoto (Anatoliy Babiy), Calgary, Alberta; **74** iStockphoto (catscandotcom), Calgary, Alberta; **75** iStockphoto (Chris Schmidt), Calgary, Alberta; **76** shutterstock (Mathee saengkaew), New York, NY; **78.1** iStockphoto (RyanJLane), Calgary, Alberta; **78.2** Fotolia.com (volff), New York; **78.3** iStockphoto (ronen), Calgary, Alberta; **78.4** iStockphoto (trgowanlock), Calgary, Alberta; **79** shutterstock (Christoph Weihs), New York, NY; **80** iStockphoto (intraprese), Calgary, Alberta; **82** Alamy stock photo (John Birdsall), Abingdon, Oxon; **83** contunico - ZDF Enterprises, Mainz; **84** iStockphoto (cmfotoworks), Calgary, Alberta; **85** iStockphoto (Yuri_Arcurs), Calgary, Alberta; **86** iStockphoto (richyrichimages), Calgary, Alberta; **87** iStockphoto (AnitaPatterson), Calgary, Alberta; **90.1** Fotolia.com (Africa Studio), New York; **90.2** shutterstock (Hadi Djunaedi), New York, NY; **90.3** Fotolia.com (Kirill Zdorov), New York; **90.4** shutterstock (lindaks), New York, NY; **91** iStockphoto (PhotoTalk), Calgary, Alberta; **92** Thinkstock (Wavebreak Media), München; **93** www.CartoonStock.com (Morris, John), Bath; **96** shutterstock (Monkey Business Images), New York, NY; **97** iStockphoto (Predrag Vuckovic), Calgary, Alberta; **99** shutterstock (pressmaster), New York, NY; **100** Alamy stock photo (Pat Tuson), Abingdon, Oxon; **102.1** shutterstock (racorn), New York, NY; **102.2** iStockphoto (goldenKB), Calgary, Alberta; **102.3** dreamstime.com (Viorel Dudau), Brentwood, TN; **102.4** shutterstock (Andrey_Popov), New York, NY; **104.2** Dream Maker Software (RF), Colorado; **104.1** Dream Maker Software (RF), Colorado; **105.1** iStockphoto (borabalbey), Calgary, Alberta; **105.2** dreamstime.com (Shchipkova Elena), Brentwood, TN; **105.3** iStockphoto (Paolo_Toffanin), Calgary, Alberta; **106** shutterstock (Tibor Duris), New York, NY; **108** iStockphoto (Feverpitched), Calgary, Alberta; **111.1** iStockphoto (Oleksiy Mark), Calgary, Alberta; **111.2** shutterstock (Pierre-Yves Babelon), New York, NY; **111.3** shutterstock (TTstudio), New York, NY; **111.4** iStockphoto (junak), Calgary, Alberta; **114.1** iStockphoto (Mark Bowden), Calgary, Alberta; **114.2** iStockphoto (artpipi), Calgary, Alberta; **114.3** Fotolia.com (Adam Gregor), New York; **114.4** PantherMedia GmbH (kadmy), München; **115** shutterstock (Dmitry Kalinovsky), New York, NY; **117** iStockphoto (Tinpixels), Calgary, Alberta; **118** shutterstock (frica Studio), New York, NY; **120** iStockphoto (miszaqq), Calgary, Alberta; **123** 123rf (Mindaugas Kaziukonis), Nidderau; **124.1** Corel Corporation Deutschland, Unterschleissheim; **124.2** Fotolia.com (Jerome Dancette), New York; **124.3** iStockphoto (Lance Bellers), Calgary, Alberta; **124.4** Thinkstock (iStockphoto), München; **126** shutterstock (milanzeremski), New York, NY; **127** iStockphoto (Krystian Nawrocki), Calgary, Alberta; **128** www.CartoonStock.com (Stan Eales), Bath; **129** Fotolia.com (industrieblick), New York; **130** shutterstock (pkchai), New York, NY; **131** iStockphoto (fcafotodigital), Calgary, Alberta; **132** iStockphoto (PhotoTalk), Calgary, Alberta; **133** www.CartoonStock.com (Morris, John), Bath; **Activity pages 1** iStockphoto (Thomas_EyeDesign), Calgary, Alberta; **Activity pages 2** iStockphoto (paulprescott72), Calgary, Alberta;

Sollte es in einem Einzelfall nicht gelungen sein, den korrekten Rechteinhaber ausfindig zu machen, so werden berechtigte Ansprüche selbstverständlich im Rahmen der üblichen Regelungen abgegolten.